The Internet For Tea... 2nd Edition

Internet Net-Speak Checklist

Get the following information from your service provider so that you have all the information you need to set up your software for Internet access. Examples of the information are shown in parentheses. (If your software comes preconfigured, you can skip all of this.)

1. Your Internet provider address (it'll look something like this: `123.456.78.90`) ____________
2. Your user name (login name): (`flintstone`) ____________
3. Your password (letters and/or numbers): ____________
4. Your broadcast address: (`123.123.255.255`) ____________
5. Your domain name: (`apple.com`) ____________
6. Your e-mail address: (`flintstone@apple.com`) ____________
7. Dial-up phone number(s): ____________
8. Mailserver name (or POP server or SMTP server): (`bedrock.com`) ____________
9. News host server name (or NNTP server): ____________ (`nntp.bedrock.com`)
10. Domain name server: (`234.00.123.0`) ____________
11. Subnet mask: (`255.255.0.0`) ____________
12. Account type (SLIP, CSLIP, PPP, shell): ____________
13. Port settings (baud rate, com/serial port #): ____________
14. Domain suffix: (`bedrock.com`) ____________
15. Ph server (not every service has one): (`bedrock.com`) ____________
16. Internet provider troubleshooting phone number: ____________
17. Software tools available with your account: ____________

...For Dummies: #1 Computer Book Series for Beginners

The Internet For Teachers™, 2nd Edition

Your Favorite Educational Sites

Site: ______________________
URL: ______________________

Site: ______________________
URL: ______________________

Site: ______________________
URL: ______________________

Site: ______________________
URL: ______________________

Site: ______________________
URL: ______________________

Site: ______________________
URL: ______________________

Site: ______________________
URL: ______________________

Site: ______________________
URL: ______________________

A+ Net Tools: Which Is Which?

E-Mail	Send and receive electronic mail
Gopher	Locate information on the Internet
Veronica	Search for titles in Gopherspace
FTP	Retrieve files from the Internet
Archie	Locate files on the Internet
IRC	Chat live across the Internet
Usenet	Search and read discussion topics newsgroups on the Internet
Web browser	Search and explore the World Wide Web
Telnet	Act as a terminal on a remote computer

Internet E-Mail

To Send To	*Use This Format*
America Online	`hamlet@aol.com`
Genie	`horatio@genie.geis.com`
CompuServe	`98765.4321@compuserve.com`
AppleLink	`BillS@applelink.apple.com`
MSN	`Shakespeare@msn.com`

Other Internet addresses (see Chapters 10 and 11):
`henry@<domain name>`

Pre-Surf Checklist

- Instructional goal(s)
- Internet resources to be accessed (gopher, Web, and so on)
- Estimated time to complete activity
- Starting URL
- Potential trouble spots
- Expected outcomes

Cheat Sheet $2.95 value. Item 0058-9
For more information about IDG Books, call 1-800-762-2974.

THE INTERNET FOR TEACHERS™

2ND EDITION

THE INTERNET FOR TEACHERS™

2ND EDITION

by Bard Williams

IDG Books Worldwide, Inc.
An International Data Group Company

Foster City, CA ♦ Chicago, IL ♦ Indianapolis, IN ♦ Southlake, TX

The Internet For Teachers™, 2nd Edition

Published by
IDG Books Worldwide, Inc.
An International Data Group Company
919 E. Hillsdale Blvd.
Suite 400
Foster City, CA 94404
www.idgbooks.com (IDG Books Worldwide Web site)
www.dummies.com (Dummies Press Web site)

Library of Congress Catalog Card No.: 96-78136

ISBN: 0-7645-0058-9

Printed in the United States of America

10 9 8 7 6 5 4 3

2B/SQ/RR/ZX/IN

Distributed in the United States by IDG Books Worldwide, Inc.

Distributed by Macmillan Canada for Canada; by Transworld Publishers Limited in the United Kingdom; by IDG Norge Books for Norway; by IDG Sweden Books for Sweden; by Woodslane Pty. Ltd. for Australia; by Woodslane Enterprises Ltd. for New Zealand; by Longman Singapore Publishers Ltd. for Singapore, Malaysia, Thailand, and Indonesia; by Simron Pty. Ltd. for South Africa; by Toppan Company Ltd. for Japan; by Distribuidora Cuspide for Argentina; by Livraria Cultura for Brazil; by Ediciencia S.A. for Ecuador; by Addison-Wesley Publishing Company for Korea; by Ediciones ZETA S.C.R. Ltda. for Peru; by WS Computer Publishing Corporation, Inc., for the Philippines; by Unalis Corporation for Taiwan; by Contemporanea de Ediciones for Venezuela; by Computer Book & Magazine Store for Puerto Rico; by Express Computer Distributors for the Caribbean and West Indies. Authorized Sales Agent: Anthony Rudkin Associates for the Middle East and North Africa.

For general information on IDG Books Worldwide's books in the U.S., please call our Consumer Customer Service department at 800-762-2974. For reseller information, including discounts and premium sales, please call our Reseller Customer Service department at 800-434-3422.

For information on where to purchase IDG Books Worldwide's books outside the U.S., please contact our International Sales department at 415-655-3200 or fax 415-655-3295.

For information on foreign language translations, please contact our Foreign & Subsidiary Rights department at 415-655-3021 or fax 415-655-3281.

For sales inquiries and special prices for bulk quantities, please contact our Sales department at 415-655-3200 or write to the address above.

For information on using IDG Books Worldwide's books in the classroom or for ordering examination copies, please contact our Educational Sales department at 800-434-2086 or fax 817-251-8174.

For press review copies, author interviews, or other publicity information, please contact our Public Relations department at 415-655-3000 or fax 415-655-3299.

For authorization to photocopy items for corporate, personal, or educational use, please contact Copyright Clearance Center, 222 Rosewood Drive, Danvers, MA 01923, or fax 508-750-4470.

About the Author

Bard Williams bought his first computer, an Apple IIgs, just two days after it rolled off the assembly line. He scooped up his first Macintosh two weeks after it was first manufactured (it took the loan sharks a bit longer to give him the money). He still occasionally uses his Apple II, even though his computer habit recently forced him to add a Power Macintosh to his computer collection and turn his old faithful Macintosh 512K into a nifty aquarium. (Anyone know how to feed a live screen saver?)

Bard is an educator, a writer, and a technology consultant who believes, like many educators, that nothing is more exciting than seeing enthusiastic teachers use technology to guide motivated learners toward new ideas and new horizons. He is the author of more than 150 articles and, in his spare time (ha!), he gets his energy from speaking at educational conferences, teaching, and consulting.

After more than 12 years teaching middle school students (the *ultimate* challenge) and a position as Coordinator of Computer Technology and Support for the Gwinnett County school district in Georgia, Bard was recruited by Apple Computer, Inc., to manage strategic education relations in the Northeast U.S.

Bard received his doctorate in Curriculum & Instruction from the University of Georgia just two weeks before the first edition of this book was published and swears that the journey was worth the reward. Now that this book and his dissertation are complete, he looks forward to reintroducing himself to his family and friends — after he gets back from Disney World.

ABOUT IDG BOOKS WORLDWIDE

Welcome to the world of IDG Books Worldwide.

IDG Books Worldwide, Inc., is a subsidiary of International Data Group, the world's largest publisher of computer-related information and the leading global provider of information services on information technology. IDG was founded more than 25 years ago and now employs more than 8,500 people worldwide. IDG publishes more than 275 computer publications in over 75 countries (see listing below). More than 60 million people read one or more IDG publications each month.

Launched in 1990, IDG Books Worldwide is today the #1 publisher of best-selling computer books in the United States. We are proud to have received eight awards from the Computer Press Association in recognition of editorial excellence and three from *Computer Currents*' First Annual Readers' Choice Awards. Our best-selling *...For Dummies*® series has more than 30 million copies in print with translations in 30 languages. IDG Books Worldwide, through a joint venture with IDG's Hi-Tech Beijing, became the first U.S. publisher to publish a computer book in the People's Republic of China. In record time, IDG Books Worldwide has become the first choice for millions of readers around the world who want to learn how to better manage their businesses.

Our mission is simple: Every one of our books is designed to bring extra value and skill-building instructions to the reader. Our books are written by experts who understand and care about our readers. The knowledge base of our editorial staff comes from years of experience in publishing, education, and journalism — experience we use to produce books for the '90s. In short, we care about books, so we attract the best people. We devote special attention to details such as audience, interior design, use of icons, and illustrations. And because we use an efficient process of authoring, editing, and desktop publishing our books electronically, we can spend more time ensuring superior content and spend less time on the technicalities of making books.

You can count on our commitment to deliver high-quality books at competitive prices on topics you want to read about. At IDG Books Worldwide, we continue in the IDG tradition of delivering quality for more than 25 years. You'll find no better book on a subject than one from IDG Books Worldwide.

John Kilcullen
CEO
IDG Books Worldwide, Inc.

Steven Berkowitz
President and Publisher
IDG Books Worldwide, Inc.

Eighth Annual Computer Press Awards 1992

Ninth Annual Computer Press Awards 1993

X
WINNER
Tenth Annual Computer Press Awards 1994

Eleventh Annual Computer Press Awards 1995

IDG Books Worldwide, Inc., is a subsidiary of International Data Group, the world's largest publisher of computer-related information and the leading global provider of information services on information technology. International Data Group publishes over 275 computer publications in over 75 countries. Sixty million people read one or more International Data Group publications each month. International Data Group's publications include: **ARGENTINA:** Buyer's Guide, Computerworld Argentina, PC World Argentina; **AUSTRALIA:** Australian Macworld, Australian PC World, Australian Reseller News, Computerworld, IT Casebook, Network World, Publish, Webmaster; **AUSTRIA:** Computerwelt Osterreich, Networks Austria, PC Tip Austria; **BANGLADESH:** PC World Bangladesh; **BELARUS:** PC World Belarus; **BELGIUM:** Data News; **BRAZIL:** Annuário de Informática, Computerworld, Connections, Macworld, PC Player, PC World, Publish, Reseller News, Supergamepower; **BULGARIA:** Computerworld Bulgaria, Network World Bulgaria, PC & MacWorld Bulgaria; **CANADA:** CIO Canada, Client/Server World, ComputerWorld Canada, InfoWorld Canada, NetworkWorld Canada, WebWorld; **CHILE:** Computerworld Chile, PC World Chile; **COLOMBIA:** Computerworld Colombia, PC World Colombia; **COSTA RICA:** PC World Centro America; **THE CZECH AND SLOVAK REPUBLICS:** Computerworld Czechoslovakia, Macworld Czech Republic, PC World Czechoslovakia; **DENMARK:** Communications World Danmark, Computerworld Danmark, Macworld Danmark, PC World Danmark, Techworld Denmark; **DOMINICAN REPUBLIC:** PC World Republica Dominicana; **ECUADOR:** PC World Ecuador; **EGYPT:** Computerworld Middle East, PC World Middle East; **EL SALVADOR:** PC World Centro America; **FINLAND:** MikroPC, Tietoverkko, Tietoviikko; **FRANCE:** Distributique, Hebdo, Info PC, Le Monde Informatique, Macworld, Reseaux & Telecoms, WebMaster France; **GERMANY:** Computer Partner, Computerwoche, Computerwoche Extra, Computerwoche FOCUS, Global Online, Macwelt, PC Welt; **GREECE:** Amiga Computing, GamePro Greece, Multimedia World; **GUATEMALA:** PC World Centro America; **HONDURAS:** PC World Centro America; **HONG KONG:** Computerworld Hong Kong, PC World Hong Kong, Publish in Asia; **HUNGARY:** ABCD CD-ROM, Computerworld Szamitastechnika, Internetto online Magazine, PC World Hungary, PC-X Magazin Hungary; **ICELAND:** Tolvuheimur PC World Island; **INDIA:** Information Communications World, Information Systems Computerworld, PC World India, Publish in Asia; **INDONESIA:** InfoKomputer PC World, Komputek Computerworld, Publish in Asia; **IRELAND:** ComputerScope, PC Live!; **ISRAEL:** Macworld Israel, People & Computers/Computerworld; **ITALY:** Computerworld Italia, Macworld Italia, Networking Italia, PC World Italia; **JAPAN:** DTP World, Macworld Japan, Nikkei Personal Computing, OS/2 World Japan, SunWorld Japan, Windows NT World, Windows World Japan; **KENYA:** PC World East African; **KOREA:** Hi-Tech Information, Macworld Korea, PC World Korea; **MACEDONIA:** PC World Macedonia; **MALAYSIA:** Computerworld Malaysia, PC World Malaysia, Publish in Asia; **MALTA:** PC World Malta; **MEXICO:** Computerworld Mexico, PC World Mexico; **MYANMAR:** PC World Myanmar; **NETHERLANDS:** Computer! Totaal, LAN Internetworking Magazine, LAN World Buyers Guide, Macworld Netherlands, Net, WebWereld; **NEW ZEALAND:** Absolute Beginners Guide and Plain & Simple Series, Computer Buyer, Computer Industry Directory, Computerworld New Zealand, MTB, Network World, PC World New Zealand; **NICARAGUA:** PC World Centro America; **NORWAY:** Computerworld Norge, CW Rapport, Datamagasinet, Financial Rapport, Kursguide Norge, Macworld Norge, Multimediaworld Norge, PC World Ekspress Norge, PC World Nettverk, PC World Norge, PC World ProduktGuide Norge; **PAKISTAN:** Computerworld Pakistan; **PANAMA:** PC World Panama; **PEOPLE'S REPUBLIC OF CHINA:** China Computer Users, China Computerworld, China InfoWorld, China Telecom World Weekly, Computer & Communication, Electronic Design China, Electronics Today, Electronics Weekly, Game Software, PC World China, Popular Computer Week, Software Weekly, Software World, Telecom World; **PERU:** Computerworld Peru, PC World Profesional Peru, PC World SoHo Peru; **PHILIPPINES:** Click!, Computerworld Philippines, PC World Philippines, Publish in Asia; **POLAND:** Computerworld Poland, Computerworld Special Report Poland, Cyber, Macworld Poland, Networld Poland, PC World Komputer; **PORTUGAL:** Cerebro/PC World, Computerworld/Correio Informático, Dealer World Portugal, Mac*In/PC*In Portugal, Multimedia World; **PUERTO RICO:** PC World Puerto Rico; **ROMANIA:** Computerworld Romania, PC World Romania, Telecom Romania; **RUSSIA:** Computerworld Russia, Mir PK, Publish, Seti; **SINGAPORE:** Computerworld Singapore, PC World Singapore, Publish in Asia; **SLOVENIA:** Monitor; **SOUTH AFRICA:** Computing SA, Network World SA, Software World SA; **SPAIN:** Communicaciones World España, Computerworld España, Dealer World España, Macworld España, PC World España; **SRI LANKA:** Infolink PC World; **SWEDEN:** CAP&Design, Computer Sweden, Corporate Computing Sweden, Internetworld Sweden, it.branschen, Macworld Sweden, MaxiData Sweden, MikroDatorn, Nätverk & Kommunikation, PC World Sweden, PCaktiv, Windows World Sweden; **SWITZERLAND:** Computerworld Schweiz, Macworld Schweiz, PCtip; **TAIWAN:** Computerworld Taiwan, Macworld Taiwan, NEW ViSiON/Publish, PC World Taiwan, Windows World Taiwan; **THAILAND:** Publish in Asia, Thai Computerworld; **TURKEY:** Computerworld Turkiye, Macworld Turkiye, Network World Turkiye, PC World Turkiye; **UKRAINE:** Computerworld Kiev, Multimedia World Ukraine, PC World Ukraine; **UNITED KINGDOM:** Acorn User UK, Amiga Action UK, Amiga Computing UK, Apple Talk UK, Computing, Macworld, Parents and Computers UK, PC Advisor, PC Home, PSX Pro, The WEB; **UNITED STATES:** Cable in the Classroom, CIO Magazine, Computerworld, DOS World, Federal Computer Week, GamePro Magazine, InfoWorld, I-Way, Macworld, Network World, PC Games, PC World, Publish, Video Event, THE WEB Magazine, and WebMaster; online webzines: JavaWorld, NetscapeWorld, and SunWorld Online; **URUGUAY:** InfoWorld Uruguay; **VENEZUELA:** Computerworld Venezuela, PC World Venezuela; and **VIETNAM:** PC World Vietnam.

3/24/97

Dedication

The second edition of this book is dedicated to my niece Ashley Cook, her brothers Jordan and Cal, Joshua Wilson, and to all the people who believe that learning is fun and teaching is an honor.

Author's Acknowledgments

Michelle Robinette, friend and teacher, deserves a whole page, but the editors wouldn't allow it. Michelle called one day and told me a story about writing a book for IDG Books, *Macs For Teachers.* Within 20 minutes, I was ready to jump on the bandwagon and crank one out myself. Since then, we've become great friends. Here's hoping *your* child ends up in Michelle's classroom.

Somewhere in Indianapolis there's a building packed full of amazingly intelligent people who help edit the content and style of my books. Christy Beck helped make a first edition into a second edition, filling pages with excellent edits and questions that helped me fill in lots of gaps. The book's first edition was edited by an amazing editor, Pat Seiler, somewhere in Virginia, who coached me through what it is like to be a "real" writer. I am forever indebted to Pat for making that first experience a joyous one.

Special thanks go to Tommy Hann of Apple Computer, Inc., who served as technical editor for both editions of this book. I chose him because I believe he's one of the best in the country at sharing the power of technology with others and because he (occasionally) laughs at my jokes. He also feeds my Internet habit with new ideas practically every week.

Bill Helling is the IDG Books "master-editor" who coached all the other editors, patiently wading through page after page of "delete this, add this", and whose professionalism and meticulous edits made working with the publisher a dream. He continues to be a great mentor and friend.

Some of the greatest people on the planet work for IDG Books. Jim Kelly had enough faith in my work to stand up in a crowd and yell, "We need *The Internet For Teachers,*" so that everyone noticed. I couldn't have created this or any of my other works without my friend, Mary Bednarek, who knows what readers want and knows how to convince me to continue to write. Megg Bonar and Suki Gear helped me translate *publisherspeak* and get a dandy deal. Joyce Pepple should get a gold star for doing all the hard work to make sure my readers got the best possible software on the CD. Special thanks to John Kilcullen, the creator of the IDG Books empire, for vision and knowing — and grabbing the brass ring. Diane Steele and Judi Taylor helped steer the IDG Books machine for this project — all on behalf of the teachers of the world. If you ever want to experience what it's like to work with a winning team, try working with IDG Books. It's wonderful.

Special thanks also go out to the hordes of people who offered encouragement and technical assistance for both editions of this work, including, Scott Tyson, Brice Vorderbrug, Sherah Carr, Sandy Ewanowski, Gayle Keresey, Ted Roth, Ed Pajak, George Bagwell, Jim Mansour, and lots of fellow educators who have told me that what I've written has changed the way they teach and learn.

Publisher's Acknowledgments

We're proud of this book; please register your comments through our IDG Books Worldwide Online Registration Form located at: `http://my2cents.dummies.com`.

Some of the people who helped bring this book to market include the following:

Acquisitions, Development, and Editorial

Project Editor: Bill Helling

Assistant Acquisitions Editor: Gareth Hancock

Product Development Manager: Mary Bednarek

Media Development Manager: Joyce Pepple

Copy Editor: Christine Meloy Beck

Technical Editors: Tommy Hann, Kevin Spencer

Editorial Manager: Mary C. Corder

Editorial Assistant: Chris H. Collins

Production

Project Coordinator: Cindy L. Phipps

Layout and Graphics: E. Shawn Aylsworth, Cameron Booker, Elizabeth Cárdenas-Nelson, Dominique DeFelice, Maridee V. Ennis, Angela F. Hunckler, Todd Klemme, Tom Missler, Mark C. Owens, Anna Rohrer, Brent Savage, Gina Scott

Proofreaders: Kelli Botta, Joel Draper, Rachel Garvey, Dwight Ramsey, Robert Springer, Carrie Voorhis, Karen York

Indexer: Sharon Hilgenberg

Special Help: Michael Bolinger, Copy Editor; Stephanie Koutek, Proof Editor

---

General and Administrative

IDG Books Worldwide, Inc.: John Kilcullen, CEO; Steven Berkowitz, President and Publisher

IDG Books Technology Publishing: Brenda McLaughlin, Senior Vice President and Group Publisher

Dummies Technology Press and Dummies Editorial: Diane Graves Steele, Vice President and Associate Publisher; Mary Bednarek, Acquisitions and Product Development Director; Kristin A. Cocks, Editorial Director

Dummies Trade Press: Kathleen A. Welton, Vice President and Publisher; Kevin Thornton, Acquisitions Manager; Maureen F. Kelly, Editorial Coordinator

IDG Books Production for Dummies Press: Beth Jenkins, Production Director; Cindy L. Phipps, Manager of Project Coordination, Production Proofreading, and Indexing; Kathie S. Schutte, Supervisor of Page Layout; Shelley Lea, Supervisor of Graphics and Design; Debbie J. Gates, Production Systems Specialist; Robert Springer, Supervisor of Proofreading; Debbie Stailey, Special Projects Coordinator; Tony Augsburger, Supervisor of Reprints and Bluelines; Leslie Popplewell, Media Archive Coordinator

Dummies Packaging and Book Design: Patti Crane, Packaging Specialist; Lance Kayser, Packaging Assistant; Kavish + Kavish, Cover Design

♦

The publisher would like to give special thanks to Patrick J. McGovern, without whom this book would not have been possible.

♦

Contents at a Glance

Cartoons at a Glance

By Rich Tennant • Fax: 508-546-7747 • E-mail: the5wave@tiac.net

page 97

"EXCUSE ME – IS ANYONE HERE NOT TALKING ABOUT THE INTERNET?"

page 7

"NOW, THAT WOULD SHOW HOW IMPORTANT IT IS TO DISTINGUISH 'FERTILIZING PRACTICES' FROM 'FERTILITY PRACTICES' WHEN DOWNLOADING A VIDEO FILE FROM THE INTERNET."

page 231

The 5th Wave By Rich Tennant

"I don't mean to hinder your quest for knowledge, however it's not generally a good idea to try to download the entire Internet."

page 309

"I did this report with the help of a satellite view atmospheric map from the National Weather Service, research text from the Jet Propulsion Laboratory, and a sound file from 'The Barfing Lungworms' new CD."

page 257

"He should be all right now. I made him spend two and a half hours on a prisoners' chat line."

page 29

Table of Contents

Introduction

Welcome to *The Internet For Teachers,* 2nd Edition. If you have a doctorate in computer science and have been an Internet user since the invention of the personal computer, you're in the *wrong* place. This book is written for those of you who just got a driver's license for the information superhighway and are ready to pull away from the curb.

Yes, there are zillions of books about the Internet, but how many are written by someone who knows the reality of being an educator? I can relate to the fact that when school's out, it takes five minutes to get an outside telephone line. I also know that getting approval for anything that costs money, whether it's Internet access or a new eraser for the chalkboard, is a major deal. I've provided lots of suggestions for getting support for an Internet connection for your class and lots of ideas from teachers around the country for using the Internet in your classroom.

Most of your ride through the wealth of resources on the information superhighway will be smooth, but you need to watch out for potholes, too. I've included information on the latest tools to use in exploring the Internet, and I've tried to make your trip easier by giving you tips, techniques, a couple hundred places to visit, and a few anecdotes that you'll especially appreciate as a K-12 or college teacher.

This second edition has provided me an opportunity to update and enhance the content presented in the first edition. I appreciate the wonderful support and input from friends and colleagues around the world. Your input shaped the changes in this edition.

So, here it is in plain English. All the techno-babble has been stripped away, and here are the basics about how to get started, how to do some cool things after you get online, and how you can harness the power of the Internet in your classroom.

About This Book

This book is designed to be used when you and your students are just beginning your trip through the Internet and for times when you get stalled on the info-way and can't find a wrecker. Just jump right into any chapter, get what you need, and jump back to the real world.

You'll find handy information, including the following topics:

- What is this Internet thing, anyway?
- Searching Internet roots
- Getting started
- Getting connected to the Internet
- Net responsibility
- Sending e-mail
- Becoming a newsgroupie
- Training Gophers and other Net-rodents
- Creating your first cyberjourney
- Ten excellent educational Web sites

How to Read This Book

Grab this book when you need a quick reference. Glance at the Table of Contents, peruse the Index, and zip right to the page that gives you the answer you need.

The book has been written so that each chapter pretty much stands alone. It's great for those five-minute reading breaks between classes.

Conventions

I love conventions. The freebies in the display area, the pressed chicken at the banquet. My favorite is the National Educational Computing Conference . . . Wait! Sorry, wrong convention.

I've done some things to make your life easier. Watch for them.

When you have to type something, it appears in **boldface** type, unless it's an Internet address. Internet addresses look like this:

```
socrates@university.edu
```

Type it in, just as it appears, capitalization and all, and then press the Return or Enter key on your keyboard.

If you make a boo-boo, just type it again, or check Appendix A for troubleshooting tips.

Exciting, huh?

Who am I talking to? (a.k.a. To whom am I speaking?)

In preparing this book for you, I've assumed the following:

- You have or would like to have access to the Internet.
- You intend to get access to the Internet through a direct network connection, an online service, or an Internet service provider.
- You are an educator who is wondering how you can learn about the Internet and how you can use it in what you do every day.
- You are responsible for arranging to bring the Internet into your school or your school system.
- You are not seeking to be the next Internet swami who, after 1,000 hours of surfing the Net, is more interested in finding out whether Microsoft's Bill Gates really does answer his e-mail than in how the Internet can reduce the time it takes to grade 35 essays.

In order to save you countless hours searching the Net for tools, I've included some of the most-often-used and most-powerful tools for accessing and navigating the Internet on the CD that comes with this book. You'll be delighted to know that it is "cross-platform" (geek-speak for "It works on both Macintosh computers and computers running Windows or Windows 95"). With these tools and others I refer to in the chapters ahead, you'll quickly become King or Queen of the NetSurfers before you can say *telecommunicate!*

How This Book Is Organized

This book has six parts. The parts are designed to be read either in sequence or on their own. You can jump in anywhere you like, but I recommend that you peek at Part I so you know a bit about the Internet before you take the plunge.

Here are the parts of the book and what they contain:

Part I: Log On: The Internet in Education

This part discusses what the Internet is, tells a bit about how it came into existence, and gives a bunch of compelling reasons why you and your school should jump onto the information superhighway.

Part II: Getting Wired

In this part, you learn what hardware and software you need to get started using the Internet, and you explore the options for getting yourself or your school connected. You also take a dip into the mysterious area of Internet responsibility.

Part III: Internet Resource Roundup

This part is the backbone of the book. It presents each Internet resource in tasty, bite-sized pieces. Find out how to send and receive electronic mail, explore online databases, receive files, and talk live to others around the world.

Part IV: The Net Meets the Classroom

What happens when it comes time to use the Internet with your students? This part gives you a glimpse into how to write lesson plans for instruction that uses the Internet, as well as some tips on your changing role as an "instructor of the 21st century" and on troubleshooting when things go nuts.

Part V: The Part of Tens: The Internet Educator

Here's the place where you find lots of cool sites for you and your students to visit after you join the Internet community. Even though this part is called "The Part of Tens," I got really carried away and gave you lots more for your money.

Part VI: Appendixes

Find out how to deal with those inevitable hardware and software problems and identify unfamiliar Internet terms. Also discover some schools that publish their own Web pages.

Icons Used in This Book

Here are the pretty pictures that can make your life easier:

Learning Link

An opportunity for your students to participate in an Internet-related educational activity.

Teacher Approved

This icon highlights items or activities that I think are a "must use" in your classroom.

Techno Terms

Vocabulary that the teacher (you!) should know to be a *true* Net surfer.

On the CD

This icon points out programs that are on the *Internet For Teachers* CD-ROM at the back of this book.

Heads Up

Handy things you should watch for or things that can make your life easier. They're time savers and frustration savers.

Try This

An activity for you to try so that you can practice using the Internet. Hands-on learning.

Net Statistics

A bunch of cool statistics collected from all over the Internet about — what else? — the Internet!

Warning!

A danger sign. Hold the mouse!

Just Do It!

Okay. You're ready to go. Learning to use the Internet is not nearly as difficult as others may tell you. You've done much more difficult things, such as learning how to handle fights in the hall and potty patrol after fifth period.

Grab this book and a cup of coffee or a can of soda (essential food groups for educators) and jump right in. You'll be Internetting in no time. Surf's up!

Feedback!

We really, really want to know what you think about *The Internet For Teachers,* 2nd Edition.

Send feedback to:

IDG Books Worldwide, Inc.
7260 Shadeland Station, Suite 100
Indianapolis, IN 46256

Be sure to log on to the official IDG "Dummies" Web site and read about other books in the ...*For Teachers* series. You find it at `http://www.dummies.com`.

Part I

Log On: The Internet in Education

"EXCUSE ME - IS ANYONE HERE NOT TALKING ABOUT THE INTERNET?"

In this part . . .

Walk over to the shelf and grab a textbook. Open it to any page. You're likely to see:

> "Some day man will go to the moon."
>
> "Let's take a look at the Soviet Union."

or

> "Modern poets such as William Shakespeare . . ."

Even your most current textbook took more than a year to get from the drawing board to your classroom. Most curriculum adoption cycles are much longer, meaning that it could be three years or more before three-year-old information is put into the hands of you and your students.

Now, don't get me wrong. After 12 years in middle school classrooms, I appreciate the value of a good textbook. They're great for offering skill and drill (or drill and kill) activities, and they do provide a good infrastructure for organizing information, but textbooks, at least in the current form, are always "old news."

Enter the Internet. Right now the Net is a lawless place in cyberspace in which bunches of information are being dumped on a daily basis. That information, however important, trite, or explicit, is, at the least, *current.* It's important for us, as educators, to work together with our students to learn to separate the gems from the junk.

When you and your students log on to the Internet, you're no longer a teacher. Both of you have become *knowledge navigators*. It's up to you to chart a course through cyberspace to find the good stuff. It's up to you to find a way to use the stuff after you find it, too.

In this part, you learn about the structure and history of the Internet, find out the cool things you can do with Internet access, read some compelling reasons for logging on in the first place, and enjoy a few success stories. All this should be painless. After all, that's what makes these books great.

If you're really chomping at the bit and already have an Internet connection picked out, go ahead and jump to Part III to find out the particulars for making your first Internet connection.

Chapter 1

What Is This Internet Thing, Anyway?

In This Chapter

- Defining the Internet
- Using the Internet in your classroom
- Success on the Net: A Beginner's Internet Journey

A friend once told me that she defined technology as "anything invented after she was born." Just when most teachers are becoming comfortable with using calculators and computers in classrooms and computer labs, this Internet thing comes along.

Never fear, though; this new form of communication and information access is becoming easier to learn as more software developers jump onto the information superhighway. Sure, the highway has some potholes, but it's my goal to help you steer clear of them.

As you read and try the activities in this book, I think you'll find that learning to use the Internet is fun and rewarding, for both you and your students.

Knocking down classroom walls and accessing information and people around the globe is what the Internet is *for.* In the next section, you get a glimpse of what the Internet *is.*

The Internet: The Textbook of Tomorrow?

The Internet is a large collection of networks that are tied together so that many users can share their vast resources. That's all. Just lots of computers tied together by high-speed telephone lines. To get onto the Internet, all you have to do is make arrangements to make your computer one of the millions already online. Easy, huh?

Learning to navigate through the interconnecting networks is as exciting as the information you can retrieve. Not only will your journeys take you around the globe, but you'll begin to appreciate the rich diversity in humanity and the wide variety of knowledge on planet Earth.

The Internet holds a wealth of information. In fact, it contains so much information that you and your students could spend your entire lives just browsing. You will learn quickly that the key to a successful and efficient session on the Internet is *good planning*.

As you plan for ways to use the Internet in your classroom, you'll also see that students need a wide variety of skills to be successful on the Net. Well-planned Internet activities tap skills in researching, problem-solving, critical thinking, communication, and data management. It's a good idea to think about how you'll reinforce those skills before, during, and after your journey into the Net.

What's the bottom line? Thanks to the information superhighway system, you and your students can now travel around the world in nanoseconds, collecting more ideas and up-to-the-minute information than you ever imagined. Sounds like something that's right for your classroom, doesn't it? Textbook? What textbook?

By mid-1996, more than 3,000 schools had registered their own Web pages, more than twice the number at the same time in 1995.

What Can I Do with the Internet?

One day last summer, I was watching an infomercial touting the latest device that could slice, dice, chop, mow the lawn, and grade papers (I wish), and I thought, "They could sell the Internet this way!" It's a great tool for lots of things, if you know how to use it.

The Internet can make a real difference in teaching and learning in your school. Not only can using the Internet effectively enhance and enrich the classroom experience, but it also has great value for you as a personal productivity tool.

Here's a sampling of what the Internet has to offer you and your students:

- **Global electronic mail:** Send a note to anyone, anywhere, anytime. Suddenly, you have the ability to build linkages between people everywhere without regard to those things that blind us from the appreciation of knowledge. Things such as race, color, creed, gender, and physical disabilities all disappear when you board the information superhighway. A teacher in my school district used electronic mail to correspond with a teacher in Alaska, who gave a play-by-play description of the Iditarod. Every day she checked to see what condition the dogs were in, who the front-runner was, and what interesting anecdotes were available about the challenges faced by the wind-blown racers. She then passed the information on to her students, who wrote articles for an "Iditarod Update," made maps of the trip, charted weather conditions, and calculated wind-chill temperatures. Is this project interdisciplinary or what?

- **Knowledge navigation:** Zip around the world via the Internet to locate documents, pictures, sounds, and even digitized movies to keep your knowledge, skills, and curriculum up to date. Glance over at the shelf and tug on the textbook that says "Some day man will go to the moon," and think about how useful it can be to have instantaneous information for use in the classroom. Got a unit on weather coming up? Use Internet resources to pop over to NASA to access ready-made classroom activities, surf to the Library of Congress (or your local library) and build a bibliography, and then head for the Jet Propulsion Lab (JPL) for digitized satellite photos.
- **File exchange:** Send and retrieve files containing documents, pictures, movies, sounds, and programs. Need the latest version of virus protection software? Jump onto the Net, hop to the vendor's file server, and retrieve your file.
- **Discussion groups:** Engage in a discussion with other Internet users about any topic you can think of. A media specialist, using a discussion group (also called a *newsgroup*), posted an electronic message asking other educators on the Net about selecting software for a media circulation system. Four weeks later, he went before the board of education with testimonials and facts from 23 school systems around the country about the system he had selected. They bought it lock, stock, and barcode.
- **Live conferencing:** Talk "live" to other Internet users. Get into a debate about outcome-based education, or Bloom's Taxonomy, or whether to have Coke or Pepsi in the faculty lounge machines.

Impressed? There's much more. By its very nature, the Internet is a *dynamic* medium. It changes just about every nanosecond as people add or delete information. The body of knowledge on the Internet is growing exponentially and the tools we use to access the Net are becoming easier to use and more powerful.

Remember the neat activity that you use to teach kids about compounding interest — the one where you offer to take as an allowance only one penny per day as long as the amount doubles each day? That's the Internet — except that it's growing *faster.* The emphasis suddenly shifts from how many resources are available to how to find the ones you need and, once you find them, how to use that information responsibly.

About half of the 23 million users on the estimated 2.6 million computers connected to the Internet in February 1996 used the Internet solely for electronic mail.

Success on the Net: A Beginner's Journey

Jenny teaches fourth grade at a rural elementary school. She has been in the classroom for more than 12 years, teaching grades 1 through 3. This year is her first year as a fourth grade teacher. She's pretty familiar with using a computer, and her pet peeve is students who get her keyboard dirty because they don't wash their hands.

A few months ago, she got a trial account from a local Internet provider. After loading the software into her brand-new Power Macintosh computer and connecting her modem, she was on her way to her first Internet cyberjourney.

In three weeks, Jenny's class would begin a study of the government. Because she'd never taught government to fourth graders, she didn't have a lot of resources, so she thought about using the Internet to find some. Was this Internet thing really worth the trouble?

She'd heard all the hullabaloo about the World Wide Web (WWW) and decided to use her *Web browser,* a tool for navigating the WWW, as a starting point. She double-clicked her Netscape icon. (Netscape is the name of a program used to browse the WWW. A copy of the Netscape Navigator browser is included with the AT&T WorldNet Service sign-on kit on the CD.) She was then officially on the Internet.

Her first step was to click Web Crawler, an Internet search tool featured as one of the menu choices on Netscape's Web page. A *Web page* is a page of pictures and text with clickable links to other Internet resources. (Because Netscape is the developer of the Web browser, when you sign on, the Netscape Web page is the first page you see.)

In the Web Crawler search window, she typed:

```
government
```

The screen listed more than 50 places to begin looking for information on the government. Yippee! Success! She clicked Government and Politics, which guided her to a WWW page that looked like the following figure:

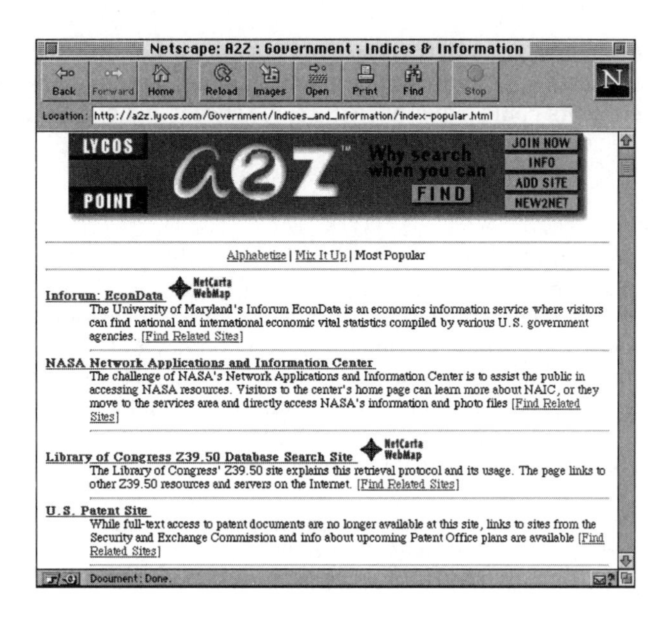

She quickly realized that her search would pay off. For the next 20 minutes or so, she browsed selected sites, cutting and pasting information from the screen into her word processor, carefully noting and citing the source of each nugget of information.

Because the Netscape browser program that she was using also gave her access to *newsgroups* (electronic bulletin boards), she spent a few minutes reading messages from other educators who were teaching government.

Next, she used Fetch, an *FTP* (file-transfer protocol) program, to *download* (copy to her computer) lesson plan files from ERIC, and she visited the White House home page (`www.whitehouse.gov`), where she clicked on an icon and heard President Clinton speak a personal welcome message. (Yes, the Net talks.) She rounded out her tour by scanning several online magazines for articles.

As she traveled through the Net, she remembered to add electronic bookmarks so she could return to the marked places later with her class. (Chapter 15 discusses how to create a bookmark.)

After about an hour, she had tons of information to use in preparing her lesson plans, as well as a list of great places on the Internet for her class to visit. As she explained what she'd experienced, the two things she'd learned from her first expedition were

- The Internet offers a huge number of resources.
- Using the Internet is easier than she thought.

Of course, she still had her work cut out for her. She had to figure out how to use all this information and how to manage and organize the lesson so that her students could experience the same success when they searched for information on the Internet.

It worked. She's hooked. Nuff said.

Not every Internet search goes this smoothly. Many Internet searches, especially for topics more narrow than "government," can take far more time. As you and your students explore, you'll encounter occasional false starts and dead ends. You'll get busy signals from computers and click in the wrong place from time to time. You'll want to throw your computer out the window and rip out the phone line at times. Never fear, though; chances are, you will find information about whatever you want, and the time you spend online will probably give you even more ideas for other activities.

By mid-1996, more than 75 percent of schools had access to the Internet through service providers or online services, but only 3 percent of classrooms were equipped with a direct Internet connection.

Chapter 2
Internet Roots

In This Chapter

- Beginnings: The first inter-network
- Connecting educators
- Merging traffic
- Continuing the transition
- Making history
- Evolving from roots to rabbit ears

It isn't really
Anywhere!
It's somewhere else
Instead!

"Halfway Down," *When We Were Very Young*, A. A. Milne

In the beginning, there was a telephone network, a bunch of wire, and a few big, blinking, data-stuffed mainframe computers. These computers lived in military, research, and educational institutions. One day, someone figured out that tying these electronic giants together would be a good idea. The Internet as we know it today came about largely because of a partnership between the military and educational institutions. Thus, the Internet isn't really in any one place, it's everywhere! As you discover in the following section, the military laid the foundation, and universities and research institutions built the building.

Where Did It All Begin?

Morse code, cellular phones, and that annoying intercom in your classroom were all developed because someone, somewhere, wanted to say something to other someones who would listen. Like these arguably vital communication pathways, the Internet began as a result of a need for *communication*.

Techno-weenie talk about TCP/IP

The set of rules that's used to move information from one server to another on the Internet is called *Internet Protocol (IP)*. (*Protocol* refers to a set of rules or a very funny movie starring Goldie Hawn.) Internet Protocol runs on computers in UNIX networks, but it can be accessed from non-UNIX computers. Of the other protocols that are used along with IP on the Internet, the most common is called *Transmission Control Protocol (TCP)*. If IP is the rules that govern the *structure* of the information, TCP is what *transmits* the information to its destination. Most of the time, people refer to this combination of protocols as TCP/IP. (More interesting cocktail talk about TCP/IP is available in *MORE Internet For Dummies*, by John Levine and Margaret Levine Young, published by IDG Books Worldwide, Inc.)

In 1969, the Department of Defense (DOD) funded a project to link DOD engineers with civilian research contractors, including a large number of universities that were doing military-funded research. Although the resulting network, called ARPAnet (Advanced Research Projects Administration Network), began with only three computers that were connected via phone lines, it quickly grew to become an essential resource for communication and data exchange for hundreds of military and research contractors.

After the foundations of the network were forged, more and more universities and research institutions jumped onto the superhighway. Eventually, the highway reached gridlock, and ARPAnet was subdivided to provide several different channels for military and research institutions. Today these channels remain linked by a dandy technical scheme called the Internet Protocol (IP). This protocol has made it possible for the Internet to grow and flourish.

The Education Connection

At the same time that the military and research communities were finding new ways to exchange information over the new information highway, colleges and universities were beginning to change from a centralized host system data management architecture to a distributed workstation-based scheme. Huh?

In plain English, the huge, expensive mainframe computers that were connected to "dumb terminals" around campus began to be bogged down with routine traffic from such things as electronic mail, file exchange, and computerized Star Trek games that bored professors and their teaching assistants were playing. Someone had the idea that if more power were moved to the teachers' desktops, the "big iron" would be free for more important work, such as calculating pi to the 10,000th significant digit.

Here's where it gets really crazy. The university workstations needed an operating system, and the bean-counters were going crazy because of the expense of changing the network scheme. Along came UNIX, an operating system that was offered to universities for next to nothing. The cool thing about UNIX is that it was designed to make it easy to connect workstations together. How appropriate, huh? Suddenly everyone with a workstation had direct access to ARPAnet. Uh oh — everyone?

Log Jam — Eighties Style

By the late 1980s, ARPAnet was overwhelmed with university traffic. Along came the National Science Foundation (NSF), which decided to unfreeze the jam by going shopping for bigger, faster computers to serve as traffic controllers for the Net. Ten million dollars and five supercomputers later, things weren't much better — mainly, as the NSF folks will tell you, because of politics. The NSF did what any respectable organization that's caught between a rock and a hard place does — it started its *own* network.

NSFNet was bigger, faster, and easier to access than ARPAnet. Within ten years, in 1990, Grandpa ARPAnet shut down because of lack of use. NSFNet thrived, but because of the expense and complexity of maintaining the finicky supercomputers and the trend toward more powerful minicomputers, commercial Internet providers began to jump on the bandwagon. People realized that they could provide the on-ramp to the information superhighway, tweaked with dandy front-end graphics software, and make money doing it. Welcome to today's information superhighway — and watch for the billboards as you whiz by them.

The Transition Continues

Today, there are hundreds of commercial Internet providers. Each provider needs only a fast computer and a high-speed, high-quality connection to the Internet to be able to license its services. To show you how far we've come, you can now use a Macintosh or PC running Windows to set up your own Internet service . . . and a Mac is a lot less expensive than a $10 million supercomputer.

An Internet server was once a $15,000 to $50,000 behemoth. Today, any platform that has a powerful CPU and lots of RAM will do. Apple Computer, for example, now offers a Communication Bundle of ready-to-use software along with its lightning-speed Power Macintosh server line. A number of other computers can be used as Internet servers as well. In general, you can do up the whole thing for about $6,500.

If the number of people signing on to the Internet continued to grow at its current rate, every person on the planet would be on the Internet by the year 2003.

History in the Making

In December 1991, the president signed the House-Senate compromise version of S. 272, the *High-Performance Computing Act of 1991*. The bill provides for a coordinated federal program to ensure continued U.S. leadership in high-performance computing, and it includes the establishment of a high-capacity and high-speed National Research and Education Network (NREN).

What does all of this mean for education? NREN includes some interesting provisions that relate directly to what could happen in the classroom. They include the following:

- Training researchers, educators, and students in high-performance computing
- Increasing access by educators and students to high-performance computing resources
- Promoting the further development of an information infrastructure of databases, services, access mechanisms, and research facilities that are available for use through the network
- Stimulating research on software technology
- Promoting the more rapid development and wider distribution of computer software tools and applications software
- Accelerating the development of computing systems and subsystems
- Investing in basic research and education and promoting the inclusion of high-performance computing in educational institutions at all levels
- Promoting greater collaboration among the government, federal laboratories, industry, high-performance computing centers, and universities
- Improving the interagency planning and coordination of federal research and development on high-performance computing, and maximizing the effectiveness of the federal government's high-performance computing efforts

The NREN will provide users with appropriate access to high-performance computing systems, electronic information resources, other research facilities, and libraries. The Network will provide access, to the extent practicable, to electronic information resources that are maintained by libraries, research facilities, publishers, and affiliated organizations.

What taking advantage of the NREN will cost schools and universities is still in question, but one thing's for sure: The information superhighway is going to get bigger and easier to use. However, the task of taming the zillion-headed monster and steering it toward enhancing and enriching what goes on in the classroom will be up to us as educators.

Get your own copy of the NREN via FTP at `gopher.es.net:70` and look for `bill-final.txt` (located in `/pub/nren/nren-bill-final.txt`). For information on how to ftp using Fetch or other FTP programs included on your *Internet For Teachers* disc, see Chapter 16.

What might the Internet look like in ten years? Ask your students to examine the NREN proposal and write an editorial describing why the classroom of the future should have access to the Net and what changes they'd like to see to make the Internet more student-friendly.

From Roots to Rabbit Ears?

Will the Internet ever emerge as a way-cool resource in every classroom? If it does, who'll bring it to schools? Telephone companies and cable television providers are working furiously to bring the Internet to your home through a variety of channels — for a fee, of course.

Yep, you'll soon be able to log onto your favorite online service or jump right into the Net through your television. (Like we need yet *another* reason to spend time in front of the one-eyed entertainment monster!?!) The real trick is figuring out when using the Net makes more sense than using a more traditional resource, such as your local library. If teachers can find compelling reasons for the Internet to be in every classroom, it'll come. We can be very persuasive at times.

But will the Net come to classrooms? Remember when the first personal computer showed up in your school? I remember huddling around the boxes as the miraculous Apple IIe computer, in all its beigeness, was lifted out and placed on the table. Everyone sort of stared. Plugging the thing in was a cinch. Then we turned it on, heard our first Apple-beep, and saw this:

```
]
```

or, if certain planets were aligned, this:

```
*
```

We've come a long way from the AppleSoft prompt. What helped make those first less-than-friendly personal computers successful in classrooms? Well, *you* did.

Technology flashback!

It's flashback time. Some of you can remember a time years ago when you first attempted to sign onto a local bulletin board service (BBS). You know, back in the dark ages when software wasn't smart and computers were just beginning to be friendly? You sat down at your Apple II or PC AT and realized that plugging in the modem and starting the software program was only the beginning. You had to learn a whole new vocabulary that included intimidating techno-weenie words such as *stop bits, parity, baud rate,* and *error correction.*

You'll be very happy to know that, for the most part, life in cyberspace is much easier now. Most software and hardware communicate well enough to do many tasks that made beginning BBS users crazy. Online services now provide "starter kits" that are preconfigured to make your first online experience successful. Recently, other independent Internet service providers have begun to ship "turn key" sign-on kits to new Internet users. In most cases, you sign on to the service, and all the software you need is there for the taking.

Now if they would just introduce a VCR that sets its own clock. . . .

—12 : 00 : 00—

In January 1996, more than 120 peer-reviewed scholarly journals were published electronically on the Internet.

The fact that you're reading this book means that you want to join the ranks of educators who are willing to explore new ways to use technology in the classroom. Plenty of other educators like you want to know more about harnessing the power of telecommunications for teaching and learning. For most teachers, just getting access to a telephone is a hassle, so you might easily think that the Internet is an impossible goal. Fear not, however, because thousands of creative educators now exchange ideas via e-mail and zip through the World Wide Web (WWW).

The most popular use of the Internet, by far, is sending and receiving e-mail. In a study conducted in early 1996, 65 percent of those people using the Net reported using it primarily for e-mail.

If I had to get out the crystal ball, I'd say that you can expect the Internet to be in most classrooms within five years — a likely spin-off of the mother lode of profit: Internet in the home. But then, maybe the classroom of the future will be at home. Or will it? Hmmm . . . makes my brain hurt just to think about it.

Chapter 3

Why Use the Internet in Schools?

In This Chapter

- Evaluating the Internet
- Six great reasons to get your class on the information superhighway
- Convincing your school board and administration
- Going to bat for the Internet

Is the Internet just another passing fad in that huge closet full of plug-in tools that we call *educational technology?* I don't think so. People said the same thing about calculators and computers not too long ago. Those tools are still around. The real question may be: Will educators be able to understand the implications of instant access to billions of bits of information in the classroom? Will anyone?

Well, we educators are a pretty shrewd bunch. We've managed to squeeze success from a lot of new initiatives and educational innovations — some that survived the test of time, and some that didn't. You know the list: open classrooms, outcome-based education, new math, standardized testing, and, yes, ballpoint pens, calculators, and computers.

Get ready to adjust your sails. The winds of the communication age are blowing. It's up to us to grab the video-game generation by the brains and use the Internet to give them something to think about.

The Internet: What Good Is It?

Remember the movie *Shane*? In one scene, Shane takes out his gun and does some fancy shooting, and then when he realizes that his greatest admirer, a young, impressionable lad, is beginning to think that guns are fun, he zaps the kid with a great lesson. He explains that a gun is just a *tool*. By itself it's neither bad nor good. The person who *uses* a gun is the one who determines whether the gun is good or bad. Don't you love those rare nuggets of wisdom in the movies?

The Internet, like many other tools at our disposal, is just a tool. It's a powerful tool, though, which offers students opportunities.

Good Internet tool users have the opportunity to do the following:

- Exchange information via global communication links
- Retrieve information "just in time" for use in the classroom (or anywhere else)
- Add to the body of human knowledge (Whoa! Think about the potential of being able to publish instantly to millions of people. Kinda gives you chills, doesn't it?)
- Have a lot of fun browsing the ideas, thoughts, and creations of others

In case you need specific education-related reasons to jump onto the information superhighway, here they are.

Six Great Reasons to Get Your Class on the Information Superhighway

This tool we call the Internet is not the single most important tool that will bring about educational reform . . . or is it? I learned everything I know about the Internet from other people. Whether I'm chatting electronically with other educators in the Electronic Schoolhouse on America Online, reading *The Internet For Dummies,* or scanning course outlines for an electronically delivered "Introduction to the Internet" course, I find new information almost daily. The following six reasons for logging onto the Net come from many conversations, both electronic and face to face, with people like you who are pondering the Net's possibilities.

The Internet presents real-world examples of integrated knowledge

The Internet provides a great deal of electronic information that's organized in different ways and represents many different topics. As students explore Internet resources, they'll discover how the information they're accessing fits into real life. They'll see that the people working at the Center for Disease Control and Prevention in Atlanta maintain medical databases as well as information about landforms and climate (science meets geography). They'll notice as they scan the files at NASA's Gopher site that its libraries are packed with technical writing that describes the design and specifications of the latest shuttle payloads (writing meets mathematics). Later, you might even challenge your students to create their own World Wide Web (WWW) page, giving them an opportunity to link resources that they believe are useful and important. The Internet is a place where electronic tools can help form the link between learning and life.

The Internet facilitates collaborative learning

You will soon discover that one of the most efficient ways for your students to use and explore the resources available on the Internet is through project-centered activities for small groups. The simple fact is that the Internet is so big and offers so many resources that teamwork makes a huge positive difference in the quality of the outcome of any Internet search.

Send four groups of students to separate Internet connections to search for information about any subject; they'll all come back with different information from different sources, written with different biases, for different audiences, and with differing levels of credibility. Bring those four groups back together and ask them one question to get the collaboration going: "What is the best (or most useful) information and why?"

Of course, there's that "excited learners are contagious" thing that we educators all understand. Put one student on the Net and watch how many others flock around. Imagine the possibilities!

The Internet offers opportunities for telementoring

Global communication means potentially connecting lots of people, each of whom has lots of ideas. This abundance of ideas translates into lots of opportunities to learn from others. I look back and marvel at those special teachers who have helped me over the rough spots in education, people such as the gifted and caring Mrs. McCue who guided me through student teaching. I think about the fact that there are probably many Mrs. McCues, just waiting to teach us all something. You can harness the power of the Internet for teaching, for learning, and even for some curbside psychiatry when the going gets rough.

The Internet is all about communicating

Editing a Supreme Court decision and posting it to the Internet takes about eight hours. Finding it takes about eight seconds. The Internet represents a communication opportunity that will probably have a profound impact on everything from politics to potato farming. Posting a message on the Internet and getting replies from Russia is cool. Logging onto the Internet and chatting live with anthropologists who are exploring Mayan ruins is an amazing experience. Students telecommunicating with their peers *no matter where in the world they live* is about as exciting a prospect as I can imagine.

The Internet can cater to different learners in different ways

Like a good library, the Internet has print, sound, photograph, and video resources. The kind of information that students choose to access and the way they choose to access it is often as revealing about the students' capabilities as the quality of the information they collect. The Internet offers opportunities to browse freely or to target information with excruciating precision. You'll find that everyone from the reluctant learner to the bookworm can find something of interest on the Net. It's up to us, of course, to help them explore their interests and channel their efforts toward furthering their educational goals. With sufficient goals and direction, virtually every student can experience success.

The Internet is a culturally, racially, physically, sexually blind medium

The first time I used electronic mail with my students, I realized that communication through the Internet was *blind.* After several exchanges of creative writing during a project designed with a teacher friend from Connecticut, my students discovered that they had been writing to other students who were from two to five grade levels ahead of them. Suddenly, they realized that they could communicate effectively with the "big kids." You should have seen the look on the middle-schoolers' faces when they saw a class picture from the Connecticut high school (and vice versa!).

The Internet is blind to many things. On some online services, the most popular online personalities have physical disabilities. Nobody knows. It doesn't seem to matter. It's pure communication.

The downside is that because much of communication is nonverbal — for example, observing facial features, silly grins and all — you can lose something in the translation. But that makes the challenge even sweeter.

That's the big six! You can surely come up with more reasons as you think about the role the Internet might play in your classroom.

What's the next step? Get busy and convince the money brokers that you need this Internet tool in your classroom. Read on!

Strategies for Convincing Your Board or Administration

A science teacher friend of mine decided that setting up a cage and raising white mice in his classroom would be a great idea. He did his homework and figured out the cost, drew up some sample lesson plans, and went to the principal for permission. At first, the principal was less than enthusiastic. After all, mice are hairy and can carry disease. They're messy (the custodians, rulers of the school, would not like that!), and they might escape and terrorize the faculty. Mr. Science plugged on, driven by the enthusiasm of a possessed mad-scientist.

Somehow, Mr. Science convinced the principal that the risk was worth taking, and two weeks later, the classroom had two new residents. Then something happened. Students began, on their own, to ask questions and express a desire to learn more about their classroom neighbors. Some went to the library to find out more about the classroom critters; others drew pictures, asked questions, and smuggled food back from the school cafeteria. Mr. Science's lessons were riveting. Other teachers came to visit. Parents began to call the school and write notes about how glad they were that the principal and teacher had allowed the mice to visit the classroom.

Two years later, the white mouse cage had grown into a condominium, and George and Gracie, the mice, had quite a few roommates. Lots, if you count the iguana, Goliath; the hamsters, Moe, Larry, and Curly; and all the rest of the zoo. Other teachers caught on, too, and the synergy that was created made for better lesson plans that kept the critters very busy.

Introducing the Internet to your administration and into the classroom isn't that different from Mr. Science's adventure.

The reason this project was so successful is that the teacher

- Had an idea
- Planned well
- Was enthusiastic
- Started small
- Expanded on the original idea

In the beginning, be sure to take the time to look at the technology and see whether it makes sense to *you*. The Internet has gotten (more than?) its fair share of criticism, much of it by short-sighted people who see it as a diversion instead of an information-rich environment. Just as some activities are best carried out with pencil and paper, perhaps the Net is the best way to accomplish some of the tasks that you and your students will attempt.

Next, think about how you and your students can use the Internet. Will it enhance instruction? Can it be a useful reference tool? Will it be a learning center or a full-time classroom resource?

Finally, think about how you will begin. Will you start with an e-mail exchange or with a search for information on your classroom's latest addition to the critter farm? Armed with a few simple plans and a bit of technical expertise to back it up, you're well on your way.

Nothin' but Net?

These days, it's not really difficult to convince your principal or district technology coordinator that networking is a great idea. The media storm surrounding the Internet has raised the consciousness of even the most Luddite educator. But in our zest to "get wired," it is easy for us to create unreasonable expectations about what teaching and learning will be like when all the wiring is finally complete.

Grab a piece of chalk at your next faculty meeting and run to the chalkboard. In your best D'Nealian, write the words "Wired for What?" and stand back. This question is a fundamental one that will haunt everyone after the fury of wire-pulling gives way to the realities of the classroom. See if anyone can really answer the question.

Here's how several educators and administrators answered the question in a recent discussion I had in conjunction with the incredible Classroom Connect conference (`www.classroom.net`). When I asked each of them to state a feature and a benefit to using the Internet in the classroom, here's what they cooked up.

Feature	***Benefit(s)***
Increased communication	Increased global awareness, more sharing of ideas, better communication with our "customers" (students and their parents)
Richer information sources	Access to more current information sources, ability to quickly and efficiently collect and compare information from multiple sources
Less isolation in the classroom	Access to people, places, and things that would otherwise be inaccessible

Feature	*Benefit(s)*
Opportunity to collaborate	Two-way medium that makes collaboration simpler, faster, and more fun
Changes teaching and learning	Helps educators, students, administrators, and everyone else review their role in light of the other benefits mentioned above and offers everyone the opportunity for a high-interest, high-content learning environment (the most powerful reason!)

Working through a "wired for what" exercise with your faculty/staff/peers is a great way to ensure that everyone understands the promises, and limitations, of this amazing medium. Take the time to answer these tough questions now, before the wire-jockeys leave town, and you and your students will reap the rewards well into the future.

Going to Bat for the Internet

The test-drive is what sells the Ferrari — at least that's what those folks who have megabucks tell me. The Internet is no different.

Set up an Internet test-drive for your administration and board members. Take advantage of one or more of the promotions from online services that offer a free hour online, or arrange to use the Internet account of someone who has a connection that enables you to use graphics-based software. (See Chapter 4 for your options for an Internet connection.) Take the crowd on a little scavenger hunt, showing resources along the way.

One more touch, just so you'll remember. Whip out Print Shop and print a banner that says, "Curriculum drives the use of technology, not vice versa." Focus your presentation on how you can use the Internet's resources in your media center and classroom, not on how to access the resources. Avoid jargon. Smile (especially at your principal, board member, and superintendent!).

Here's a dandy statistic that you can use in your Internet presentation: As of early 1995, more than 2,000 schools regularly published information to the Internet in the form of a home page on the World Wide Web. A *home page* is an electronic Internet document that presents information and gives the user options for jumping to other information resources that the author deems to be interesting or useful. (See Chapter 15 for more information about the Web.)

The amount of money spent on advertising on the Internet in 1995 is estimated at $33,000,000.

It's reality time. Textbooks become outdated before they are published. Budgets for educational materials continue to be thin. Libraries and media centers can't keep up with the continued flow of new information. Can your school afford *not* to investigate the Internet as a source for educational content?

Part II
Getting Wired

"He should be all right now. I made him spend two and a half hours on a 'prisoners' chat line."

In this part . . .

In this part, you learn what kind of hardware, software, and connections you need to begin your adventure on the Internet. I also discuss your connection options, some advantages and disadvantages of using popular online services as your Internet on-ramp, cool tools for traveling the Internet, and (last but not least) the responsibility that you and your students hold as members of the telecommunication community.

If you've already connected to the Internet, jump to Part III, but be sure to check out the chapter in this section about Internet responsibility.

Chapter 4
Getting Started

In This Chapter

- Building an Internet shopping list
- Selecting the right hardware
- Choosing your gateway to the Net
- Getting with the programs!
- A modem is a modem is a modem
- Searching for a phone line
- Budgeting for Internet access
- Getting your Macintosh or Windows PC ready for connection to the Net
- Installing Netscape Navigator

You can relax. You're about to realize that collecting only five simple things can get you on your way to Internet access. The good news is that between the software that accompanies this book and the hardware that's already in your school, you probably have 90 percent of what you need to be connected to the Internet.

In this chapter, you'll find the "five easy pieces" you need to begin surfing the Internet, a few ideas about budgeting for telecommunications, and the low-down on what you need to do to get your computer ready for logging onto the Net for the first time.

What Do I Need?

This section describes exactly what you need to make an Internet connection. First, look at this basic diagram that shows the "big five" items you need: hardware, software, a modem, a phone line, and an Internet account.

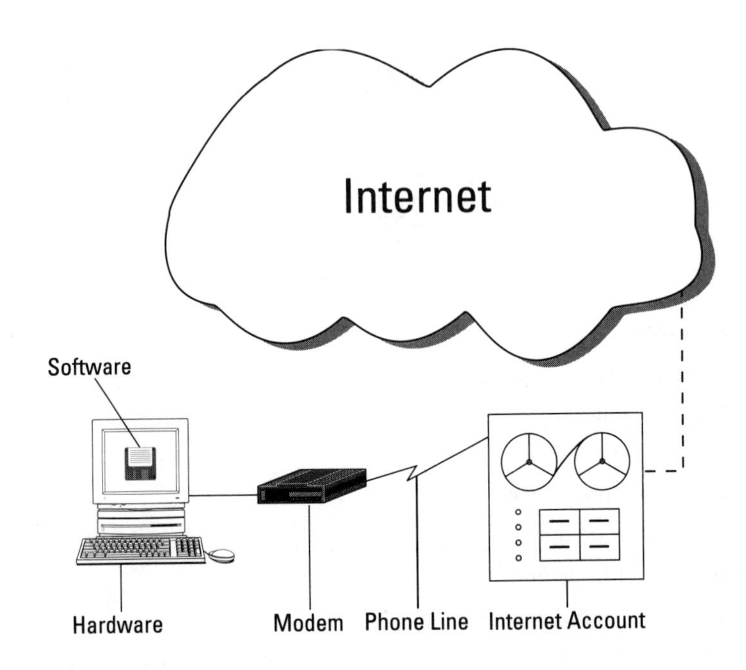

You probably already have a computer and a modem. The software provided with this book will get you well on your way to surfing the Net, and you'll find step-by-step instructions for getting lots of other free tools or tools for other operating systems. All that's left is a phone line (groan) and an Internet account. Take a look at each section that follows to see how to build the vehicle for your first trip on the information superhighway.

All those chips and no place to go

In March of 1996, nearly 4 million computers were connected to the Internet. They ranged from Amigas to Apples, IBMs to Dells, Sun workstations to dumb terminals, mainframes to minis. Some of these machines (usually, but not always, big ones) are service providers (*hosts*), and some are regular desktop computers (*clients*) that extract information from the host computers.

The great news is that you can use just about any computer to connect to the Internet. The only caveat is that you have to have enough memory (RAM) to unpack large files or to process and view pictures that you download.

If you're using a Macintosh or a PC that's running Windows, I suggest 8MB (megabytes) of RAM. (RAM memory is the electronic holding area where your programs and documents live while your computer is turned on.) Having more RAM enables you to work more quickly and efficiently as you process the information that you've retrieved from the Net.

The moral of this story? You can never have too much RAM or too large a hard drive. Remember when you thought you could *never* fill a 5 1/4-inch floppy? Now I'm wrestling with where to put the 3 gigabytes of data that I use on a regular basis.

About passwords

Whether you're using an online service, a university network, or an Internet service provider, you should *never*, repeat, *never* give your password to anyone else. It can be just as valuable (and as potentially dangerous) as your PIN number for your automatic bank teller machine. Here are a few tips for protecting your password:

- Change your password regularly: The majority of students will respect your right to keep your password private. However, some students will make it their life's quest to discover your password. Foil them by changing it regularly. And please, *don't* write it down under the blotter on your desk, tape it to the bottom of your keyboard, or write it on the corner of your grade book. They'll look there. If you have a really rotten memory, just write it down and stick it in your wallet or purse. But, just to be safe, split the password on two tiny pieces of paper.
- Use a combination of alphabetical and numeric characters: You'll be tempted to use the principal's name or the initials of the school as a password — don't. That's the first thing someone trying to gain unauthorized access to your account will try. Make up a password that combines letters and numbers that have some meaning to you but not to others. Try the number of years you've been a teacher and the first and last letters of your two sisters' names, for example (15SCLW).
- Look over your shoulder before typing your password: Just as teachers have eyes in the back of their heads, students have razor-sharp vision when it comes to getting their teacher's password. Most programs show your password as ••••••••• when you enter it so it's protected from prying eyes, but remember, students can see your fingers on the keyboard, too.
- Resist the temptation to use an autologin program: Autologin settings in your software enable you to access the Internet with a simple mouse click, *without* having to remember the password. With autologin, you pre-enter your password and save it to disk. This method is very handy when you're in a hurry, but it's also a cinch for others to use when they want unauthorized access to your account. I'd say that you should use autologin *only* if you, or members of your family, are the *only* users of your computer *and* unauthorized users are never anywhere around your computer. (In other words, it's the computer that's in your home or in some other very controlled environment.)

Now, I know this must seem like overkill, but I've seen what happened when a student got hold of a commercial online account and used more than 100 hours in a week. A word to the wise . . .

If you're in the process of making a decision about what computer to use in your classroom and you want an awesome resource, check out *Macs For Teachers,* by my good IDG Books buddy and teacher friend Michelle Robinette, or *PCs For Teachers,* by Pam Toliver (both published by IDG Books Worldwide, Inc.). Both are fact-filled, and you'll laugh your way to becoming the computer guru in your school.

Your gateway to the Net

Perhaps the most important choice you'll make is which Internet provider to use. The provider supplies your gateway to the Internet and your very own Internet e-mail address. (More and more people are putting their e-mail addresses on their business cards. You're a professional — you should have a business card too. Get one and put your e-mail address on it.)

How you access the Internet determines, in large part, what resources you have access to, as well as whether you operate from a graphical interface or suffer from command-prompt disease. You need to ask some essential questions before you select a provider. They are so important that I've devoted an entire chapter to them. Check out Chapter 6.

Get with the program

The software that you need for Internet access depends on how you're connected. If you get connected via an online service, all the software you need comes on the disk you'll get in the mail with your subscription kit. Users of university networks or UNIX shell accounts can use off-the-shelf telecommunication packages such as Microphone (Macintosh) or CrossTalk (DOS/Windows) to access host-based programs.

If you connect via an Internet service provider, most providers send you a disk that's preconfigured with all the necessary software when you subscribe. Simply install the programs on your computer, and you're on your way!

If your information provider doesn't send you any software, you're in luck. Simply use the programs that are on the CD in the back of this book. (See Appendix D for details about the CD.) You find information about how to get other useful software and software updates throughout this book. (See "Getting Your Computer Ready for Connection to the Net," later in this chapter.)

A modem is a modem is a modem

A *modem* is the hardware device that translates the electronic signal from your computer into a form that's transmittable over a telephone line. (Modem stands for *modulator-demodulator,* in case anyone asks in the teacher's lounge.)

Modems generally come with two cables, one to connect to the serial or com port on your computer; the other, a standard telephone cable, to connect to your telephone wall jack.

You have only two decisions to make when you purchase a modem:

- Do you want an internal or external modem?
- How fast do you want to travel the information superhighway?

When you think about internal and external modems, think about the future. Your choice may depend on whether you're a nomad or a settled soul. If you're likely to purchase a new computer within the next year or two or will need to use the modem somewhere other than with your computer, consider an external modem. If you're using a laptop or a computer that'll be in a place where desktop space is limited, an internal modem will do.

One neat thing about external modems is that the only real difference in modems for Macs and PCs is the cable that runs from the computer to the modem, and you can change that. So purchasing an external modem ensures that you'll be able to switch platforms should the "gotta buy a new computer bug" hit you anytime soon.

Because the whole point of owning a modem is to move data back and forth through the telephone lines, the faster you can move that data, the better. When shopping for a modem, always get the fastest modem you can afford. Modem speeds are expressed as *baud rate,* with numbers such as 2400, 9600, 14.4 (14,400), 28.8 (28,800), and 33.6 (33,600) *bps* (bits per second).

The industry standard now is 28.8 (28,800 bps) but it's quickly creeping up to the next level. If you're buying now, don't settle for less than a 28.8 Kbps modem.

Make sure the modem is Hayes compatible. The folks at Hayes pretty much invented the modem as we know it today and established a standard for how modems talk to one another. Most every modem you purchase today bears a "Hayes compatible" label.

The Hayes Modem Communications Companion (published by IDG Books) is a comprehensive, easy-to-understand computer communications guide. Hayes also has some terrific deals for educators purchasing a modem. For information, call the Hayes fax info line at 800-429-3739 and request document #801.

You knew there was a catch!

Teachers have chalk. Teachers have textbooks. Teachers do not have telephones. Even as we approach the year 2000, teachers are one of the few professionals without easy access to a basic communication tool — the telephone. Some schools built by forward-thinking school districts have a telephone in every room. Hooray for that!

If there is any catch in getting hooked up to the Internet, it's getting easy access to the phone line. There are basically two reasons for this problem:

- Phones cost money to install.
- Phones cost money to maintain.

It's that money thing again. Luckily, there are ways to save money and still get your phone line. Here's how.

Your school probably has two kinds of phone lines: integrated and dedicated. Most schools that are large enough to have more than a couple of lines have signed contracts with telephone companies to install *integrated* custom phone systems that give you everything from intercoms to voice mail. Although this kind of system has some great features, it may present a problem for telecommunications.

The problem with integrated systems is that along with your phone call, your telephone handset sends signals through an electronic switchbox before your call exits the building into the real world. Because you're dialing out with a modem rather than with an especially configured handset, sometimes the modem has difficulty getting a dial tone. (If you have to dial 8 or 9 to get an outside line, you may have an integrated phone system.) Unless your phone system is configured specifically for modem communications, dead air is all you'll hear when your modem attempts to connect. The answer is to either have the phone company make an adjustment for one or more of your current lines or get a dedicated phone line.

A *dedicated* phone line is a standard phone line like the one in your home. (The phone company calls it *POTS* for *plain old telephone service* — really!) It goes straight from any telephone to a junction box that transmits the signal, unchanged, to the lines outside your building. In general, if you can plug a telephone from home into a jack and it works, a modem will work there too. Dedicated phone lines are the best bet for schools, especially because you don't have to share the line with 28 other teachers who are trying to call to let Johnny's parents know how well he's doing in school.

Your Internet phone line needs to be convenient if you're going to integrate it into the classroom. You need to locate it in the media center, computer lab, or, in the best case, in your classroom.

One way to save money on phone lines is to install *extension* lines. One dedicated line to the media center can be split and run to classrooms. The downside? Only one user can dial out at a time. Someone will always be waiting.

Here's a tip for avoiding the "I'm on the phone" problem. Visit your local electronics store and pick up a phone-line-in-use light for each extension. They're under $20 and well worth the money.

If you want to investigate Internet connections at faster than dial-up speeds, you have several options. Your school can pay for the installation of a super fast line, called a *T-1* or *T-3 line,* or an almost-as-fast 56K line (ISDN), if you have the money. (Super fast lines are sometimes known as a *leased line* because you pay a premium to lease the line from the phone company.) You'll need a T-1 or T-3 line if you want to become *your own* Internet service provider (that is, have a *direct,* 24-hour, hard-wired connection to the Net).

Budgeting for Telecommunications

How much you need to budget for telecommunications depends, obviously, on the deal that you strike with your service provider. If you're connecting to the Internet through an online service such as America Online or CompuServe, you'll pay a bit more for the all-in-one interface. If you purchase time through an Internet service provider, you'll have to consider how much time you'll use each month or get an unlimited time account. If your school is in a rural area, you may also have to contend with long-distance charges from the school to the nearest service provider.

The best way to estimate your budget costs is to try to find a school that's already connected and ask how much they spend. In my school system, one school that's connected through a PPP account to an Internet provider pays $60.00 per month for a dedicated phone line and $20.00 per month for unlimited access time for one account.

If there are large service providers in your area, you may be able to wrangle an account for free because the account is for a school. See Chapter 6 for strategies for dealing with an Internet service provider.

Commercial online service access can range from $15 to more than $80 per month, depending on usage and the deal you get when you sign up. Shop carefully!

If your school chooses to get a direct connect and purchase a leased (high-speed) line, expect monthly charges to top $300 (down from almost $1,000 at the time of the first edition of this book!). Remember, however, that with a leased line, many users can use the same single line to connect simultaneously, so the cost per user may actually be less expensive.

Getting Your Computer Ready for Connection to the Net

Before your personal computer can "speak" to the Internet, it needs to have access to the programs that make that connection. On the Macintosh, you need two programs to make the connection: MacTCP or Open Transport and either MacPPP, MacSLIP, INTERSLIP, or an equivalent. On a Windows machine, the program you need is WinSLIP. In the following sections, I outline, step-by-step, how to get your computer online. Doing so is not really difficult, only a couple of steps on your Mac and only a few more on your Windows PC. Well, then again, it's easier than re-doing your classroom bulletin board — and it takes far fewer steps.

CyberMacintosh

If you're a Macintosh owner, you're in luck. Most of what you need to connect to the Net is built right into your machines. Assuming that you've got an Internet service provider, all you need to do is enter some information into a program called MacTCP (or TCP/IP if you've got a Mac running System 7.5.2 or up) and spend a minute or two entering some information into the software that controls your access, called MacPPP or MacSLIP.

MacTCP is an extension that enables your Macintosh to speak the language of the Net: TCP/IP. MacPPP and MacSLIP are the control panels that enable TCP/IP to work over a serial connection (as with modems).

Here's a screen shot of MacTCP. You get the IP Address from your Internet provider. Clicking the More button reveals lots more blanks to fill in.

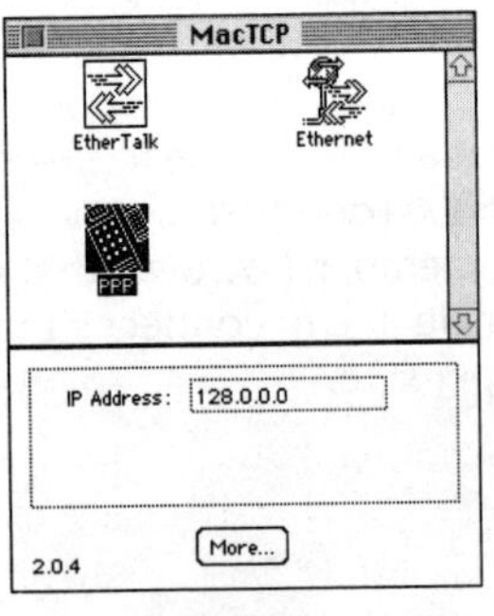

MacTCP

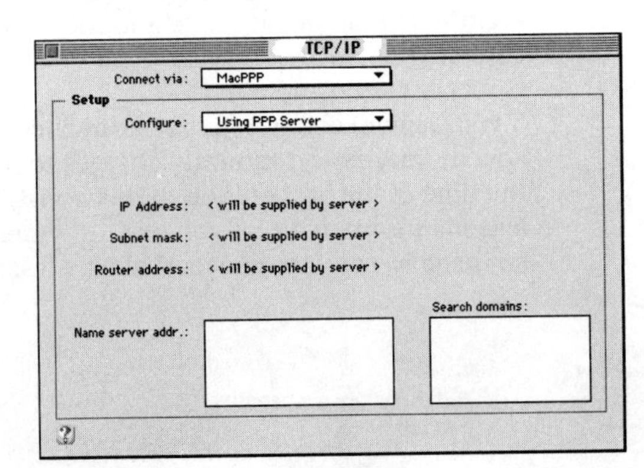

TCP/IP

The control panel (MacPPP, MacSLIP, or the equivalent) is where the specific information about the computer that you're connecting to is stored. The following figure shows the MacPPP control panel configured for an internal modem connected to an Internet service provider called Mindspring.

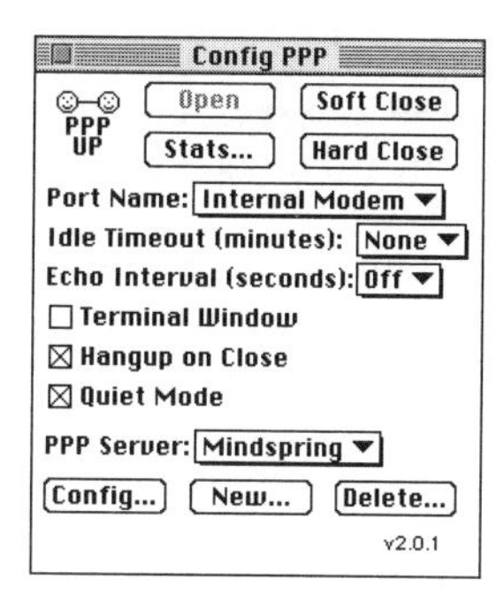

If you're connecting to the Internet via most information providers or through a local area network, these programs will probably come to you preconfigured. (Ask your system administrator to give you a hand.) All you have to do is drag them into your Control Panel's folder on your Macintosh hard drive.

You don't need MacTCP or a driver if you're connecting to the Internet through an online service such as CompuServe or America Online — those things are built into the front-end software.

Window(s) on the Net

In order to access the Net with a PC running Windows, you need two pieces of software: SLIP or PPP software and TCP/IP software. The TCP/IP software helps your computer speak the language of the Internet, while the PPP or WinSLIP software manages the pipeline.

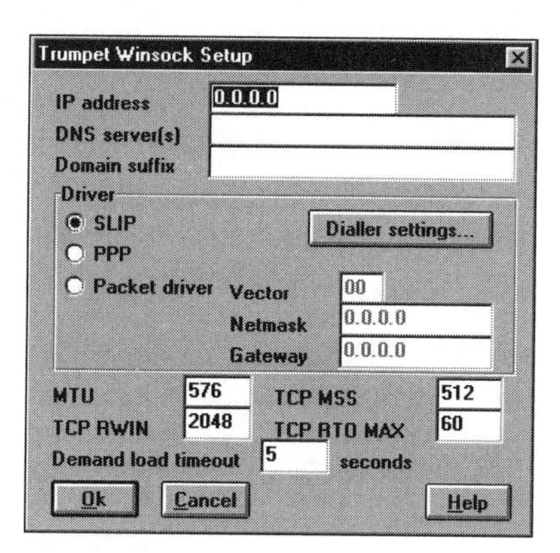

If you have Windows 95 or OS/2, what you need may be already built-in. If you're using MS/DOS or Windows 3.*x*, you need to get shareware or commercial software to run TCP/IP. Luckily, most Internet providers give you all you need when you sign up. If not, grab a copy of *The Internet For Windows For Dummies* Starter Kit (published by IDG Books Worldwide, Inc.), and you'll be on your way!

You don't need WinSLIP if you're connecting to the Internet through an online service such as CompuServe, America Online, or MSN — those things are usually built into the front-end software.

To make your life even easier, we've included the configuration tools you need for both Macs and Windows in a special Internet sign-on kit from AT&T WorldNet Service. Just insert the CD and follow the configuration instructions on the screen!

What next?

Okay, you've got your SLIPs and PPPs in order. Now here's a checklist of items you need to get from your service provider so that you can fill in all the blanks in your MacTCP and MacPPP/MacSLIP or WinSLIP software. (I've put some samples in parentheses so you know what to look for.)

If your software comes preconfigured, skip all this!

Forget your sock(et)s?

Way back in 1991 (that's a hundred years in PC terms), a bunch of networking vendors got together and decided they were tired of the fact that each of them was writing toward a different networking standard. So they got together and came up with a common set of functions for a typical Windows Internet application. Every Internet software vendor agreed to support this new progeny they called "Windows Sockets," or "WinSock" for short. (It's called sockets because it began life as a UNIX package and that's the design the Windows program was based on.)

What does all this mean to you? In theory, it means that Windows Internet applications like Netscape Navigator and Microsoft Explorer work on your PC without too many additional software tweaks. In practice, stick to the "big guys" (like Netscape, Spyglass Mosaic, and Internet Explorer) and you won't be disappointed. The most popular "sockets" software for Windows is called Trumpet WinSock. It's shareware (from Tasmania, no less), and most ISPs will give you a copy of the program when you open an account.

Internet Information Checklist

1. Your Internet provider address: (it'll look something like this: 123.123.78.90) ______

   (This number is sometimes called a *dotted quad.* Is that techno-speak or what?)

2. Your user name (login name): (`flintstone`) ______
3. Your password: (letters and/or numbers) ______
4. Your broadcast address: (`123.123.255.255`) ______
5. Your domain name: (`apple.com`) ______
6. Your e-mail address: (`flintstone@apple.com`) ______
7. Dial up phone number(s): ______
8. Mailserver name (or POP server or SMTP server): (`bedrock.com`) ______
9. News host server name (or NNTP server): (`nntp.bedrock.com`) ______
10. Domain name server: (`234.00.123.0`) ______
11. Subnet mask: (`255.255.0.0`) ______
12. Account type (SLIP, CSLIP, PPP, shell): ______
13. Port settings (baud rate, com/serial port #): ______
14. Domain suffix: (`bedrock.com`) ______
15. Ph server (not every service has one): (`bedrock.com`) ______
16. Internet provider troubleshooting phone number: ______
17. Software tools available with your account: ______

Installing Netscape Navigator

All that's left to do is to install your Web browser (a tool you can use to access the Internet), and you're off and running!

Netscape Navigator is the browser tool of choice these days. You've got a couple of options for using Navigator. A special version of Navigator for Mac and Windows PCs is hidden inside the AT&T WorldNet Service sign-on kit on your *Internet For Teachers* CD — it's designed specifically for use with AT&T WorldNet Service. To use it, just insert the CD in your CD-ROM drive and follow the installation instructions on the screen.

If you already have a service provider who has supplied you with Navigator, or if you've downloaded a copy of the browser from the Internet, follow the next instructions for either Macs or Windows.

If you've got a Macintosh, locate the copy you downloaded or received from your ISP and double-click Install Netscape Navigator. Your Mac unpacks and installs all the necessary files. If you've got a PC running Windows, set your sights on the copy you've downloaded or received from your ISP and follow these steps:

1. **Create a directory called \NSINST**

   This directory is just temporary. From the Windows File Manager, choose File⇨Create⇨Directory. From Windows 95, use My Computer and choose File⇨New.

2. **Copy the Netscape distribution file (installer) into that directory.**

   The file's name begins with N16 (for Windows 3.*x*) or N32 (for Windows 95). Drag it to the directory in File Manager, My Computer, or Explorer.

3. **Run the program called SETUP.EXE**

   This file starts the installation process. SETUP.EXE asks you a bunch of questions, but the default answers for all of them are okay. Netscape is installed in a directory called \Netscape (unless you direct your computer to do otherwise).

Ready to Ride

The buggy's configured, and you're ready to coerce the horses into their first ride. Believe me, the configuration of the Internet is getting easier. In the early days of computing and the Internet, you needed many more programs and much more knowledge of the dreaded TCP/IP and other bedazzling acronyms to get logged on.

Computer manufacturers and the makers of operating system software have finally figured out that the Internet is just as important a basic tool as your Program Manager or Finder, so they're beginning to build in Net accessibility. Watch for a whole warehouse-full of easy-to-use, preconfigured tools for your television, backpack, and lawn chair to begin eating up even more of your precious leisure time. Hmmm . . . does that mean I can attend my next class reunion from my lawn chair on the Cancun coastline? (We can all dream, can't we?)

Chapter 5

Getting Connected: You've Got Options!

In This Chapter

- Choosing your Internet connection
- Speeding on the I-Way: direct connections
- Dialing for resources: dial-up connections
- Locating an information provider
- Finding funding for your Net connection

Choice is good. Whether you're choosing a vegetable in the school cafeteria — why do they always serve corn with pizza? — or a new style for the football team's jerseys — be sure to consult the student fashion police before trying that one — it's nice to have lots of options.

As with any other choice, you need to know the facts before you make a decision about the best way for your school to access the Internet. Doing some research can keep you from getting caught in the bog of administrative bureaucracy. The decision about how your school will connect to the Internet boils down to three things:

- **Money:** How much money does your school or district want to commit to an Internet connection now? In the future?
- **Speed:** How fast do you want to travel the superhighway? Is speed an issue?
- **Need:** What do you need, in terms of information, access, and support, both now and in the future?

Direct or Not?

The two ways to get connected to the Internet are by a *direct connection* or by a *dial-up connection*. These connection methods vary widely in cost, ease of access, and the amount of support needed to maintain the connection.

Before you read on, I'll go ahead and tell you that I've provided a table toward the end of the chapter that gets right to the heart of the matter. If you have only a minute before your technology committee meeting, read the table. Otherwise, read on for some hints, and hazards, that will help with your choice of connection to the Internet.

Go direct

In a *direct connection,* your computer or your local area network (LAN) is connected to the Internet all the time. To achieve a direct connection, your computer or LAN is connected to a magical box called a *router,* which carries a signal that has been translated from your computer's language into the official language of the Internet, TCP/IP (which stands for Transmission Control Protocol/Internet Protocol — just a term to throw around to impress your friends). The router is then connected via special high-speed telephone lines to the nearest Internet gateway, usually a university, research institution, or commercial Internet service provider (ISP).

Why choose a direct connection?

A direct connection has many benefits. Because you're always connected, the Internet becomes just another resource on your network. A direct connection is also very fast, so you don't have to wait for files to transfer, and your e-mail zips along faster than you can lick a stamp.

Another benefit is that a direct connection supports multiple users at the same time. This means that you and several other users in your school can gain access to the Internet over the same single high-speed line. Because you control the network, you can easily control which Internet resources are available to users. This feature is especially nice for restricting certain newsgroups or limiting those inevitable naughty-file transfers.

What's the bad news? Cost. Direct Internet connections cost big bucks in the short term but may save you money in the long run. You have to buy the router (which can cost several thousand dollars) and get the thing installed (more money). But the biggest cost is the installation and maintenance of the high-speed lines. These lines are priced according to the speed of the connection. A 56K (fast) ISDN connection costs much less than a T-1 or T-3 connection (very fast). Super-fast phone lines can cost from $200 to $1,000 or more per month to maintain.

Over the long haul, however, a direct connection may be the most cost-effective route for most schools. Not having bunches of phone lines saves some money. You're also not paying a service provider a monthly fee for each Internet account as you do with most dial-up accounts.

Also, don't forget to consider the potentially large hidden cost of a direct connection: support. With other types of connections, the Internet provider is responsible for troubleshooting the system. With a direct connection, you need a Net-savvy person to maintain the gateway, assign and maintain user accounts, and troubleshoot. Luckily, the technology is moving toward easier-to-manage and more trouble-free connections.

Take a good, hard look at this type of connection if you're looking at ten or more connections from your school or at some type of countywide or districtwide network. Think about what you'll need now and in the future.

With a direct connection, by the way, you can request your own *domain name*. The domain name is the part after the @ symbol in an Internet address, and it tells the receiver of your message where your computer is located. If you hail from Lexington High School, for example, your address could be

```
yourname@lexington.edu
```

The `edu` identifies the address as one for an educational institution. (For more information about domain names and addresses, see Chapter 10.)

Establishing a direct connection

Here are the general steps to take if your school decides to establish a direct connection to the Internet:

1. **Determine your school's needs.**

   How many concurrent users do you want to be able to support, and how fast do these connections need to be?

2. **Contact the operator of the nearest Internet gateway host.**

   Call a local university's computer center.

3. **Plan and design your Internet connection.**

   Get help from the university or from another school that has been through this procedure. Don't forget to think about how you'll handle the maintenance and support of equipment and Internet accounts.

4. **Apply for an IP address.**

   You need to fill out lots of forms; find out how from your university contact. Note that the university or your ISP can probably do this for you.

5. **Have an experienced person install the hardware and phone lines.**

   Companies such as Apple Computer now offer Internet server bundles that are very easy to assemble. (The company claims you can be up and running within minutes.) Nevertheless, you can never have enough gurus around for the tough parts.

6. **Set up your Internet gateway accounts, do some general housekeeping, and set up an acceptable use policy (see Chapter 9).**

   Surf's up!

Remember money, speed, and need? A direct connection to the Internet makes sense if you have a good size startup budget (including money for monthly lease fees), want the fastest available connection, and need to support many simultaneous users.

Dial it up

The second type of connection is a *dial-up connection*. In a dial-up connection, you use your computer to dial another computer or server where your account is established. That *host* computer is directly connected to the Internet. It's kind of a direct connect, once removed.

Dial-up connections can be made through a local bulletin board service (BBS), an Internet service provider (ISP), or a commercial online service (COS — I just made up that acronym because these acronyms are everywhere!).

A dial-up connection is great because it has a very low initial cost. You can use all the dandy graphical interface tools that directly connected users do, too. Dial-up connections are also very handy for home users and for users who are occasional surfers.

The downside is that because a dial-up connection uses POTS (plain old telephone service), it's slower than a direct connection. You can still whiz along at 14,400, 28,800, or 33,600 baud though, and that's plenty fast for most of us . . . for now.

Another problem that you'll occasionally run into with a dial-up service is a busy signal. Depending on the time of day, it can get mighty frustrating. You know the drill — 40 students sitting on the floor impatiently waiting for you to dial into the Net for a demonstration. You get a busy signal. Luckily, most service providers limit the number of subscribers based on a ratio of subscribers to phone lines. Check this ratio when you choose an ISP. (For more about wheeling and dealing with service providers, see Chapter 6.)

Because you are dialing into another computer, you may not have as much access control as you would in a direct-connection scenario. ISPs and BBSs and most of the online services offer some kind of parental control options.

Need another "pro" to balance the "cons"? With a dial-up connection you can rely on someone else (the service provider) to troubleshoot when things go wrong. Because you're not maintaining your own Internet server or gateway, those nightmares fall to someone else. Mighty convenient if you don't have time to teach six periods, grade papers, *and* manage a network node.

SLIP or PPP

Yep. Another couple of acronyms. These are pretty simple ones, though. I'll spare you the techie-talk and get right to the point.

If you're dialing into the Internet through an Internet service provider, you'll most likely be offered a choice of what *type* of dial-up account you want. Remember, choice is good if you're an informed decision maker. You can generally choose between a couple of kinds of accounts:

- SLIP accounts (Serial Line Internet Protocol accounts). CSLIP, compressed SLIP, is its close cousin.
- PPP accounts (Point to Point Protocol accounts).

A SLIP or PPP account is the next best thing to a direct connection. You can use all the software tools, such as World Wide Web (WWW) browsers and e-mail packages, very easily. You also can immediately store transferred files on your local hard drive. Other connections, such as those usually provided through a university dial-up account, first store files on the host computer — requiring an extra step to move them to your home or school computer.

SLIP and PPP accounts cost less, too. You can get one of these accounts for about $20 per month with unlimited online time. A bargain! Remember, you need one phone line for every account.

If you have a PC that is running Windows, you may want to consider a SLIP connection. You can run a dandy program called WinSock (Windows Sockets), a standard way for Windows programs to work with SLIP. WinSock applications, such as Trumpet and Chameleon, are great for Net-surfing. Several PPP options are available, too, many built into Windows 95.

If you have a Macintosh, you should choose a PPP account if you have a choice. Although the Mac will run both SLIP and PPP, PPP is a newer type of account that's generally more dependable and works best if you're using the WWW, which sends lots of graphics in short bursts.

What about an online service?

Commercial online services, such as America Online, CompuServe, MSN, and Prodigy, offer a dial-up option that's also attractive to schools. Not only do you get Internet access through a single, easy-to-use interface, but many other resources are available through the service itself. If you're a casual user or want a great way to learn to Net-surf, try an online service. They're easier to install, and, in general, easier to use than some other Internet software programs.

Another plus is the number of educational activities and resources that are available through the online services. America Online offers tons of online projects, ready-made for teachers, in its online Electronic Schoolhouse. The service also makes contacting other educators very easy. The Internet isn't so friendly.

What's the downside of a commercial online service? Here's that money thing again. Online services most often charge a flat monthly fee, and then the meter runs by the hour. If your students get lost in the Web or stuck in a Gopher hole, the meter could ring higher than the national debt. Luckily, a couple of the online providers enable users to prepay for blocks of time each month. After the limit is reached, the service shuts you out until the next month. Easy cost control.

As with the dial-up service, you may also get a busy signal from time to time. America Online runs more than 2,000,000 sessions a day. Not even Alexander Graham Bell could have prepared for that. Remember, too, that you need one phone line for each connection unless your online service provides for direct TCP/IP connection.

One glance at a newspaper and you no doubt see that lots and lots of the "big players" in the Internet industry are beginning to form alliances. CompuServe inked a deal with Microsoft. AOL's working with both Microsoft and the Netscape folks. Where will it end? Will McDonald's become an Internet provider? (Just think, drive-thru Internet!). We'll see.

Accessing the Internet via a university network or BBS

If you use a telecommunications program to dial into a BBS or university computer for Internet access, you have what's generally referred to as a *shell account.* When you dial in, you get only a computer letter (like a DOS prompt) or a symbol prompt such as % or >. You can do most anything other Net users can do, but the environment is strictly a text environment, and you have to deal with UNIX, a computer language that only a serious computer programmer could love.

This kind of dial-up access enables you to do FTP (file transfer), telnet, and search for documents with WAIS. By using a host-based program called Lynx, you can get a text front end to the graphically stunning World Wide Web. Using Lynx is kind of like going to a movie blindfolded. You get access to some information but miss all the online maps, diagrams, logos, and pictures. Of course, it's better than nothing!

In some cases, files you download get sent to your host computer and not directly to your own hard drive or floppy. Then you need to go through the extra step of transferring the file from the host computer to your computer at the end of your session. It's a bit confusing, but it works. (All Internet traffic used to work this way.)

Sometimes, local BBSs or university nets offer users a limited tier of Internet services, like e-mail, Gopher, and telnet. This kind of account (sometimes referred to as a *Limited shell* account) is the one that's the least expensive (often free) and most restricted. But, if the price is right . . .

Establishing a dial-up connection

Here are the general steps to take if your school decides to establish a dial-up connection to the Internet:

1. **Determine the needs of your school.**

   How many concurrent users do you want and how fast do these connections need to be?

2. **Install phone lines (one per dial-up connection needed).**
3. **Buy a modem and a computer (any computer and the fastest modem you can afford).**
4. **Get an Internet service provider, online service, or the number for an Internet-ready BBS.**

   They'll give you the details, such as the number you should dial and your account name.

5. **Build a collection of freeware, shareware, and commercial Internet tools (for SLIP or PPP accounts), or request front-end software from a commercial online service.**

   Note that many of these online service start-up kits come with a bit of free time for you to use in evaluating the service.

6. **Do some general housekeeping and set up an acceptable use policy (see Chapter 9).**
7. **Dial, and you're in!**

As of April 1996, almost 320,000 commercial domains (`.com` sites) were on the Net.

Decisions, Decisions

Is your head spinning yet? That's okay. A friend once spent two hours in a teacher supply store trying to figure out how to cover a classroom bulletin board with a colorful background and border for less than $5.00. She came out with a roll of decorative trim ($4.95) and 30 shopping bags (marked "ABC & Me") donated by a generous store clerk. (Don't laugh, it worked!) The decision about what type of connection your school needs may require just as much ingenuity, especially since your budget might be just as tight.

I'll sum up all the stuff for you. Table 8-1 compares dial-up accounts to direct accounts.

Table 8-1 Dial-Up versus Direct Internet Accounts

Factors	*Dial-Up Connection*	*Direct (dedicated) Connection*
Capacity	Limited to number of telephone lines	Unlimited
Short-term cost	Low	High
Long-term cost	High	Lower (the more users, the more savings)
Access control	Information provider allows limited control	You determine what resources users use
Speed	2400 to 33,600 baud	Faster than a speeding bullet (56 kilobytes and up)
General recommendations	Great for single-user (you) and limited school use (until you can afford a direct connection)	Great for schoolwide connection to the Internet

Locating an IP

After you decide what route to take to connect to the Net, you will need to contact an information provider. If you've decided to use an online service, all that's left for you to do is to make a phone call to the online service's toll-free number and request your software. (For information about online services and their telephone numbers, see Chapter 7).

If you're dialing up a local BBS, you need a computer, a modem, a communications program, and the BBS's phone number. Many free or inexpensive communications or *terminal programs* are available. A terminal program is a program that allows your computer to shift the burden of number crunching to a remote computer and act as a "dumb terminal." Contact a local user group or dial in to a BBS to find one.

If you decide to locate an Internet service provider (ISP), you have two low-tech options and one high-tech option. High-tech folks can use a couple of online methods to find out how to get online. First, ISPs on the Net regularly contribute information about dial-up Internet access to a directory compiled into a text file called *PDIAL.* PDIAL lists providers predominantly connected directly to the Internet, but much can be explored through BBSs and commercial providers as well.

One way to get a copy of PDIAL is to send an e-mail request to the Info Deli server. Your message gets you a regularly updated list (file) of many commercial Internet providers. To get a PDIAL list, send e-mail to the following address:

```
info-deli-server@pdial.com
```

In the body of the message, type the following if you want to get new PDIALs as they are published to the Internet:

```
subscribe PDIAL
```

Or type this to get the entire PDIAL text file:

```
send PDIAL
```

Two "low-tech" choices for getting PDIAL are

- Let your fingers do the walking. (Check your local *Yellow Pages* under "Telecommunications.")
- Check magazines and other popular press for advertisements. *MacWorld, PC World,* and *Internet World* are all great sources for Internet provider listings.

A second (easier) method of locating a service provider is to point your browser to THELIST (`thelist.iworld.com`) on someone else's computer. There you find an extensive list of providers and lots of statistics to help you make an informed decision.

Going for the Bucks

How will your school pay for Internet access? The first thing to do is check with your district office and state department of education to find out whether they have a source for free access to the Internet. Colleges and universities are also a potential source of free Net time. Be sure to ask for a SLIP or PPP account (as described previously), or you'll get attacked by the UNIX prompt monster.

Grants are also a great source of funding for telecommunications. Quite a few grant databases are available on the Internet. For information about them, point your WWW browser (Netscape, Mosaic, and so on) to one of the following addresses:

```
http://galaxy.einet.net/GJ/grants.html
http://infoserv.rttonet.psu.edu/gweb.htm
http://magnet.educ.monash.edu.au/Education_Foundation/
        edfound1.htm
http://fdncenter.org/2book/2egg.html
```

Even with grants and free Net time, using the Internet costs money. Here are some teacher-tested ideas for raising the money you need to go online:

- Work with your PTSA to conduct fund-raisers. (Sell bits and bites for chips and bytes.)
- Seek business partner sponsorships.
- Sponsor a computer camp.

  A local college makes big bucks each summer with a Tennis and Computer Camp. Students spend half a day with a tennis pro and half in the computer lab. The charge is $100 per student for a week, and the waiting list is a mile long.
- Offer pay-as-you-learn courses for parents.
- Sponsor an adopt-a-phone line campaign.
- Organize a software fair and invite parents and teachers from other schools. Charge $2.00 at the door.
- Sell computer services to your community.

  An elementary school once raised $600 making banners for parents. The same school raised another $300 by volunteering to enter data into a database for a local business. The possibilities are endless!
- Offer to create newsletters (or Web pages!) for community groups, churches, and so on.

If you need tips on selling telecommunications, check the section in Chapter 3 on how to convince your administration or board to support the Internet in your school.

The day will come when all schools will be directly connected to the Internet. The big decisions concern who will pay for it and how the connections will be maintained. You'll be much happier if you keep it simple in the beginning. Get a dial-up SLIP or PPP account and see how much, and how effectively, your staff and students use the resources available on the Internet *before* you go to the expense of establishing a direct Internet connection. The data you collect will probably be invaluable in helping you argue for greater Internet access in your school.

A Word about NetDay

The latest phenomenon to hit the education world is NetDay. The concept of NetDay was born in California, but like Elvis, NetDay sightings are popping up everywhere! Well-meaning business coalitions have decided that the way to get schools wired is to stage a "high-tech barn raising" and get local businesses to underwrite the cost and supply the labor to pull wire through the halls of learning. As with any initiative, this kind of barn-raising has good points and not-so-good points.

The good news is that NetDays

- Provide the beginnings of the necessary infrastructure for the next level of interactivity in classrooms (the Internet)
- Draw attention to the lack of networking and connectivity in today's schools
- Create coalitions of school and community that can strengthen interest and involvement for years to come

The not-so-good news is that NetDays typically

- Don't include adequate staff development for educators
- Don't invest time in helping teachers and administrators answer the question "Wired for What?"
- Don't provide the technical and financial support necessary after the wires are installed
- Don't (typically) wire an entire school, just a portion of it
- Don't prepare schools for the ongoing costs associated with the use of the wiring installed
- Don't take into account the fact that our aging schools lack the power resources to support the computers to be attached to this new "plumbing"

So . . . how will you take advantage of the boost in awareness of the needs in the area of technology and ensure that NetDays now and in the future will be successful? Think about these five tips:

- Think of NetDay as a catalyst, not a one-shot deal. Make plans for several NetDay-like events throughout the year. Be sure the NetDay effort is integrated into, and helps support, your school and/or district's technology plan and your *curriculum.*

(continued)

(continued)

- Spend some time thinking and planning for the infrastructure necessary to support your new Net connections. Think about staffing, maintenance, facilities (including electrical service), computer hardware, software, and training.
- Suggest that your NetDay partners broaden their support to include funding for staff development, awareness seminars, or continued partnerships with your school or district. This is one coalition that could make a huge difference in the quality of teaching and learning in your school!
- Set expectations precisely. Will your community think that, after NetDay, your school won't need other funding for technology? Do the educators and technical coordinators in your area really know what the NetDay effort will do for your school — and what it won't do? (Will every classroom have a connection — or just a few? Will Internet access be free — or will the school have to pay for it?)
- Find out what other states are doing. Just about every NetDay effort has a Web page explaining the process, the purpose, and the result (after the fact). Take a virtual field trip to California and see what schools there have done; learn from their first year's experience with NetDay to make your life easier.

Here's to a very successful, sustainable, scaleable NetDay! Happy wiring!

Chapter 6

Wheelin' and Dealin' with Internet Service Providers

In This Chapter

- Swimming with the sharks
- The Wheeler-Dealer's ten tips

If you've made the decision to use an Internet service provider (ISP), as opposed to jumping onto the information superhighway via a commercial service such as America Online or Prodigy, or if you've been unable to weasel some free accounts out of a local college or ISP, you need to put on your wheelin' and dealin' hat and go to town.

Choosing an Internet Service Provider

Choosing an ISP is a little like choosing food in the school cafeteria. Most of the choices look good, but when you get around to actually sampling them, you're liable to get something that's hard to swallow. Somehow, that lunch that the fifth grade teacher down the hall brought from home always looks much better. Fact is, the number of ISPs is growing quickly, and each of them is dangling a carrot — some better than others.

The moral to this food-filled story (are you getting hungry?) is *buyer beware!* If you're careful, and note the Wheeler-Dealer's questions that follow, you're much more likely to end up with something that's easy for you and your administration to enjoy.

The Wheeler-Dealer's Top Ten Questions for an Internet Service Provider

Think of yourself as a reporter on the information superhighway. Get a comfortable seat, your best #2 pencil, and a telephone, and go to work. Get the names of information providers by searching current magazines or your local telephone book, by dialing into a commercial online service and downloading PDIAL, a list of Internet service providers around the world, or by using THELIST. (See Chapter 5 for how to access PDIAL and THELIST.)

#1 How many toll-free telephone lines do you control?

A busy signal is the electronic equivalent of a traffic jam on the information superhighway. The number of telephone lines that a service provider controls is very important. That $15 per month "unlimited access" won't do you much good if you spend all your time redialing and listening to Ma Bell's busy symphony. Ask the ISP how often users can expect a busy signal. If they get really quiet, run, don't walk, to another provider.

Several providers offer Internet access via a long-distance phone call. They promise you the world, as long as you pay 90¢ per minute. The best providers offer local access or access via a toll-free number. (Note that toll-free access is often accompanied by a "convenience surcharge.")

Don't be too concerned if an ISP says that it has only 10 or 20 phone lines. If you're a bit antsy, remember that the Internet is an ever-changing beast, so be sure to follow up your inquiry about phone lines with the obligatory "What are your growth plans?" question. It's really the ratio of phone lines to users that matters.

#2 How many users currently use your service?

Think of what the hallway in your school looks like seconds after the last bell of the day rings. Hundreds of book-totin' bodies running for the nearest door, pushing and shoving. If your ISP has more users than its phone lines can accommodate, sooner or later you'll end up as the last one out the door and miss your Internet bus!

A good way to quantify "how many is too many" is to think about the relationship between the number of users and the number of free phone lines. A reasonable ratio is about 1 phone line for every 10 users. 1 to 100 might sound like an awful lot, but remember that every user won't log on at the same time on the same line.

#3 What kinds of accounts do you offer?

Here's your chance to recall those TLAs (three-letter acronyms) you read about in Chapter 5. Most Internet carriers offer three types of accounts: shell, PPP, and SLIP. If you're just looking for e-mail, a shell account may work fine, but you'll have to put up with some UNIX shenanigans. Some shell providers offer menus for easier access. If you want a shell account, seek out the ones that provide front-end software. Shell accounts are usually a few dollars a month cheaper than their feature-rich cousins, PPP and SLIP accounts.

If you want to mount the ultimate surfboard and get easy access to the World Wide Web (WWW), then a PPP or SLIP connection is the way to go. I always recommend PPP accounts because they offer better error correction and are supported by more nifty shareware or freeware tools.

#4 What does establishing an account cost?

The fine print is what often kills a sweet deal. Whether you're negotiating for yourself or your school, watch for hidden fees. Although most Internet service providers charge a fee to cover the establishment of the account, the amount they charge varies greatly. I've seen initial charges of from $10 to $75. An average is about $30. Most providers even throw in a dandy book (like this one!) or some handy software.

Wait! I've already *got* an account — how do I know what kind it is?

If you use a program that's a terminal emulator, such as CrossTalk, Microphone, or Z-term, and you see a UNIX command line after you're connected, you probably have a shell account. Most shell accounts cannot access the World Wide Web (WWW) or use some of the slicker data retrieval programs.

If you dial by clicking on a MacPPP, MacSLIP, or WinSLIP icon, or by simply double-clicking an Internet application icon, you have a dial-up or direct access account.

#5 How much time do I get for my monthly fee?

Imagine for a moment that you've been waiting all afternoon to see the sun set over the waterfront. You spend all afternoon finding the place you want to sit where the viewing is best. Seconds before the big event, everything goes black. A booming voice comes from nowhere and says, "Sorry, your time is up."

Unless you and your students want to experience the unsettling and inevitable "information interruptus," go for an unlimited use account. The few extra dollars per month saves you much heartache and many heated discussions with the teacher down the hall who surfs more than Gidget at Malibu.

#6 How many and what kind of newsgroups do you carry?

Because the number of newsgroups you can access has to do with the capacity of the equipment that your Internet service provider owns, some services don't offer many newsgroups. If you and your students rely heavily on this information, you want to maximize the number available. Most providers give you access to 500 or more.

Some ISPs choose not to carry certain eclectic newsgroups, such as the notorious `alt` groups. Chapter 13 has a discussion of the potential and some of the pitfalls of newsgroups. Look for the section on saving your job. Get the hint?

#7 Can I spin my own Web (page)?

Want to build your own Web page? Many providers offer you space on their hardware to create your school's own Web page. Often they even give you a template to fill in with your school information until you've had time to discover *HTML* (hypertext markup language), the scripting language that enables you to create really cool Web pages.

Be sure to check to see how much space the provider will allow. Depending on the number of graphic images that you include, you can use up a few megabytes of memory very quickly. Try for about 4MB of Web space in the beginning. Most providers allow you to pay a bit more and get a bit more space.

Check out this screen shot from the home page of a very talented elementary school teacher:

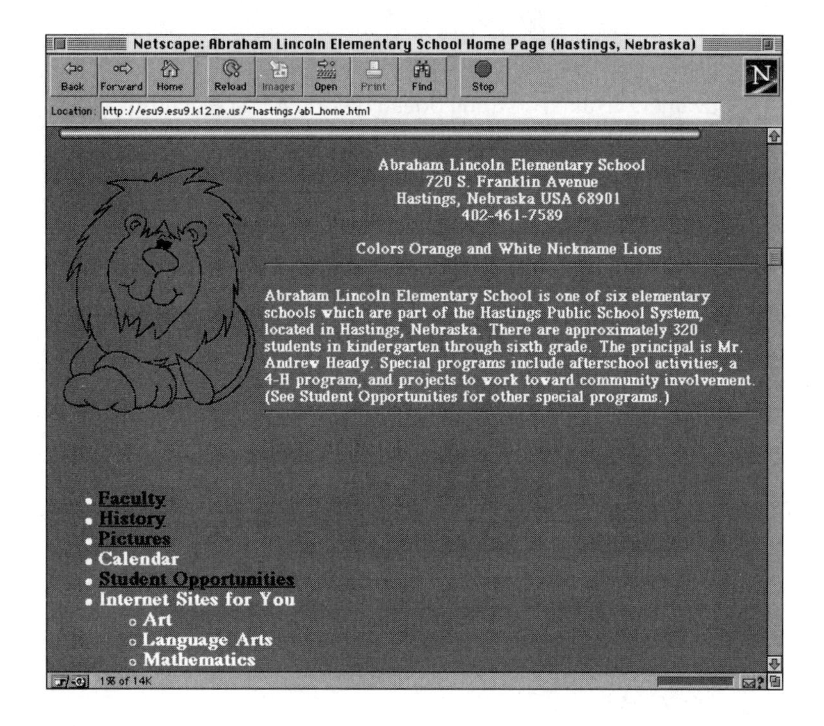

This page comes from an elementary school in Nebraska and is a great overall picture of the school and community. This page, while simple, contains all the information you need to get an idea of what's up in the Hastings, NE, school, and it contains many links to other sites. Visit the page for yourself by pointing your Web browser to

```
http://esu9.esu9.k12.ne.us/~hastings/abl_home.html
```

#8 How is your customer support?

Don't you just love the commercial where the lady calls the customer support line of a major aerospace and appliance company and asks how to remove the elephant from her dishwasher? Like any technology — especially technology where students and newbie teachers are involved — things are bound to go wrong.

Just for fun, don your best British accent and call the customer support number of your ISP with a question such as, "What's the URL for that Coke machine at Carnegie Mellon University?" or "What do Archie and Veronica have to do with the Internet?" If they answer correctly, they're doing their job. If you get a recording asking you to leave a message, go to another provider. A recording just doesn't cut it when you're demonstrating Internet access to your class, with the principal sitting quietly in the back of the room conducting your evaluation, and the thing doesn't work. A voice mailbox won't get you tenure.

Oh, and be sure that when *your* elephant gets caught in the dishwasher you only have to make a *local* call to customer support!

#9 Do you have any special deals for educators or schools?

Ever see educators at a trade show? My favorite thing to do is get freebies. You know, those nifty pens, disks, magnifying glasses, posters, catalogs, and, of course, the mother of all freebies, the umbrella. Everyone likes free things — especially when money is tight.

Many companies know that we're using the Net and related technology to help children just like theirs, so they're very often glad to cut you a deal. Having your district office do the negotiating also can bring the price down. Remember, negotiating for a few bucks off the per month fee is, in the long run, better than getting a complimentary sign-up fee. Don't be shy. If you don't ask, they aren't likely to offer!

#10 What kinds of front-end and tool software do you supply?

Entering the Net without tools is a little like trying to teach without books and paper. A lot of great Internet tools are available, many for free on the Internet itself. Check to see whether your ISP provides you with tools; it will save you the trouble of downloading them. Here is a short list of tools, all of them available for free (or inexpensively) on the Internet. A few basic Internet tools that Macintosh and Windows users need are included with this book. (The boldface items in the list are included on *The Internet For Teachers* CD.)

Anarchie	**Eudora Light**	InterSLIP	MacPPP
MacWAIS	MacWeb	**TurboGopher**	MacTCP Watcher
MacWeather	Blue Skies	**NCSA Telnet**	**Netscape Navigator**
Talk	WinSLIP	NewsWatcher	Trumpet WinSock

Spyglass	Mosaic	AppleSearch	Fetch
Nuntius	**IRCle**	Sound Machine	**StuffIt Expander**
MS Explorer	**WinZip**	Chameleon	

Note that some software resides on the Net servers themselves. UNIX mail tools such as elm and pine are an example. These programs are run directly on the host computer and don't have to physically reside on your computer's hard drive.

Most Internet providers nowadays save you a few gray hairs by giving you a disk, as part of your sign-up fee, that comes preconfigured and makes your first Internet sign-on a breeze. Configuring your software initially can be at least twice as confusing as programming your VCR, so having it all done for you means a lot. You and your students merely copy the software, click the mouse, and start surfin'!

Chapter 7
Online Services and the Internet

In This Chapter

- Weighing the benefits of online services
- Surfing the Net with America Online
- Cruising the Net with CompuServe
- Browsing the Net with Prodigy
- Checking out other online services
- Looking at the bottom line

When I taught earth science to seventh graders, I just couldn't wait until we reached the point in the year when we learned about geology. The students and I could go outside and find rocks and minerals and play Sherlock Holmes as we tried to identify them.

One day, a student brought up the concept of *abrasion.* (That's what happens to rocks when wind, water, or other natural forces wear away at a rock's surface.) Remembering that I had a huge collection of nifty river rocks in the science workroom just down the hall, I turned to my best science student, Mitchell, and asked him to "go get me a river rock." He nodded happily and left the classroom.

About 15 minutes passed, and Mitchell still hadn't returned. I was concerned, so I asked the teacher next door to watch my class, and I set off to the workroom to find the wayward student. The tub filled with river rocks was still nestled in the corner, in plain sight, but Mitchell was nowhere to be found. I dropped by the office and alerted an assistant principal, who said she'd look for him.

Twenty more minutes passed, and I wondered whether my dependable student had gone AWOL. Just as I was ready to call out the cavalry, in walked Mitchell, covered from head to toe with mud. In Mitchell's hand was a most magnificently smooth river rock, still dripping (and so, by the way, was Mitchell). Mitchell had gone across campus and hiked through the woods to a nearby creek to find the rock.

My point is that there's a hard way and an easy way to do just about anything. For the most part, accessing the Internet through an online service is the easy way.

Big Plusses?

The major online services are jockeying to be your on-ramp to the information superhighway. The four things that may make you choose one online service over another are

- Interface (ease of use)
- Level of Internet access
- Content and organization
- Cost (the clincher)

Basically, when compared to direct access to the Internet through an Internet service provider, online services

- Present a friendlier Internet interface than does "raw" Internet access
- Currently offer a more limited level of Internet services
- Organize content so that finding what you want is much easier
- Charge more to access Internet services, but offer you more than just Internet access

Virtually all the major online services offer something that approximates full Internet access by the time you read this book, so what's a teacher to do?

Read on! This chapter takes a look at the "big three" online services, America Online (AOL), CompuServe, and Prodigy, and gives you a quick look at the Internet services that each of them currently offers so that you can decide which online services make the grade.

Each of the big three commercial online services offers connection at 28.8 Kbps (28,800 baud). AOL and CompuServe are also testing ISDN (really fast) connections.

The Internet on America Online

America Online, born in 1989, has spread like wildfire. As of early 1995, the service passed CompuServe as the largest online service, and it now has over 6,000,000 subscribers and more than 2,000,000 sessions a day. It has been a virtual circus at AOL headquarters trying to keep up with increasing user demands, but they're managing it well. (Couldn't resist the circus metaphor since AOL's headquarters in Vienna, Virginia, is right next door to Ringling Brothers' headquarters.) Because information providers are flocking to AOL like kids to an ice-cream truck, the quantity and quality of information available continues to grow.

The interface

Like most online services, the folks at AOL ship you a front-end program that provides a *graphical user interface* (GUI). From the very beginning, AOL's clean, friendly interface is the very thing that sets it apart from the other guys. The AOL gurus ensure that what you see is visually pleasing and intuitive.

The opening screen gives you easy access to the myriad of resources that AOL has to offer. Clickable buttons for an Internet Connection, Learning & Culture, and Reference help educators get where they want to go quickly. As the creative folks at AOL continue to evolve the interface, I suspect that you'll see even more bells and whistles. Whether you're a Windows or Macintosh user, you can already click your way through short online movies, vivid graphics, and integrated Internet access. These services are only a hop, skip, and a much faster connection away from full-length video!

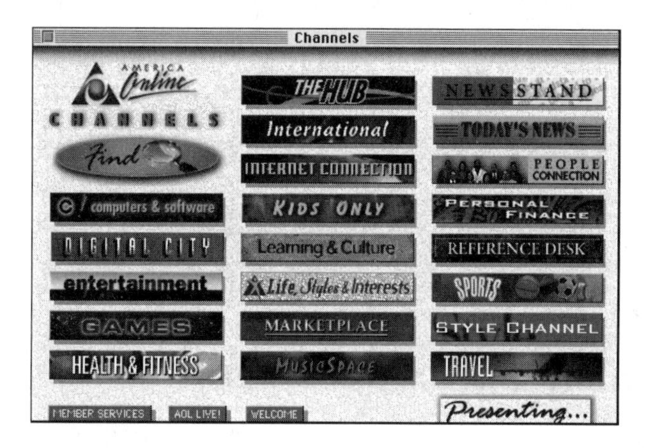

Internet access

AOL currently offers many Internet resources to users. They include

- A seamless e-mail gateway that enables you to send and receive e-mail from Internet users as easily as you send and receive messages from other AOL junkies.
- World Wide Web: A powerful, integrated Web browser makes mining the Web as easy as jumping around on AOL.
- A Gopher/WAIS interface that's easy to use (and the Gopher icon has cheeks that'll make you giggle).
- FTP (file transfer protocol) via a point-and-click metaphor that's as easy as clearing the hallways at the last bell of the day.

- Usenet newsgroup access — you pick 'em, you read 'em. (AOL doesn't censor which newsgroups you can subscribe to, so watch for students who stray down forbidden paths.)
- Mailing lists: An easy way to fill your mailbox with lots of tips and ideas from users all over cyberspace.

You reach all these resources through the Internet Connection menu (Keyword: Internet). In addition to links to the Internet, you'll also find other Internet resources, such as online magazines, message boards, and Internet tutorials. Telnet on AOL, incidentally, is "in progress" and should be available soon.

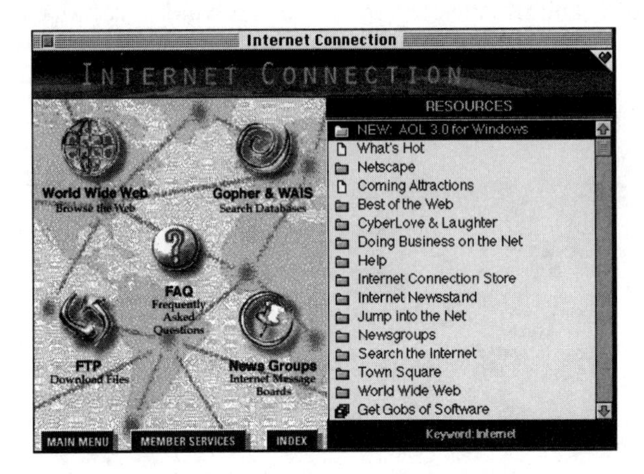

Content and organization

AOL offers a virtual cornucopia (Did I really say that?) of educational resources. From online conferences to school-to-school projects, you'll find lots to browse. The nifty Exam Exchange and Lesson Plan Exchange libraries provide tons of fresh ideas, and the education libraries are brimming with software for you to download.

You'll find Internet resources ranging from "Zen and the Art of the Internet" (the UNIX lover's guide to the Net) to FAQ (frequently asked questions) files. A very active message board area where even newbies can get their questions answered rounds out AOL's Internet support resources.

The intuitive interface provides a good organizational scheme for educational and Internet resources. Here are a few must-visit locations and the AOL keywords that you'll want to remember:

- **ESH:** the Electronic Schoolhouse
- **TEN:** The Education Network

- **TIN:** Teacher's Information Network
- **KIDS:** Kids Only Online
- **Internet:** Internet connection (WEB, FTP, and NEWSGROUPS also work.)
- **Reference:** Reference sources, including links to Internet resources

AOL is also doing something I wish the other guys would think about: incorporating Internet resources into its regular online areas. In the "politics" area online (Keyword: Politics), for example, you'll find links to Internet Gopher servers nestled in between AOL resources. You'll even stumble upon applicable WWW pages there, too. That makes sense. Bravo, AOL!

Cost

AOL offers a couple of different schemes for purchasing online time. Schools can take advantage of an offer from CNN Newsroom to purchase blocks of online time (a great budget-control option) or bulk-purchase hours directly from AOL.

One thing that sets AOL apart from the rest is that AOL charges no gateway fees. Other online services have "plus" or "gateway" charges that they add to your initial monthly fee when you access certain areas; AOL doesn't. AOL's one-price-fits-all scheme prevents you from ever having to say, "You can't do that; it costs extra."

The only downside to AOL's pricing is that, like the other services, it can get expensive, particularly if your school is a heavy user. If you're budgeting for AOL use, figure your average monthly cost for about 20 hours to be around $40 to $60.

One way to control your costs is to use "stop time" billing. AOL enables schools to buy ten-hour blocks of time at a discounted rate for blocks of ten hours. When you use up the time you have purchased, the service won't let you sign on until the following month, when your hours are again available. It's an excellent way to control cost, but frustrating when you need more time for a major project. Estimate wisely, though, and you and the people who budget for your school will be happy.

Get a free America Online sign-on kit by calling 800-227-6364. The sign-on kit gives you and your students ten free hours to explore and evaluate AOL. To find out about special deals for education or to arrange for stop-time billing, call 800-344-6219.

The bleeding edge

Being in the online service business must be tough. Everyone expects you to have the latest and greatest tools available, all wrapped in a clean, easy-to-use interface. Nowadays, all the large online services are close to offering the full suite of Internet services, but not without problems. In early 1994, one service lost more than 4,000 e-mail messages while trying to make things better. Another service experienced a catastrophic 19-hour outage in 1996, wreaking havoc among businesses and personal communication and an all-too-dependent public.

If you stop and think about it, being the first out of the starting block with anything is risky, especially with technology. Being on the leading (or is it bleeding?) edge of telecommunications is fraught with peril. Competitors snapping at your heels. Users screaming that they want it *now!* Not that I feel sorry for the online services, mind you; they're making billions of dollars.

My job enables me to visit lots of schools that also are on the bleeding edge. You know what? Those are the places where I see a staff that's enthusiastic about technology. That's where the excitement seeps from school to community. Sure, you may get nicked now and then, but the ultimate rewards are far greater. Be on the bleeding edge; it's worth it. End of sermon.

The Internet on CompuServe

CompuServe (CompuServe Information Service, or CIS) is the granddaddy of all online services. It began in 1979 as a text-only online service aimed primarily at business and, after being swallowed by H & R Block, grew into one of the "big three" players with more than 2,000,000 members around the world.

CompuServe's strength is its truly international flavor. Although America Online and Prodigy users only recently became able to access their accounts through special arrangements with international Internet providers, CompuServe has been international for years. Being *international* means not only receiving e-mail from abroad (you can do that on any service), but also being just as likely to run into a person logged on from France as one from Florida. Kinda neat, huh?

The interface

Although CompuServe began as a text-only service, the wizards soon whipped up CIM, CompuServe Information Manager, a graphical interface that moves you from cryptic text to point-and-click ease of use.

CompuServe's dandy graphical front-end software, available for PCs that are running Windows and for Macintosh computers, gives you a BOW interface. (BOW stands for *Bunches of Windows.*) CompuServe is both flexible and

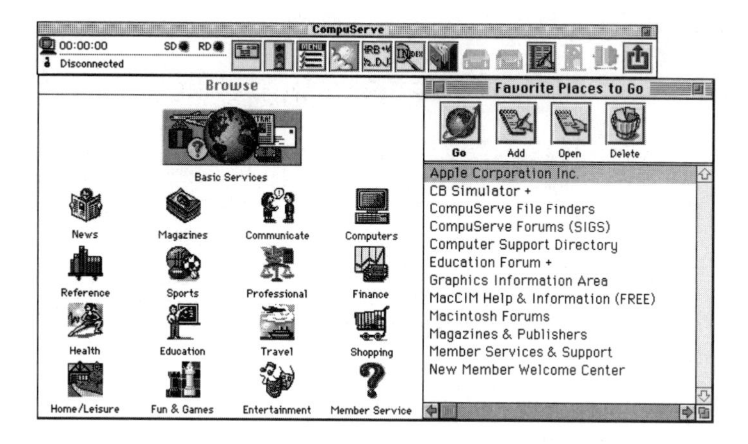

frustrating. Being able to open lots of windows all over your screen for different things, instead of generally navigating from one point, is a customizer's dream and a beginner's nightmare.

One other pet peeve is the CompuServe member address. On AOL, you can have screen names such as "GayleK" and "Tooter," but on CompuServe, the mainframe in the sky chooses your member number and assigns it to your account. Your address looks like this: 12345,6789. Sigh. It works, of course, but I like the more personal approach to communication. "Have you seen 98765,4321 online lately? I just spoke with him yesterday."

I don't want to slam the CompuServe folks too much for their numerical screen names, though. Rumor has it that a substantial update to the service software will soon cure that digital disease.

Internet access

CompuServe has a great way of surrounding the very unfriendly UNIX Internet language with friendly point-and-click decisions. The service offers access to Telnet, Gopher, Internet e-mail, Web access and FTP.

The newsgroup reader is easy to use and intuitive, as are the file downloading menus in FTP. Sending Internet e-mail is easy, but receiving a message via the Internet costs extra. CompuServe charges ten cents a message for incoming Internet e-mail. The charges can be high if you subscribe to a mailing list.

Here's an example of what you see as you investigate newsgroups on CompuServe:

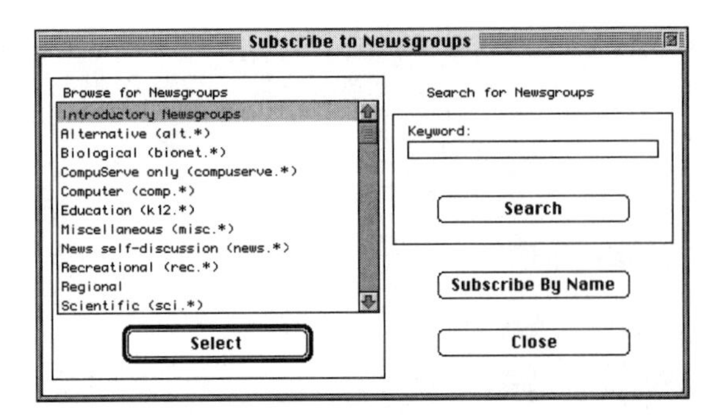

One major plus for CompuServe is that you can now access the service via PPP, bypassing the front-end software altogether in favor of your favorite browser. This development is a great option, one that will, no doubt, soon be recognized by the other players in the online service market.

To access Internet services on CompuServe, choose Go from the Services menu and type **Internet**.

Content and organization

Even though CompuServe's focus leans toward financial information and news, the service provides lots of great stuff for education. The reference areas offer everything from online magazines to encyclopedias. The Education Forum (a "plus" service) gives educators a chance to exchange ideas, do online projects, and download tons and tons of freeware and shareware software.

The sheer amount of information in CompuServe's coffers is amazing, but sometimes it's difficult to find. Use the Go command or the search function to find what you need so you won't get lost in a sea of windows. A monthly magazine provides a good source of information about what's new on the service and helpful tips for new users.

Cost

CompuServe, like the other guys, charges a monthly fee (currently $9.95) for a subscription and then extra bucks for "plus" or "$" areas. Unfortunately, most of the good education stuff is a "+" service, so you have to watch your charges carefully. It can get really expensive really quickly.

As you navigate around CompuServe, watch for the plus sign (+) or dollar sign ($) immediately following the name of a forum or online location. These symbols indicate that the meter's running and you may be racking up a higher bill.

Because of the rather convoluted charging scheme, budgeting for using CIS in schools is a bit difficult, but the vast array of information that's available still makes CompuServe a wise choice for some people, especially for colleges of law or business.

Navigator software, available for an extra charge for computers that are running Windows and for Macintosh computers, enables you to make decisions about what you want to see or retrieve *before* you log onto CompuServe and the meter begins to run. I highly recommend the CompuServe Navigator if you intend to use CIS in a media center as a reference tool. It will save you a great deal of time and money.

For a free CompuServe trial membership, call 800-848-8119. Take it for a test drive today.

More than 10 million Web users a day logged into the 1996 Atlanta Olympic Web site during the 19 days of the Summer Olympics.

The Internet on Prodigy

Prodigy was born in 1990 through a joint venture between IBM and Sears. With more than 2,000,000 user IDs, it certainly deserves a place in the big-players' market. Prodigy positions itself in the online market as a family network, and it has lots of topics, games, and news that are aimed at parents and children.

The Prodigy service is, overall, easy to use, and it offers lots of education-related content. Classroom Prodigy, a commercial-free version of the Prodigy service, is a great place to start in the online service market.

According to a survey in mid-1996, about 60 percent of those with a computer also have a modem.

The interface

Prodigy offers users an easy-to-navigate welcome menu with big, clickable buttons. Each button takes you to another screen that offers more choices. The Education areas are hidden away in the Home/Family/Kids section.

Some screens seem to take a long time to redraw (even at 14.4 Kbps), but the time is acceptable. The screen font, Zartron, looks as strange as it sounds. The graphics aren't terrific compared to AOL, but the Prodigy folks have recently released a software update that takes care of that problem. The wizards at Prodigy certainly won't stand still and let the other guys pass them by!

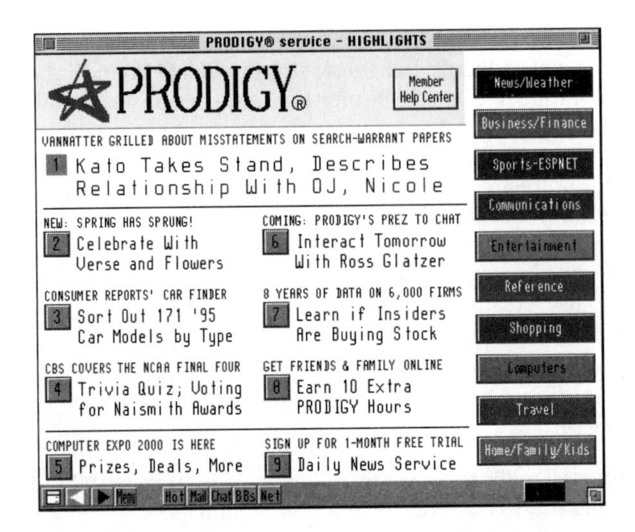

One major complaint from parents and educators is that every so often while you're surfing around Prodigy's menus, an on-screen commercial pops up. Although this visual interruption may seem minor, I've found that students spend lots of time clicking the LOOK button to find out more about the trip to Jamaica or the newest sport utility vehicle from Ford. It's fine for home but not so good for the classroom. Luckily, Classroom Prodigy offers schools a commercial-free environment.

Internet access

There's good news and bad news when it comes to Prodigy's Internet resources. Prodigy was the first out of the box with a browser for the WWW for Windows users, and they recently unveiled a working browser for the Mac users out there. Prodigy's Web interface is also the way users access FTP and Gopher. Watch closely, though, for some dynamite Internet access and interface improvements from the folks at Prodigy. Here's a glimpse at newsgroup access via Prodigy:

Your USENET Newsgroup List

Your Newsgroup List (Subscribed) Total Unread

news.announce.newusers
k12.chat.elementary
k12.chat.junior
k12.chat.senior
k12.chat.teacher
k12.ed.tech
k12.news

Go to Newsgroup
Description
Remove (Unsubscribe)
Find Newsgroups
Options
View Articles Since: 3/14
Cancel
Help

To access Internet services on Prodigy, from the Jump menu choose Jump to and then type **Internet**. You can get to the World Wide Web browser (Windows users) by "jumping" to Keyword: Web.

Content and organization

The education areas on Prodigy are easy to find. Clicking the Home/Family/Kids button from Prodigy's main screen takes you to another screen that has an Education button and lots more education and reference resources. Like the other major services, Prodigy offers a large number of reference resources, education bulletin boards, and places for teachers to exchange ideas.

Prodigy's point-and-click-the-buttons organizational scheme is fairly straightforward, but you'll quickly learn that it's light years faster to "jump" from one place to another with a keyword.

Prodigy doesn't offer files for download, except through FTP and the Internet.

Cost

Like CompuServe, Prodigy has a scheme for charging extra for many things. E-mail, for example, can get costly and complicated. Prodigy has different rates for sending and receiving e-mail messages from within the service and outside the service (through the Internet).

The service does a pretty good job of warning users when something they're about to do costs more money (a handy little blue box in the screen's lower right displays your current charge status), but it's very easy for a novice user or curious student to click their way to a hefty charge.

Classroom Prodigy is an extension to the Prodigy service that offers commercial-free screens and a slew of student activities and teacher resources — for a fee. If you choose Prodigy, Classroom Prodigy is definitely the way to go. The activities are great, and the resources are high quality.

For a free sign-on kit, dial 800-PRODIGY. Ask about Classroom Prodigy, too.

A Word about the Other Guy(s)

New services are popping up practically every day. The Microsoft Network and a host of other, smaller players also offer Net users lots of options. In general, it's the content and the organization that set these services apart. The key to selecting a service in the future will probably depend upon which service is most configurable to the way you work, learn, and play. If I had to stare into the crystal ball, I'd say personalization will become more important than the pipeline in the near future. Soon "fast enough" will be replaced by "useful enough."

Fact is, the online world is very, very competitive. The "here today and gone tomorrow" adage definately rings true. We've seen eWorld and a host of other online services try to compete and get lost in the shuffle. By the time this book is published, yet another shakeout will no doubt have happened. In general, sticking with the services that have some history seems safest.

The number of "shop by computer" sites is skyrocketing. By early 1996, more than 200 mail-order catalogs were posted on the World Wide Web. The growth of the industry will really explode when the gurus figure out a better way to protect credit card numbers that are sent via the Net.

The Bottom Line

My advice on selecting an online service for use in your school is to get the free trial accounts and sharpen your red pencil. Grading the services on ease of use, content and organization, Internet services, and cost helps you make a wise choice. For the purpose of this book, I've used all the services discussed in this chapter for a while — my credit card bill looks like the national debt — but I'll probably keep two or three just because of the neat stuff on them.

Remember that no online service currently offers access to all Internet services, so there's still a definite advantage to dialing into the Net directly. Internet dial-up accounts tend to cost less, too.

Chapter 8

The Right Tool for the Right Job

In This Chapter

- Surfing with the Mac
- Doing Windows
- Software that makes surfing easy

This chapter provides a brief glance at some of the more popular Internet software tools that are available as commercial software, freeware, or shareware. It also includes information about the tools that are on the *Internet For Teachers* CD.

Internet software tools are great. They enable you and your students to surf the Internet without ever seeing any of those unfriendly UNIX prompts. Knowing what to do when you see this

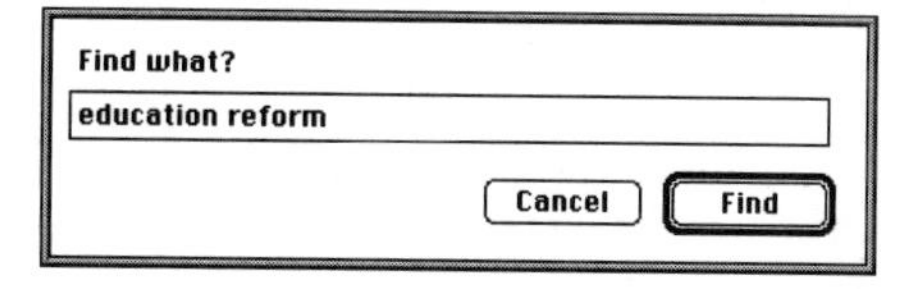

is much easier than knowing what to do when you see a prompt like this

```
%
```

Wanna hear some really great news? The vast majority of the easy-to-use software tools that you need are available *free* for educators. Not only that, but I've included a set of the most popular Macintosh and Windows software on a CD in the back of this book to get you started. The other programs that you need are available through FTP (file transfer protocol), and they are only a mouse click away. (Refer to Chapter 16 for information on FTP.)

All the tools described in this book work pretty much the same way whether you have a Macintosh or a PC that is running Windows. Most Internet service providers offer a starter set of software that gets you online so you can download the other tools you need. It's easy — really! I'll even tell you where to get the free tools you need.

Occasionally, you'll get a busy signal when you try to fetch (ftp) files. The best strategy is to try several times, and then, if you're not successful, to try to access the site during off hours (after 5:00 p.m. at the accessed site). Because the software discussed in this chapter is so popular, many of the programs are also available at other sites (called *mirror* sites) that have similar software. To find other sites that may have the software you need, visit a Web search site (such as WebCrawler or World Wide Web Worm) and search for the title or use Anarchie to search FTP sites for titles.

The Net is a great source for Internet software for all platforms. Several sites always seem to have the latest and greatest software. To get to one of them, launch your Web browser and surf to

```
http://www.jumbo.com
```

Batteries Included: Surfing on the Mac

Because the Macintosh has had built-in networking capabilities practically since it was born, it's no wonder that most of the Internet utilities for the Mac are powerful, easy to use, and fully featured.

If you're connecting via modem, you need two pieces of software to help your Macintosh communicate with the Internet: Apple's MacTCP and a SLIP or PPP control. You can obtain programs such as InterSLIP or MacPPP from most Internet service providers.

To install MacPPP/SLIP or MacTCP, simply drag the icons (from the disk) on top of the closed System folder icon on your computer's hard disk. Your Mac's operating system does the rest. After the basics are installed, restart your computer, and you're ready to harness powerful Internet software tools.

If you're connecting directly to the Internet through a schoolwide network, all you need is MacTCP. See your network administrator for details on making your Internet connection.

In 1996, an estimated 7.7 percent of adults in the U.S. were using the World Wide Web.

Batteries Also Included: Surfing on a PC That Is Running Windows

Before you can go surfing, you need to wax your board. To prepare your Windows machine, you need to get your hands on SLIP or PPP client software. Your Internet service provider will usually provide one at no charge. Simply install the SLIP software, and then you can use bunches of graphical interface software packages that make Net-surfing a breeze.

If you have a DOS machine, a freeware program called UMSLIP is available via FTP at `boombox.micro.umn.edu` in the directory `/pub/pc/slip`

Trumpet WinSock (ftp to `ftp.cs.umn.edu` in the directory `/users/riedl/CS-5113/Slip`) is an excellent shareware package that handles all your SLIP needs in Windows. This dandy program dials into a SLIP server and establishes a low-level network connection.

Windows Sockets (WinSock) is a set of specifications that enables programs to interface with Microsoft Windows. Developers who are creating Internet access programs for machines that are running Windows follow the WinSock guidelines to ensure that their programs will be compatible. If you're running Windows, be sure to look for the words "Windows Sockets Compliant" in the information about programs that you download to be sure things will run smoothly.

A+ Net tools: Which is which?

With all the tools available for the Internet, how can you remember what's what? Here's a quick listing of Internet resources and the general category of software tool that you use to access them.

Tool	*Task*
E-Mail	Send and receive electronic mail
Gopher	Locate information on the Internet
Veronica	Search for titles in Gopherspace
FTP	Retrieve files from the Internet
Archie	Locate files on the Internet
IRC	Chat live across the Internet
Usenet newsgroups	Search and read discussion topics on the Internet
Web browser	Navigate the World Wide Web
Telnet	Act as a terminal on a remote computer

Software That Makes Surfing Easy

The following sections describe some of the Internet software that's available today for SLIP/PPP or direct-connect access. (See Chapter 5 to review your options for connection to the Internet.) The CD icon indicates which software is included on the *Internet For Teachers* CD. After you install the software, establish your connection to the Internet, double-click the icons, and you're on your way.

Note: To get your hands on the software listed in the next sections or to snag some updates to your current software, point your Web browser to one of these two sites:

```
http://www.jumbo.com
http://www.netscape.com
```

You'll find links to thousands of other sofware sites and access to search engines that allow you to enter the name of a program and find out where you can get it with the click of a mouse.

E-mail

Electronic mail (e-mail) software tools are designed to make sending and receiving e-mail, with or without attached files, as easy as sharpening a pencil. E-mail is quickly becoming one of the most common methods of communication for people around the world. (For lots more information about using electronic mail, see Chapters 10 and 11.)

For the Macintosh

- **Eudora Light for Macintosh:** A full-featured, user-friendly, freeware e-mail application that enables Macintoshes to communicate across TCP/IP networks, such as the Internet. A commercial version of Eudora Light is available in Version 2.0 and above. The commercial version contains higher-end features such as spell-checking and the ability to filter (analyze) e-mail.

  Point your browser to http://www.qualcomm.com

- **TCP/Connect II:** A commercial product that integrates electronic mail, Usenet news, FTP, and telnet services into a single program.

  Point your browser to http://www.intercon.com

For PCs that are running Windows

- **Eudora Light for Windows:** A close cousin to Eudora Light for Macintosh.

  Point your browser to http://www.qualcomm.com

  A more fully featured commercial version is also available.

- **Elm:** Originally available only for UNIX systems; text-based.

  Point your browser to `http://www.contra.org/elm`

- **TCP/Connect II:** A commercial product that integrates electronic mail, Usenet news, FTP, and telnet services into a single program.

  Point your browser to `http://www.intercon.com`

- **Pegasus Mail:** Available from the University of Alabama, Pegasus has lots of useful features. It can also be integrated into a Novell network.

  Point your browser to `http://www.pegasus.usa.com`

On September 19, 1993, author Stephen King published a short story to the Internet — days before it reached the bookstore shelves.

Web browsers

The World Wide Web (WWW) is the name that the Internet gurus have given to a network of interconnected computers, accessed through software that presents a graphical front end that enables you to click words (hypertext) or pictures and be transported from place to place on the Net. The software that makes this all happen is called a *Web browser.* Besides browsing the Web, browsers usually enable you to read newsgroups, access Gopher (databases), and send and retrieve files. Some browsers even enable you to send e-mail. (For a detailed look at browsing the Web by using Netscape, see Chapter 15.)

The great news is that you have several options in the browser market, and most are free for educational use. I recommend Netscape Navigator for both Macintosh computers and PCs that are running Windows.

For the Macintosh

- **Netscape Navigator:** A powerful commercial navigator for the Internet. Although Navigator is primarily designed as a Web browser, you can also use it to send e-mail and begin Gopher, telnet, and FTP sessions. Netscape Navigator provides a common feature set and graphical user interface for computers that are running Microsoft Windows, Windows NT, or Macintosh and Power Macintosh operating systems. The program supports Web access, Gopher, and FTP, and it even includes basic e-mail functions.

  Point your browser to `http://www.netscape.com`

- **Internet Explorer:** Microsoft's entry into the browser war, Internet Explorer provides a set of powerful, integrated Internet tools for your Macintosh. The program allows you to surf the Web, send e-mail, ftp, and do most anything else you'd like on the Internet.

  Point your browser to `http://www.microsoft.com`

- **MacWeb:** A full-featured Web browser that includes features such as bookmarking and easy file transfer. MacWeb is available in 68K and Power Macintosh versions.
- **Spyglass Mosaic:** A next-generation version of the trend-setting NCSA Mosaic browser.

  Point your browser to `http://www.microsoft.com`

Because Web access is a hot property these days, many browsers are on the drawing board, including some that may be built into the operating system (OS) of future Macintosh computers.

For PCs that are running Windows

Here's a list of Web browsers for those of you who are using a PC that is running Windows. Many of these programs are also available in OS/2 and UNIX formats.

- **Netscape Navigator for Windows:** A Windows version of the most fully-featured Web browser on the market today. It is also available for UNIX machines at the same address.

  Point your browser to: `http://www.netscape.com`

- **Internet Explorer:** Microsoft's entry into the browser war, Internet Explorer provides a set of powerful, integrated Internet tools for your Windows PC. The program allows you to surf the Web, send e-mail, ftp, and do most anything else you'd like on the Internet.

  Point your browser to `http://www.microsoft.com`
- **WinWeb:** An easy-to-use graphical interface makes this program a good basic Web browser.

  FTP source: `ftp.cc.utexas.edu` in the directory `/pub/AI_ATTIC/ATW/programs/pc/windows`
- **Mosaic for Windows:** Easy to use Web browser and sister to Netscape. A bit buggy, though.

  FTP source: `ftp.ncsa.uiuc.edu` in the directory `/Web/Mosaic`
- **Cello:** A very simple browser for Windows. It supports World Wide Web, Gopher, FTP, ph, and Usenet news retrievals.

  FTP source: `ftp.law.cornell.edu` in the directory `/pub/LII/Cello`

America Online handled more than 2,000,000 sessions in an average day in early 1996.

Gopher/WAIS

Gopher is the tool that everyone used before the World Wide Web appeared and made file transfer a bit easier. A Gopher search shows you a hierarchical menu of database resources and provides point-and-click access to documents, search engines, and other resources.

Gopher's cousin, WAIS *(Wide Area Information Server),* is a tool that searches indexed database documents that contain information you are seeking. Like Gopher, you first supply WAIS with a search word. WAIS then displays a list of related retrievable documents. For more information on Gopher and WAIS, check out Chapter 14.

For the Macintosh

- **TurboGopher:** A terrific Gopher client that runs on almost any Macintosh computer. TurboGopher enables you to keep a list of favorite sites (bookmarks) and to navigate Gopher sites with ease.
- **MacGopher:** A simple Gopher client that runs on all Macintosh computers, even those with 512K.

For PCs that are running Windows

- **HGopher:** A Gopher+ program that enables you to navigate the various Gopher and Gopher+ servers on the Internet. It is menu-based, with each selection bringing up either a file (information, a program, a picture, whatever), a link (telnet or tn3270 terminal session), or another Gopher(+) menu.
- **WinSock Gopher:** Another excellent gopher client.
- **EWAIS (EINet WinWAIS):** A shareware WAIS search client featuring automated installation and two graphics viewers.
- **USGS WinWAIS:** A WAIS that's courtesy of the U.S. Geological Survey and which features automated installation, online help, and a separate (optional) SLIP dialer.
- **WAIS Manager:** A WAIS client that features online help and start-up instructions.

Telnet and remote logins

Telnet enables you and your students to log onto other people's Internet-connected computers. You can use telnet to access searchable databases and much more. The telnet applications that follow enable your computer to become a *dumb terminal* that emulates an on-site computer that's plugged into a host computer. (This feature is known as *terminal emulation.*) Chapter 17 has more information on telnet.

For the Macintosh

- **NCSA Telnet:** Enables your Macintosh to connect to remote computers using MacTCP.
- **Comet:** Another telnet program that allows TCP connection to telnet hosts.

For PCs that are running Windows

- **Ewan:** A great telnet client that provides full vt100 terminal emulation.

  FTP source: `ftp.lystaton.liu.se` in the directory `/pub/msdos/windows`
- **COMt:** Can be used to turn your favorite terminal package, such as Procomm Plus for Windows or Windows Terminal, into a telnet client.
- **Windows Telnet (NCSA WinTel):** Enables your PC to connect to remote computers via TCP. Provides another telnet client interface that has decent vt100 emulation.

File transfer protocol (FTP)

FTP (file transfer protocol) programs are tools that enable you to send (upload) and retrieve (download) programs, pictures, sounds, and movies from remote computers at the click of a mouse. For oodles of FTP ideas and more about the process of downloading files, see Chapter 16.

For the Macintosh

- **Fetch:** A Macintosh shareware program for transferring files. It uses file transfer protocol (FTP) and enables a networked Macintosh to transfer files with any connected machine that supports FTP.

  Point your browser to `http://www.dartmouth.edu`

For PCs that are running Windows

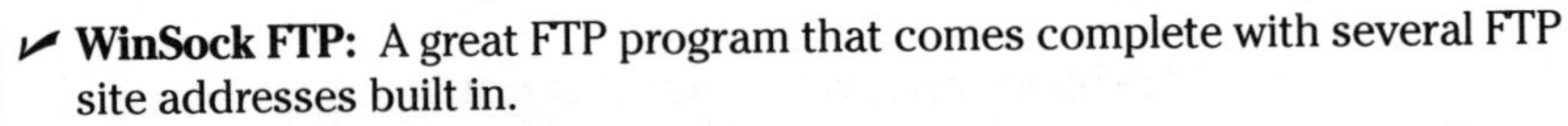

- **WinSock FTP:** A great FTP program that comes complete with several FTP site addresses built in.
- **Chameleon:** Part of a larger, integrated package that includes Chameleon mail, Ping, FTP, telnet, SLIP, and more. Chameleon is a commercial product, but a demo version is available for download at the FTP source site.

Hello, Archie

While you're fetching programs, you'll no doubt want a program that makes it easy to locate the file you need to fetch. Luckily, a program called Archie runs on many host computers (you can reach it through Gopher) to help you find those files based on a keyword search. Learn more about Archie in Chapter 16.

> **Hyper-database?**
>
> I'm always looking for tools that help me find new resources on the Internet. This one gets its own place in this chapter because it's so useful. Hytelnet is Peter Scott's Hypertext database of publicly accessible Internet sites. Hytelnet currently lists more than 1,800 sites, including libraries, campus-wide information systems, Gopher, WAIS, WWW systems, and more.
>
> Hytelnet software for the PC, Macintosh, UNIX, and VMS systems is available via anonymous FTP from `ftp.usask.ca` in the directory `/pub/hytelnet`

For the Macintosh

- **Anarchie:** You can make Archie-ing easier by using this great software program written especially to search the Internet for files. Anarchie, in addition to searching for sources for Internet files, also allows file transfer (like Fetch).

  Point your browser to `http://www.amug.org`

For PCs that are running Windows

- **Archie:** Makes finding files on the Internet easier.

Reading newsgroups

Newsgroups are the Internet equivalent of topic-centered bulletin boards. Newsreader programs make reading and contributing to these newsgroups a cinch. To learn how to use a newsreader, visit lucky Chapter 13.

For the Macintosh

The Mac has some of the most powerful and easy-to-use newsreaders of any platform.

- **NewsWatcher:** A Usenet newsreader for any operating system. Freeware for teachers. (See Chapter 13 for more information.)
- **InterNews:** A close competitor to NewsWatcher. Includes on-the-fly file decompression.
- **Nuntius:** A useful and free Usenet newsgroup reader.

You can find other newsreaders for the Mac, including TheNews, NetNews Grazer, and Newshopper, by using Archie or Anarchie.

For PCs that are running Windows

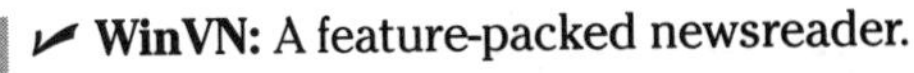

- **WinVN:** A feature-packed newsreader.
- **Free Agent:** A powerful newsreader that sets new standards for Windows Internet programs.

  Point your browser to `http://www.forte.com`
- **Trumpet News:** Another tool from the Trumpet series. A simple interface makes this very easy for the beginner and powerful enough for a veteran surfer.

Other Windows newsreaders include News Express and WinNews.

Chatting live

Internet Relay Chat (IRC) programs put a friendlier front-end on the process of live conferencing via the Internet. Chapter 18 has lots more information about using IRC.

For the Macintosh

- **IRCle:** A very simple IRC front end that enables you to choose UNIX commands from a pull-down menu.
- **Homer:** A humorous, offbeat IRC program that even has speech synthesis capabilities if you have the Mac Sound support. Users pass silly pictures of themselves so you can see them as you chat.

For PCs that are running Windows

- **mIRC:** A very powerful, much-used Windows IRC client.
- **WinSock IRC:** An easy-to-use graphical IRC front end.
- **IRC II for Windows:** A descendant of the powerful IRC II UNIX program.

Graphics and sound utilities

You need one or two utilities to help your computer read the different types of sound and graphics files on the Internet. Literally hundreds of utility programs are available, both commercially and on the Internet.

For the Macintosh

- **JPEGView:** A fast, powerful image viewer for both 68K and Power Macintoshes. JPEGView can open and display images in JPEG, PICT, GIF, TIFF, BMP, MacPaint, or Startup Screen formats.

- **Sound Machine:** Freeware that enables you to play and record sounds that you download from the Internet. Sound Machine has lots of cool buttons that you can use to change the speed, play backwards, loop sounds, switch formats, and so on, while the sounds are playing. There is no restriction on file size, and playing can take place in the background.
- **Sparkle:** A shareware program that enables Mac users to view MPEG movies. (MPEG, like QuickTime, is a file format for movies that are in digital format.)
- **GIF Converter:** Another graphics viewing program that enables Mac users to view, edit, and resave graphics in different formats. GIF Converter is shareware.
- **Simple Player:** A shareware program that uses the QuickTime movie controller to play and edit movie files.

For PCs that are running Windows

- **ACDSee:** A GIF/JPG viewer for Windows.
- **VuePrint:** A great tool for viewing, translating, and printing your favorite graphics from the Internet.
- **QuickTime for Windows:** Enables you to view QuickTime movies by using the Windows Media Player.

  Point your browser to `http://www.apple.com/QuickTime`

- **Paintshop Pro:** A fullfeatured paint program that's perfect for converting and touching up graphics.
- **MPEGPlay:** Great for viewing MPEG animation. Requires a machine capable of running Win32 applications.

Graphics with a UNIX shell?

Never fear. The wizards of technology have come up with a couple of interesting utilities that enable you to use graphical Internet software, such as Netscape and Eudora Light, with a standard UNIX shell account.

- The Internet Adapter (TIA) (Macintosh): Converts a shell account into a pseudo-SLIP account the same way an electrical adapter converts a two-prong outlet into a three-prong outlet. (For more information on The Internet Adapter, see Chapter 15.)

  Web source: `http://marketplace.com/tia/tiahome.html`

- SlipKnot (Windows and Macintosh): A graphical Web browser that, like TIA, does not require SLIP, PPP, or TCP/IP.

  Web source: `http://www.interport.net/slipknot/slipknot.html`

Both of these commercial software products work "acceptably well" when compared with a true SLIP or PPP connection.

File compression and decompression

In order to make the transmission time shorter, files on the Internet are often squished (compressed) before they are sent. Here are a few tools that you can use to unsquish stuff, as well as to compress your own files for transmission.

For the Macintosh

- **StuffIt Expander:** Expands files that are compressed before they are sent over the Internet. StuffIt Expander is a scaled-down version of Aladdin Software's popular StuffIt Deluxe program.

  Point your browser to `http://www.aladdin.com`

- **Acrobat Reader:** A very useful program that reads Adobe Acrobat (.pdf) files. Acrobat allows application-independent saving of documents and retains all layout and design on both Mac and Windows PCs.

  Point your browser to `http://www.adobe.com`

For PCs that are running Windows

- **WinZip:** Software utility for file compression and decompression.
- **Acrobat Reader:** A very useful program that reads Adobe Acrobat (.pdf) files. Acrobat allows application-independent saving of documents and retains all layout and design on both Mac and Windows PCs.

  Point your browser to `http://www.adobe.com`

Finding people

Here are some tools to use with Windows when you want to find out who has an account on the Internet. See Chapter 11 for more information on using Finger and other people-finder programs.

For the Macintosh

- **Finger:** Search servers on the Internet for information about specific users.

  Note that Finger and its cousin Ph are also incorporated into Eudora Light and are accessible through many Web browsers and mail programs.

For PCs that are running Windows

- **WS Finger:** A program that works with WinSock (Windows Sockets) and helps you locate other users on the Internet.
- **WinWhois:** A whois client for Windows. (Whois is a UNIX command that helps you locate a known user on a known server.)

  Note that Finger and its cousin Ph are also incorporated into Eudora Light and are accessible through many Web browsers and mail programs.

All-in-one tools to use with Windows

The Chameleon suite of applications (`http://www.netmanage.com/netmanage/nm3.html`) for Microsoft Windows is a ready-to-run package that includes both applications and the TCP/IP protocol stack. It can be installed and up and running in about five minutes. Applications include: Mail, Gopher, News Reader, FTP, FTP Server, Telnet, TN3270, TN5250, Finger, Whois, Visual Script Editor and Player, Bind, Phone Tag, NewtPROFS, LPR/LPD, TFTP, Ping, and SNMP Agent. Chameleon also includes both LAN and dial-up support.

Other cool Net tools for Macs and for PCs that are running Windows

Other tools let you do everything from live videoconferencing via the Internet to checking the weather in Peoria. The following programs begin to give us a glimpse of future uses of the Internet.

- **CU-SeeMe:** A conferencing tool for the Macintosh and PCs running Windows; used by elementary schools, individuals, and other organizations around the world for low-cost video communications.
- **Blue Skies for Macintosh:** Recipient of one of Apple Computer's Cool Tools Awards for Internet Programming Efforts, this Macintosh application offers a graphical interface to weather and environmental information that features interactive graphics and user input features.
- **Macweather:** Great for finding out what the weather is in Peoria.
- **MacTCPWatcher:** An Internet troubleshooter that monitors and reports information about your TCP/IP connection.
- **Maven:** A tool that brings real-time audio-conferencing to the Internet. A fast, direct connection to the Internet is recommended.

Other Goodies!

The update from the first edition to this software-packed 2nd Edition of *The Internet For Teachers* allowed me to include some other goodies I've found recently that are terrific examples of cutting-edge Internet software. On the CD you find

- **Claris E-mailer (Windows/Macintosh):** A full-featured e-mail program that allows you to sort, filter, and file e-mail from one or more Internet accounts. The easy interface and powerful add-on tools (like a spelling checker) will make your Internet e-mail exchanges a pleasure and a breeze!

- **Claris Home Page (Macintosh):** A really cool program that walks you through the process of producing a home page on the World Wide Web *without* any knowledge of HTML code. A Windows version will hit the shelves by the time you read this book.
- **Internet Coach/Mission to Planet X (Macintosh/Windows):** A self-paced guide to using the Internet from the very creative folks at APTE.
- **Surfboard (Macintosh):** An amazing program that makes accessing bookmarks for your Web browser as easy as using your TV remote.
- **SiteMarker (Macintosh):** Another tool for organizing bookmarks. You and your students will love this one!
- **Webphone (Windows) and Internetphone (Macintosh):** A couple of programs that'll make your long distance carrier angry and your phone bills plummet. The voice quality is still not there, but it's cheaper to call Chile than to buy some at a restaurant!

The Future

The Internet is still an infant. As it grows and changes, so will the tools that you use to access its resources. Internet tools are already being integrated into higher level operating systems, like Macintosh OS and Windows 95, and into applications (such as word processors and databases). In fact, a tool called CyberDog, from Apple, allows the incorporation of powerful Internet tools into practically any OpenDoc-aware application. Pretty soon, it'll all look like one seamless network. Right now, though, look around for the best tools for the job that you need to do, and look for ease of use when you select tools for teachers and students. Don't forget to plan for the future. Net-baby is likely to need new clothes (hardware) and different food (software) in the not-too-distant future.

Chapter 9

I Told You So: Net Responsibility

In This Chapter

- Avoiding potholes on the information superhighway
- Introducing the Internet
- Thinking ethically
- Taking out a contract on your kids

My mother taught me to drive in a bright red Pinto wagon (with wood-grain sides) in a church parking lot not far from our home. Before she would release me to terrorize the world, she wanted to make sure I was prepared for some of the hazards I might encounter. We parallel parked, we backed in circles, we even made believe there were stop and yield signs. Before long I was the best parking-lot driver you've ever seen.

You know how the story goes. Not long after I got my license, I made an unfortunate decision to take a unfamiliar shortcut on a very rocky dirt road on the way home from the grocery store. I'm not exactly sure what happened, but I know I ran over something that dented the fender (and probably more), and that the "something" was nothing like I had encountered in the church parking lot. That day I learned a lesson — there are some things a Pinto wagon just wasn't designed to do. At the least, I should've driven more slowly, looked ahead, and chosen a better route.

As you and your students navigate the Internet, you need to know where the potholes are and have a strategy for steering around them. As you see in the sections ahead, a little preplanning for your Internet excursions makes the trip much smoother.

Controversy Knocks

Most educators know that sooner or later controversy follows any innovation or change. The introduction of global resources to the classroom is no exception. As access to databases, electronic mail, computer art, and programs increases, so does the anxiety of your peers and members of your community who don't understand what you're doing.

Surf-Watch

Currently, more than 200 Internet newsgroups contain sexually explicit material. Some sites on the Web also contain pictures and text that depict sexual situations. Until recently, no easy way to control access to this information existed.

Surf-Watch is a software product for Macintosh and PCs running Windows that enables you to block access to sexually explicit (or other objectionable) sites from individual computers or through networks. A password-protected on-off switch enables you to allow or prevent access.

Surf-Watch comes with an initial listing of hundreds of sites that the folks at Surf-Watch believe may be inappropriate for children. They also offer a subscription program that adults can use to update the list of unwanted sites periodically. Their standards for site selection are admittedly subjective, but you can request a customized list for your particular setting. Currently, changes to the site list can be made only by the Surf-Watch programmers.

The software controls access to specific WWW, FTP, Gopher, and chat sites and can restrict access to selected newsgroups. Surf-Watch works with any Macintosh that is running System 7.*x* or higher and with any modem, ISDN, or high-speed Internet link. It is not designed to work with commercial online services.

Some people will say that this program is a form of censorship; others will say that it is a useful tool for blocking inappropriate material from the classroom. You make the call. If this program interests you, contact Surf-Watch, via e-mail, at `info@surfwatch.com`

As in the real world, you and your students will likely stumble on attitudes and opinions that are very different from your own — sometimes even disturbing. The Internet, after all, is a confederacy of single-minded users in a multicultural society. The only thing that governs the content on the Net is the good sense of those who place information there. And, as educators especially understand, not everyone has good sense.

So what's a teacher to do? Do you put all the cards on the table before you introduce the Internet to your school, or do you just stand by and wait until the controversy monster rears its ugly head?

I think the answer is . . . well . . . both. I've developed a plan to help introduce Internet technology to the three R's. It's called the three I's!

Want a great place to find statistics about the growth and use of the Internet? Try pointing your Web browser to `http://www.ed.gov/NCES/`

The Three I's

The former president of Apple, John Sculley, once said, "The journey is the reward." In some cases, your efforts to introduce the Net to your school in a planned, educational way will both strengthen your resolve and help you appreciate how others think about and learn about the Internet. As you approach the beginning of your journey, check out these three tips:

- Invite
- Introduce
- Integrate

Invite your fellow teachers and community members to sample the water

When I make a presentation at a parent-teacher association meeting or to a faculty, I try to focus the group's attention on positive uses of the Internet, not on its pitfalls. Nothing is more dangerous than entering a discussion without all the facts. Most people learn what they know about the Internet from the media or from "urban legends" that float around and grow into amazing stories of Net use or abuse. What you (and your community) need are facts. After your peers and community have firsthand experience of the wealth of resources available on the Internet, they'll have a better idea of its potential uses in the classroom and firsthand factual information to help them continue the dialog about the Internet in your school. Chapter 21 has some dandy cyberjourneys that you can try out as you answer questions from the crowd.

Of course, the best way to have people sample the waters is to conduct an afterschool class about the Internet. Allow small groups to wander the Net or create cyberjourneys of their own. As you discuss their task, suggest that the focus in using the Internet in the school is both learning *about* the Internet and learning *with* the Internet. Find out what their opinions are about the value of each strategy.

Whichever method you use to help folks see what the Net is all about, be sure to shoot straight. Colleges and universities, for the most part, have erased objectionable graphics from their servers. The Net *is,* in a way, policing itself. But quite a few things on the Net will give you goose bumps when you read, see, and hear them. Be honest about what you've personally witnessed, if anything, that some people may be uncomfortable with.

After the people who want to dive in and get wet have had their fill, look to your media and technology committee (You *do* have one, don't you?) to move on to the next step. Be sure that your committee has a broad representation — especially student and parent representatives.

Introduce a set of guidelines

Have you ever driven up to a very busy intersection where the stoplight isn't working? This situation is the quintessential example of how a set of community guidelines — in this case, traffic laws and courtesy — helps things run more smoothly. Sure, the occasional bozo zips through the intersection — and usually pays a dear price, both physically and to the repair shop. But, for the most part, people get through without a scratch. You can, too.

Setting guidelines for the use of the Internet is a great way to ensure that you and your students don't end up as casualties on the information superhighway. The guidelines that you set will help guide administrators, teachers, and students as they find ways to use the technology.

After the decision-makers in your school have taken a test run on the Internet, think about what's important to make the implementation successful. What cost-control issues need to be considered? Equity issues? Content issues? Training issues? Support issues?

In some cases, schools have to worry about cost considerations. If the call you're placing to log onto the Internet is a toll call, or if you're using a commercial pay-as-you-go service, creating a set of guidelines that relate to your budgetary restrictions is critical. Some online services, such as America Online, enable schools to purchase time in increments of 10, 20, 30, or more hours per month. When the time is up, no more Internet time. Simple, and great for budgeting. But these restrictions make some people very nervous. What if you have a really exciting and innovative project, but you have only 30 minutes left this month? What's a teacher to do? The answer is something teachers are all too familiar with — advance planning.

Equity is also an issue. Are you comfortable with the inevitability that Mr. Jones or Mrs. Smith will be surfing all the time and others will become jealous that they're missing all the great waves of knowledge? Think about finding ways, either through increasing the access to Internet-capable computers or by monitoring time, to maximize access to this exciting technology. Think "out of the box" and try schemes such as issuing time vouchers or rewarding teachers with Internet time for innovative instructional plans.

If your school wants to control the content accessible through the Net, you have some options. Depending on how you access the Net, varying amounts of control are available. Many universities, for example, lock out access to the much maligned "alt" (alternative) newsgroups. The universities aren't concerned about content so much as they are about whether anybody will get their regular schoolwork done because they've turned into Net-addicted cyberjockeys. Some commercial services offer "parental control" features that may or may not meet your needs. If you're concerned about control issues, contact your Internet provider and find out about your options.

Protecting us from our cyberselves

A number of organizations are thinking about policies and about ethics issues that are related to the Net. Among these organizations, the Electronic Frontier Foundation (EFF) is perhaps the one that has the highest profile. Its goal is to "ensure that the principles embodied in the Constitution and the Bill of Rights are protected as new communications technologies emerge." Founded by such high-profile folks as Lotus founder Mitch Kapor, Sun Microsystems founder Bill Joy, and Grateful Dead lyricist John Perry Barlow, the EFF has been very effective in getting the ear of people in Washington who matter. The EFF already has an impressive record in protecting citizens from government interference and helping the computer-using community become aware of issues related to data security, ethics, and free speech. The EFF maintains online support on America Online, CompuServe, and other online services, and it has its own Internet node. For more information, send e-mail to `info@eff.org`

The EFF isn't alone. Here's a short list of a few other groups that are concerned with issues relating to Internet policy and ethics. As you'll no doubt realize if you request information, each takes a slightly different slant on the issues at hand. All of the groups, however, promote free speech and equal access to electronic communications.

Group	*Address*
Americans Communicating Electronically (ACE)	e-mail: `info@ace.esusda.gov`
Center for Media Education (CME)	e-mail: `cme@access.digex.net`
The Digital Freedom Network (DFN)	e-mail: `gopher.iia.org`
Libraries for the Future (LFF)	e-mail: `LFF@phantom.com`
National Public Telecomputing Network (NPTN)	e-mail: `info@nptn.org`

How about training and support? How will teachers learn about the Internet? Should students use valuable time if they haven't been shown the ropes? (The last question is one that only you, as the responsible adult in charge, can answer.) Suffice it to say that this whole Internet business is like a four-legged stool, with a hardware leg, a software leg, a training leg, and a support leg. Leave out a leg and see what happens to the stool. And you thought surfing was hazardous?

Integrate

My friend and school technology coordinator, Dr. Sherah Carr, always says, "The curriculum should drive the use of technology and not the other way around." Nowhere is this statement more true than in using the Internet. The Net, after all, is a *huge* place. You and your students can spend time wandering aimlessly and get absolutely nothing accomplished. Or you can use the time wisely, enriching and enhancing the curriculum. The choice should be a conscious one.

Now before you jump out of your chair, know that there *is* something to be said for "playing" on the Net. That's pretty much the way I learned. I got my learner's permit on the information superhighway by getting in and out of places that I'd never heard or thought of. It is important, however, to plan. Showing your students that there's a valid purpose for the terabytes of information that are floating around out there is essential. It's also important to know when using the ragged-edged encyclopedia or sorting through old magazines is *better* than using the Internet.

Integration means working the wonders of the Net into the parts of the curriculum where they best fit. In some cases, the Internet can be the missing piece in your curriculum puzzle. Integration means setting curriculum goals and using the Internet as a *tool* to enhance or enrich instruction. Model this to others and your journey into the Internet will be richer, as will the students you mentor.

Well, there it is. Of course, no plan is perfect. And your school may never be faced with controversy concerning the Net. But if it does, the I's (ayes!) have it!

The first K-12 schools connected to the Internet in 1988.

InternEthics

Even though the Internet is still the "wild, wild west" of cyberspace, a virtually lawless and totally free environment, people have been talking about Internet ethics and rules since the Net's inception. Groups such as the Division Advisory Panel of the National Science Foundation's Division of Network Communications Research and Infrastructure (Is that a mouthful or what?) have formalized thoughts about unethical and unacceptable activities. They define these activities as those that purposely do any of the following:

- Seek to gain unauthorized access to the resources of the Internet
- Disrupt the intended use of the Internet
- Waste resources (people, capacity, computer)

The top ten ways to be a good Internet citizen

1. Never knowingly post or forward information that's not true.
2. Have good manners.
3. Tell people when you like their work.
4. Be creative, not destructive.
5. Always obey copyright laws.
6. Think before you send.
7. Be yourself.
8. Don't use someone else's account or password.
9. Ask for help when you need it.
10. Think before you upload.

(adapted from "Ten Commandments for Computer Ethics," Computer Ethics Institute)

- Destroy the integrity of computer-based information
- Compromise the privacy of users

Pretty straightforward, no? It's a great idea to schedule time to read and discuss these statements with your students and talk with your school's technology committee about the issue of ethics on the Internet.

After you've taken your students on a tour of the Net and discussed the above list of Internet don'ts, ask them to work in small groups to develop their own Code of Internet Ethics and post each group's work in your classroom. Focus on what effective Internet citizens should *know, do,* and *be like*.

You can find a great three-part series entitled "Internet Ethics and Behavior" for students in grades 5 through 8 at the Software Publishing Association's Gopher site. Gopher to `kids.ccit.duq.edu` (for information on Gopher, see Chapter 14).

Take out a contract on your kids

Don't worry, the contract I'm talking about is a simple agreement between you and your students (and their parents) about how, when, and why the Internet is used in the classroom. Having the little piece of paper around will make you feel better, and it will make what's OK and not OK when surfing the Net very clear to all involved.

Creating a 40-page document that covers all possible angles would probably be pretty easy, but you really don't need that. A brief, well-constructed, well-thought-out document, *collaboratively* developed by parents, students, administrators, and fellow teachers, is the best bet.

Here are a few questions that you may consider answering as you build your Internet use contract:

- Is it necessary to keep a log of student time and purpose?
- What are the expectations about adhering to federal, state, and local laws?
- How about school policies? Should you mention them?
- What kinds of information (if any) are off-limits?
- What about copyright laws?
- What constitutes an "authorized use" and an "authorized access"?
- What about commercialization and the Internet?
- How about privacy? Passwords?
- What are specific expectations for student behavior? What should be done about students who misuse the Net?
- What are the parent, teacher, and administrative responsibilities related to the contract?
- Who grants the rights to use the Internet in your school, and who can rescind those rights?
- Are there time limitations?
- What happens if someone violates this contract?

I hope that you'll reread my comments about being brief that appear before this too-long listing. You don't, after all, want to scare the students away. They're not buying a house or writing a book. Keep it simple.

After creating your agreement, be sure to develop a plan to inform your students about the contract and decide how it will be signed. Think about enforcement as well. Be as swift with punishment for misuse of the Internet as you are with praise for proper use.

You know your school better than anyone on the outside. Get your media and technology committee together and discuss whether you feel you need policies, guidelines, or contracts for Internet use. Check magazines, online services, and the Internet itself for examples of completed contracts. (I purposely didn't give you a completed contract. Yours will be much better than mine, anyway!)

Going through the exercise of writing a contract is worth the time and effort. You'll all learn something new, and your journey into the Internet will be much smoother.

Remember, however, that although a little forethought and open discussion about responsibility, ethics, and the proper use of the Internet can save you and your students much grief, no contract can replace close supervision if you're concerned about what students will find.

Part III

Internet Resource Roundup

In this part . . .

In this part, you take your first steps onto the information superhighway. As your coach, I offer bunches of helpful tips and step-by-step instructions on how to use popular shareware and freeware programs (some included on the CD with this book) to make your journey on the Internet more pleasant and productive.

The Internet is a vast, lawless place, full of knowledge just waiting to be used. These chapters give you the basics, step-by-step, for becoming a top-notch knowledge navigator, plus a glimpse into the near future as multimedia meets the Web.

Chapter 10

E-Mail: You'll Get Hooked!

In This Chapter

- What is e-mail?
- Working with e-mail
- Getting started
- Finding your own address
- Can we talk?
- Dissecting e-mail
- Sending and receiving e-mail
- Internet 101: Eudora Light
- Using 'da browser for mail
- Worldwide shopping basket

My teacher friend Cathy came flying down the hall one day, waving a piece of paper. It was a recipe for pecan fudge cookies. Big deal? You bet! That recipe was her very first e-mail (electronic mail) message. And the coolest part? It came from a home economics teacher in Alaska who teaches in a remote K-12 school with 20 students, and Cathy had never had any contact with her before. Great, huh? There are lots of great ideas out there, and electronic mail is a great way to share them.

I have a prediction. The very first time you receive an e-mail message from a fellow teacher hundreds of miles away, you'll be hooked, too. If you're like most educators, you spend precious little time communicating with other teachers. I mean, we're kind of isolated in our classrooms, aren't we?

Don't believe me? Try to call a teacher friend during the day. Bus duty, homeroom responsibilities, and faculty meetings, not to mention teaching five or six periods a day, leave little time for using traditional methods to communicate with the outside world. Just as mastering global communications is becoming a standard work skill for our students, the same is certainly true for teachers. Electronic mail (e-mail) may be the grand equalizer that finally knocks down the walls of our classrooms and enables us to get to the resources we need. With access to e-mail through a classroom or media center phone line, a schoolwide network, or from home, we can finally have a clear line of communication with parents, friends, relatives, and students.

What Is E-Mail?

Any message sent over a network, regardless of whether the message stays in your school's local area network (LAN) or passes through an Internet provider to the Australian outback, is e-mail. It is the electronic equivalent of a 32¢ stamp, only faster, usually.

Think of electronic mail as the sledgehammer that enables you to begin knocking down classroom walls. We teachers have been somewhat restricted to ideas and resources that are housed within our own school. Sure, we grab a moment now and then to discuss ideas with fellow staff members and visit the media center, and we store classroom resources like pack rats. Still, our resource base is pretty much within the walls of the school.

Using e-mail, you and your students can exchange ideas with people all over the planet. It's awesome to think that, through the power of telecommunications, you can communicate directly with everyone from research scientists to rock stars. Electronic mail is a great way to begin your exploration into the Internet from your classroom.

What can I do with e-mail?

It slices, it dices, it . . . oh, sorry. It's just that e-mail is very versatile. Just versatile enough to get you connected with the world or offer a grand opportunity for kid mischief. But look on the bright side: With access to electronic mail, you and your students can

- Send and receive electronic letters. Mail a note to a local politician or to your best friend who's on another commercial online service. By using e-mail, you can reach virtually everyone on the Internet — all 23,000,000+ of them. The letter arrives almost instantaneously — complete with misspelled words and happy thoughts. Oh, and by the way, you can send one letter to lots of different people with the click of a mouse. Wait . . . is that good?
- Send and receive files. I can whip up a lesson plan on ClarisWorks, save it to disk, and attach it to a letter. Then friends around the world can experience the wonders of my fifth-period science class. I can get pictures from the Internet, too, and programs — even sounds. Most for *free.* Is this awesome, or what?

- Receive regular mailings from topic-based mailing lists. *Subscribing to* (applying to receive) any one of a bunch of electronic newsletters and topic-based discussion groups is a snap if you're using e-mail. Subscribe to too many, however, and your mailbox will quickly look like the front hall at the last bell.

The Internet is growing by more than 10 percent each month.

Okay! I'm convinced! What do I need to do first?

To send electronic mail, all you need is a computer, a modem, a connection to the Internet (see Chapter 5 to explore your connection options), and access to a computer program that sends and receives mail. You can connect through a commercial online service, an information provider, or a college or university. The way you send and receive messages depends on how you are connected to the Internet.

Your personal e-mail address is granted by your Internet provider when you make arrangements for Internet access. After you have your connection and your address, the rest is as easy as ABC. Read on!

What's my address?

Knock, knock. Who's there? Before you send a letter to someone, it's probably a good idea to know your own address. An Internet address is assigned by your Internet provider and has three parts: the *username* (a series of letters and/or numbers that form your unique identity as an Internet citizen), the *domain name* (the name of the one [or more] computer[s] to which the account belongs), and the *top-domain name* (which describes the type of location from which the message is sent). An @ sign separates the username from the domain name and top-domain name.

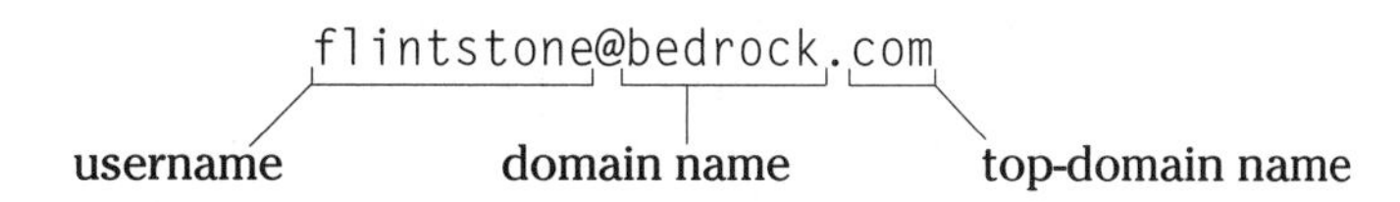

Your username (the first letters and numbers to the left of the @ symbol) is assigned to you by your Internet provider. Depending on the size of your organization, sometimes usernames can get really lengthy. You may, for example, see something like this:

```
george%george.jungle@bananaman.com
```

Some are strictly numeric, as in this CompuServe address:

```
72344.1234@compuserve.com
```

The first letters and/or numbers in the domain name (to the right of the @ symbol) describe the name of your Internet server.

An America Online (AOL) address, for example, might look like this:

```
socrates@aol.com
```

If you are on CompuServe, your address could be the following:

```
98765.1234@compuserve.com
```

The `98765.1234` is the user's ID, and `compuserve` is the name of the online service.

A Prodigy address might look like this:

```
VWXY123@prodigy.com
```

If you're connected through a university or commercial information provider, your address could be this:

```
barney@university.edu
```

or

```
bananaman@bigshack.jungle.com
```

The last few letters, referred to as the *top-domain,* or *zone,* are separated from the Internet computer's name by a period and help you determine what kind of organization sent the mail — business, government, education, and so on — and in some cases the country of origin. In the following address, `.edu` (the top-domain name) indicates that the mail originated from an educational site, such as a college or university:

```
mapleleaf@canada.edu
```

Table 10-1 lists some common country codes that you use to identify the country of origin.

Table 10-1 Country Codes (Zones)

Zone	*Country*
au	Australia
at	Austria
be	Belgium
ca	Canada
cz	The Czech Republic
dk	Denmark
fi	Finland
fr	France
de	Germany
in	India
ie	Ireland
il	Israel
it	Italy
jp	Japan
nl	Netherlands
no	Norway
ru	The Russian Federation
es	Spain
se	Sweden
ch	Switzerland
tw	Taiwan
uk	The United Kingdom
us	The United States (optional)

Breaking the Internet's secret code

You may see any one of a number of different endings (called *top-domains or zones)* in an Internet address. Here are the six most common:

- **.com:** a commercial service (example: socrates@aol.com, an America Online address)
- **.edu:** an education or education-related organization (example: quarterback@uga.cc.uga.edu, which gets you a touchdown at the University of Georgia)
- **.gov:** government and/or government contractors (example: president@whitehouse.gov, one of the president's e-mail addresses — the mailbox is always full!)
- **.mil:** the military (example: patton@army.mil, one of our nation's finest)
- **.org:** other organizations that don't really fit into another classification (example: greentree@manatee.org; a fake address, but my friend Nita loves manatees, and I think it sounds cool)
- **.net:** network resources (example: chiphead@mainframe.net, for chipheads only)

You also see endings such as .uk and .fi. These endings are *country codes* (refer to Table 10-1). These examples are from notes that came from Buckingham Palace and Helsinki, respectively. What? You've never received a letter from the Prime Minister?

Now don't go sending a bunch of mail to the addresses in this sidebar. They're all figments of an occasionally fertile imagination — except for the president's address, that is.

Can we talk?

Well, you've gotten this far, and I know what you're thinking: "Wait! I have a Zebra 9000 computer, and my friend has a Peach 6150. Can we talk?" Luckily, the answer is yes. Because the Internet works in a *standard protocol* (that's techno-weenie for *common language*), virtually any machine can send and receive e-mail. The only hitches come when you exchange pictures, sounds, or programs, as discussed in Chapter 16. So don't worry; I've sent e-mail from my Apple IIe to an Acorn computer somewhere in Britain without a hitch. (They're nuts about computers over there.)

On occasion, you'll be asked to give your Internet address to someone else over the telephone or in person. To sound like an Internet veteran, remember one rule: When you say your address, the familiar period becomes "dot." So, if your America Online e-mail address is `socrates@aol.com`, you say, "Socrates at A-O-L dot com." Isn't techno-babble wonderful?

In January of 1996, the Internet carried more than 21 *trillion* bytes of information (21,233,433,431,110 bytes, to be exact).

Mail anatomy

Before you learn to send a message, here's a little mail anatomy: E-mail has two parts, the header and the message.

The *header* may contain information about you (the sender), the receiver's electronic address, the date, and a subject. The *message* part contains your birthday wishes, requests for information about your spring break trip to Florida, or anything else you feel like writing. Easy as pie!

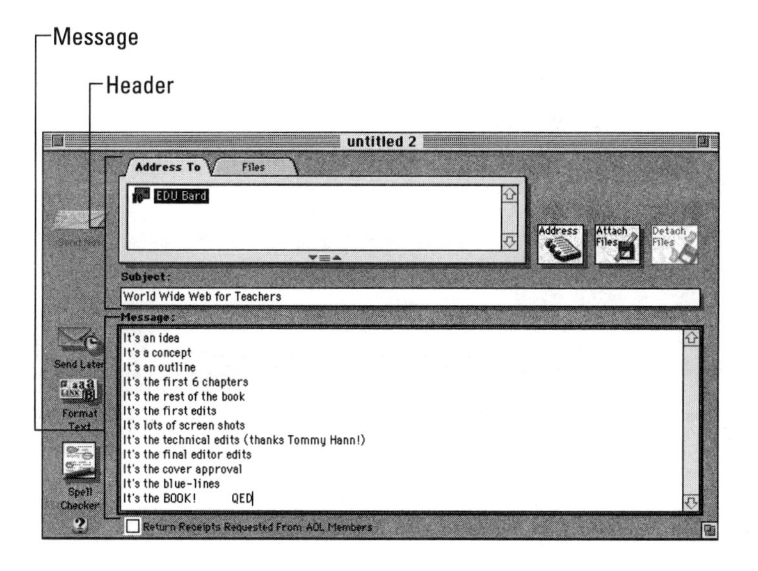

Sending and Receiving E-Mail

Commercial online services and accounts furnished by Internet providers (SLIP or PPP accounts) offer the easiest and most user-proof method of sending Internet mail. The graphical interfaces and (more or less) intuitive commands are a bit easier to handle than *mailers* (programs running on a UNIX network that enable you to send e-mail).

Sending and receiving Internet mail via an online service

All the major commercial online services offer users the option of sending electronic mail through the Internet. Most services only require you to enter a full Internet address (`username@domain name`) in the address field and send the message on its way.

On America Online, for example, sending and receiving Internet e-mail is a cinch.

Note that these examples are based on AOL Version 3.0 for Macintosh and AOL 3.0 for Windows and Windows 95. If you have an earlier version, some of these screens may look a little different. Get a FREE upgrade to Version 3.0 of AOL by signing on to the service and entering Keyword: Upgrade.

1. **Sign onto America Online.**
2. **Choose Compose Mail (⌘+M /Ctrl+M) from the Mail pull-down menu on the menu bar.**

   You are presented with a blank message screen that looks like this:

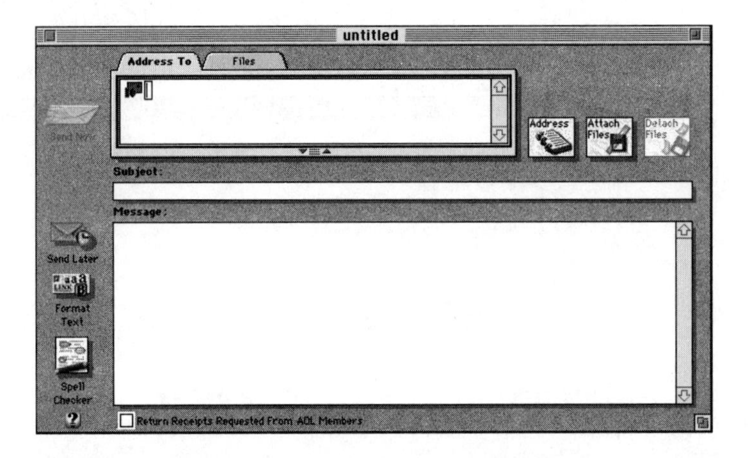

3. **Enter the full Internet e-mail address of the recipient in the Address To box and press Tab to move to the next box.**

   Note: If you're sending e-mail to someone on the same online service, you don't need the `@domain name` part of the address. If you use it, the mail will still get through, but it's a little like calling your basement from your attic via Mozambique.

4. **Add a subject in the Subject box and press Tab to move to the next box.**
5. **Enter your message.**
6. **Click Send Now (to send immediately) or Send Later (to ask AOL to send your message another time).**

Here's what an e-mail message, ready to be sent to a CompuServe user, might look like:

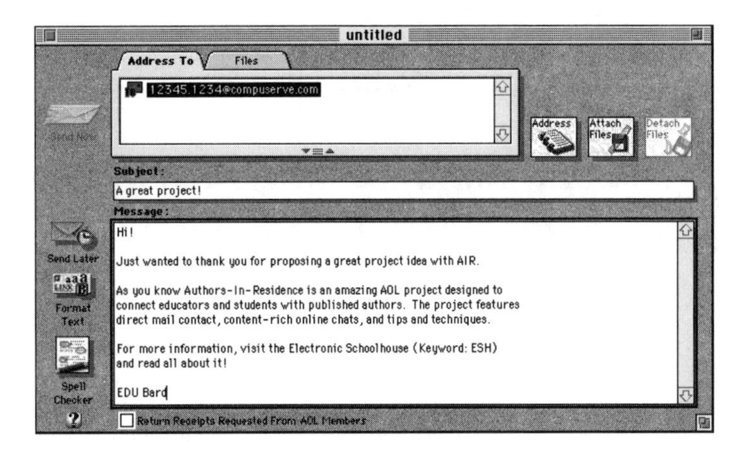

The e-mail message zips through America Online's Internet gateway computer out onto the Internet and roots around until it finds a destination. This long journey, by the way, takes milliseconds. That's faster than a teacher can duck a flying eraser (an important survival skill taught and practiced in teacher preparation programs everywhere)!

Other commercial online services, such as CompuServe and Prodigy, offer similar graphical interfaces. Incoming mail comes right to your electronic mailbox, and you are notified with audio or visual online cues. Just select Read new mail from the Mail menu and double-click to read your incoming messages.

How do you know whether you have mail? On AOL, you see a mailbox, and if you have a Macintosh or a computer that is running Windows and has a sound card, your computer proudly announces, "You've got mail," and you see the flag go up on your online mailbox. Talk about addressing multiple learning styles!

By mid-1996, there were seven Internet providers in Egypt.

Claris E-mailer to the Rescue!

Sooner or later, you'll have more than one e-mail account, and you'll wish you had some way to manage all these e-words so you don't go e-crazy. Thank goodness for Claris E-mailer. E-mailer not only offers automated access to multiple accounts, but it's also a full-featured e-mail sending and receiving program. That's not all: It sorts and filters your mail, has a great address book, and even has a dandy built-in spell-checker. The Macintosh and Windows interface is a dream, and the setup is so easy you'll wonder whether you've missed something. This program's a winner, folks. Try it — you'll love it!

Sending and receiving Internet mail via a university/UNIX network

If you are connected via a university network, you have access to server-based programs, called *mailers,* that have names that sound environment friendly, such as *pine* and *elm,* or names that sound technical, such as *x-mail* and *mail/mailx* (Berkeley mail). These text-based mail programs are just as functional as their online service counterparts, but you have to use somewhat cryptic commands to read and send messages instead of merely clicking an icon with your computer mouse.

To access a mailer from your computer workstation, sign onto your network and at the prompt type **elm** or **pine.** The rest is menu driven.

Here's a sample message ready to be sent by using pine:

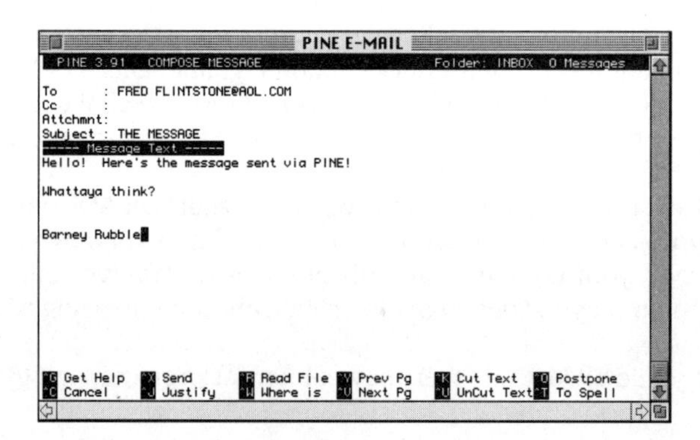

See what I mean? It's hardly as friendly or as fully featured as its graphics-based relatives, but it works quite well.

Several other e-mail programs are available for UNIX-class users. One of the most common is called pine. Someone once told me that pine is an acronym that stands for *pine is not elm.* I guess elm stands for *electronic mail,* but it could stand for *everybody's limited mail.* Sorry, elm-people.

Luckily, most information providers and some universities provide a great way to avoid the hassle of using elm or pine. Say hello to Eudora Light.

Internet 101 Eudora Light

Eudora Light is a computer program that you can use to send and receive electronic mail if you're connected to the Internet through a SLIP or PPP account. (If SLIP and PPP are Greek to you, check out Chapter 5.) Eudora Light and its big sister, Eudora Pro, are available for both Windows and Macintosh computers. The program has an easy-to-use front end for sending, receiving, and managing mail. As with most other programs these days, it has lots of useful bells and whistles, too.

The version of Eudora Light included with this book is freeware for educators. The folks at QualComm, makers of Eudora, also have a commercial version that has an enhanced feature set. For purchasing information, send e-mail to `eudora-info@qualcomm.com` or check the Read Me file on the accompanying CD-ROM.

The manual accompanying Eudora says that the program got its name when the programmer was inspired by Eudora Welty's "Why I Live at the P. O." Isn't it wonderful that great writing still moves people . . . to write programs? Long live Eudora!

Okay. To get down to business, here are the basics. . . .

Sending mail with Eudora Light

You're in luck! Freeware versions of Eudora for the Macintosh and for PCs running Windows are on the CD that comes with this book. Eudora for Windows operates very much like Eudora for the Macintosh, so the directions below work virtually identically for whatever computer you're using. You can use any FTP program (Fetch, wsFTP, and so on) to retrieve a more current version of Eudora Light for your computer via FTP from `ftp.qualcomm.com`

Using Eudora Light to send a message is very simple. Basically, you launch the program, type your message, and send it.

Here's a set of step-by-step instructions for you to follow to send an e-mail message:

1. **Double-click the Eudora Light icon.**

   Note: If this is your first time using Eudora Light, the configuration window pops up automatically on the Windows version and on some of the Mac versions of the program. If the configuration window doesn't pop up when you first launch Eudora Light, choose Settings from the Special menu, choose Personal Information from the icons on the left of the dialog box, and enter your account information in the following screen before moving to Step 2.

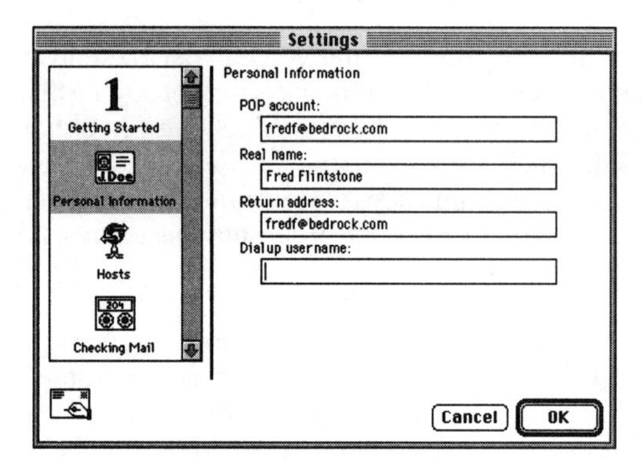

2. **Log on to your Internet service provider.**

   You don't have to be logged in to create your message. You can complete Steps 4 through 8 and *then* log on (see Steps 2 and 3) and click on Send.

3. **After you log in, enter the password furnished by your Internet provider when you are prompted.**

4. **Choose New Message from the Message pull-down menu.**

   If all goes well and the planets are lined up just right, you see this:

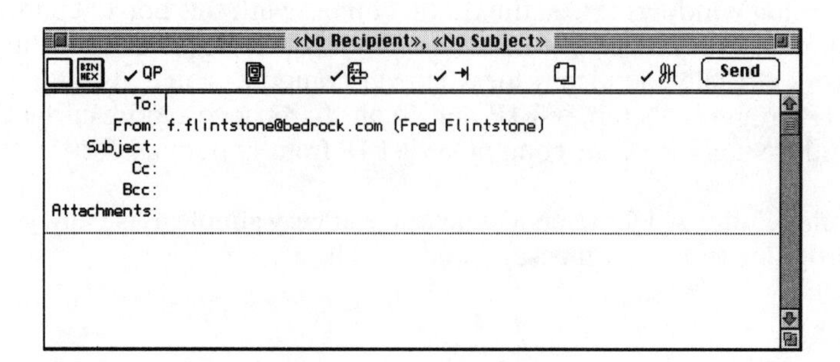

5. **Click just to the right of the word *To* and enter the full Internet address of the person to whom you're sending your letter.**

   (Example: `ashley.jordan@cook.com`).

   You can type more than one Internet address in the To line. Just separate them with a comma, like this:

   ```
   addressone@domain.com, addresstwo@domain.edu
   ```

   Eudora also has a Nicknames option that enables you to save lists of frequently used e-mail addresses to save you time. Just think, you and your students can publish your own online newsletter and send it to hundreds of people with the click of a mouse! Now there's a scary thought!

6. **Press Tab to move to the next line.**

   Note that the cursor "leapfrogs" over the From line because it's already completed for you.

7. **Next to the word Subject, enter what your message is about and press Tab.**

8. **Enter one or more other Internet addresses next to Cc (carbon copy) or Bcc (blind carbon copy) if you like.**

   When you send a blind carbon copy, the original recipient does not know that you sent it. Sneaky, huh?

9. **Press Tab to move to the next line.**

   Note that the cursor makes another jump, this time over Attachments. Attachments enables you to send a file (a program, a picture, sound, or text) along with your e-mail message. To send an attachment, choose Attach Document from the Message menu and select the file you want to attach from the dialog box.

   Attached files don't always translate properly between commercial online services and accounts with universities or Internet service providers, or vice versa. Sending files from one member of a commercial online service to another member on that service, or sending an attached file from one university or ISP account to another, however, usually works without a snag.

10. **Write all you want.**

    A very long message (more than five pages or so) may be clipped or segmented when it is received by other Internet mail servers.

11. **When your masterpiece is complete, click the Send button to send it on its way.**

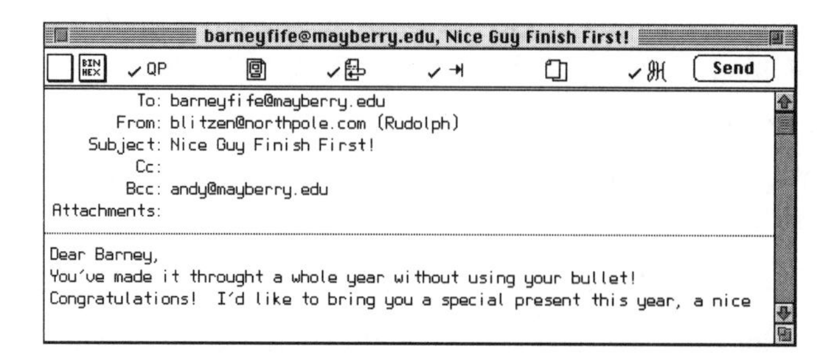

You see a dialog box containing a progress bar that lets you know the message is being sent. It looks like this:

12. **After your message is sent, choose Quit from the File menu.**

    Note that you've just quit the Eudora Light program, but your Internet connection is still active. You can relaunch Eudora Light to send or receive more e-mail, or you can use another Internet software tool, such as TurboGopher/HGopher or Netscape Navigator (which are discussed in Chapters 14 and 15, respectively), or terminate your Internet connection from your SLIP or PPP control panel.

Now you can fool around with all those buttons that are displayed across the top of Eudora's mail screen. You can use them to get to other Eudora goodies. For example, the JH button (on the far right) enables you to add a customized signature (see Chapter 11). Use other buttons to add a nickname, forward mail, and so on.

Getting organized

Stop right now and think about how you want to organize your list of favorite e-mail addresses. Because some e-mail addresses are pretty long, it pays to store 'em so you don't lose 'em. Eudora Light enables you to create "nicknames" that match e-mail addresses for your personal use, but a more visible record may be more appropriate for your class. Ask your students to begin a class list of the most helpful or most interesting Internet e-mail addresses. Post it prominently in your classroom. These addresses will come in handy when you begin to put together Internet projects. Now, what was the President's address? (Try `president@whitehouse.gov`)

Receiving and reading a message with Eudora Light

When someone else sends you e-mail, it automatically arrives in your Internet e-mail box, if they use the correct address. Here's how to read your mail after it arrives:

1. **Double-click the Eudora Light icon to launch the program.**

   Eudora talks to your computer, and if you're not already logged onto the Internet, it launches MacPPP, MacSLIP, or WinSLIP and dials your Internet service provider.

2. **After you log in, you are presented with a dialog box where you can enter your password.**

   Use the password furnished by your Internet provider. Eudora Light also enables you to automate the password entry function.

3. **Choose Check Mail from the File pull-down menu.**

   If you have no mail, Eudora Light presents you with a dialog box in which a happy snake accompanies a "no new mail" message. (Try sending e-mail to *yourself* so you can see how Eudora Light handles incoming mail.)

   If you do have incoming mail, you see Eudora Light's "In Box," which looks something like this:

In

	newaccounts@wired.com	2:00 AM 2/7/95 +0	7	Welcome to HotWired!
	BITNET list server at UNMUMA (1.8	6:52 AM 2/18/95 -	2	Output of your job "bardw"
	BITNET list server at UNMUMA (1.8	6:52 AM 2/18/95 -	23	File: "TEACHER3 CONTACTS" 1/9
	Netsurfer Digest	12:31 AM 3/3/95 +	7	Welcome to Netsurfer Digest
	Netsurfer Digest	12:31 AM 3/3/95 +	10	Netsurfer Digest FAQ
	Netsurfer Digest	12:31 AM 3/3/95 +	25	Your First Netsurfer Digest (HTML
R	US Dept. of Education	2:08 PM 3/4/95 -0	2	Re: Your Input Needed! New Inter
R	fred.flintstone@bedrock.com	8:33 AM 3/6/95 -0	3	Internet Book
R	Wentworth Worldwide Media	4:42 PM 3/6/95 -0	2	back issues of Classroom Connect
•	Internet for Teachers	4:16 AM 3/9/95 -0	5	Cover Art Ready to Go!
	Scott Tyson	8:23 PM 3/13/95 -	1	We're Going to Disney World!

12/82K/0K

See all those messages? A bullet (•) in the message status column to the far left means that a message hasn't been read. An R means that a reply has been sent.

Here is a full list of the codes Eudora Light uses for both incoming and outgoing messages in the message status column:

Code	Meaning
•	Unread/Sendable
	Read/Unsendable (blank)
R	You've replied to this message.
D	You've redirected this message.

F	You've forwarded this message.
Q	You've queued this message to send later.
S	This message is sent.
–	This message is waiting to be sent.

4. **To read a message, just double-click it.**
5. **After you've read a message, delete it by selecting the message (single click) and pressing the Delete key (or choosing Delete from the pull-down Message menu) or take no action and the mail item stays in your Eudora In Box.**

   You can also print, reply, forward, redirect, or save your message by using commands from the pull-down menus at the top of the screen.

One word of warning about the Reply function. If someone writes you a note and copies it to 20 others and you simply use Reply, your reply is also sent to all 20 original recipients. It doesn't take a math whiz to figure out that everyone's mailbox can quickly be stuffed with a bunch of unnecessary "me too" messages. To avoid this sometimes embarrassing moment, always check the To Box to make sure it contains only the e-mail address of the person or persons to whom you want to send a reply.

Not too tough, is it? Easy as pie. After you're comfortable with manually checking your mail, visit the Special menu in Eudora's menu bar and choose Settings to explore Eudora Light's automatic options.

Eudora Light and Eudora Pro (the big-sister commercial application available from QualComm) has lots more features, such as a gong that sounds automatically when something is in your mailbox and the ability to snip off, on the fly, all the annoying extra information in the header of an e-mail message.

See you at 4 p.m.

I once received a message that said simply, "See you at 4 p.m." Unfortunately, I had no idea what the message referred to. Was it a faculty meeting, a happy hour, or a tax audit? It's courteous to remind folks of their message to you when you reply. Just snip out the important parts of the message that you're replying to and paste them in your reply. Eudora does this automatically when you choose Reply from the Message menu. The "quoted" text is signaled with a greater-than sign (>). Feel free to delete parts that aren't important to the essence of your message before you add your reply and mail your letter.

For chipheads only

Here's an example of one of those annoying headers. With a degree in Computer Science and a secret decoder ring, you may be able to figure out what's what. It all means something important to someone.

Received: from piaget.wired.com [140.174.72.1] by socrates.mindspring.com with ESMTP id VAA19763 for <plato@mindspring.com>; Mon, 5 Jun 1995 21:02:35 -0500

Received: from bruner by piaget.wired.com (8.6.9/8.6.5) with ESMTP id SAA08919; Mon, 5 Jun 1995 18:01:36 -0800

Received: by bruner (940816.SGI.8.6.9/930416.SGI)for plato@mindspring.com id CAA03978; Tue, 7 Feb 1995 02:00:14 GMT

Date: Tue, 6 Jun 1995 02:00:14 GMT

From: benbloom@taxonomy.edu

Message-Id: <199582070200.CBA03978@bruner>

To: plato@mindspring.com

Eudora Light is a great compromise between the graphical interface of a commercial service and the kludgy server services. You can get updates to Eudora Light from `http://www.qualcomm.com` or get the commercial version, complete with a ton of new features, a 150+ page manual, and other stuff by sending e-mail to `eudora-info@qualcomm.com` or by telephoning QualComm at 800-2-EUDORA.

Okay. Now you're ready to e-mail the world. You can use Eudora or your favorite online service to reach out and e-mail someone with the click of a mouse. Because e-mail is quick and easy, it's a great way to introduce yourself and others to the Internet. Now, where is that Alaskan pecan fudge cookie recipe that was forwarded to my e-mail box?

Using Netscape Navigator for E-Mail

New versions of Netscape Navigator now (finally) support e-mail. Navigator needs a nudge or two to get it ready to send and receive e-mail.

To prepare Netscape Navigator to send and receive e-mail:

1. **Choose Mail and News Preferences from the Options menu.**
2. **Select the Server tab.**

3. **Fill in the blanks with information given to you by your Internet service provider.**

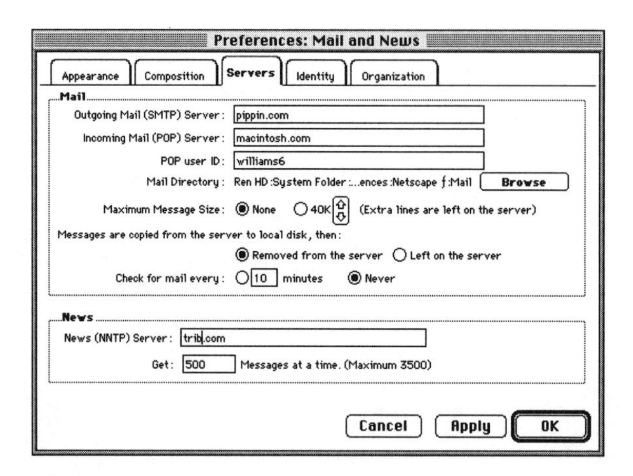

4. **Click the Identify tab.**
5. **Enter information about your name, e-mail, and reply-to address.**
6. **Click OK or press Return/Enter to accept your changes.**

Note that you have a ton of other related options to play with after setting the options I've mentioned above. Things like signature files (see the Identity tab) allow you to add custom name and address information automatically to the end of your e-mail message.

There are two ways to send mail on the Web using your Web browser:

- Choose a link that automatically opens the e-mail response window (meaning you click on a mailto command — HTML for I'll-supply-the-return-address-for-you. This option is what happens when you click someone's e-mail address on their Web page)
- Use the New Mail Message command in the File menu (make a brand new mail message and send it to whomever or several whomevers)

Navigator's mail system works just like Eudora Light's — you simply "fill in the blanks" (see the following figure for a Netscape Navigator e-mail screen). Note that you can attach files, cc to others, and use the address book, too (click on the Address button).

Receiving e-mail is easy. First, double-check to make sure you've entered Server and Identity information into the Mail and News Preferences dialog boxes (accessible through the Option menu).

Next, click on the envelope icon in the bottom-left corner of your Navigator browser window. Naviagator launches a mail-reader application, logs on to your Internet service provider's e-mail server, and retrieves your mail.

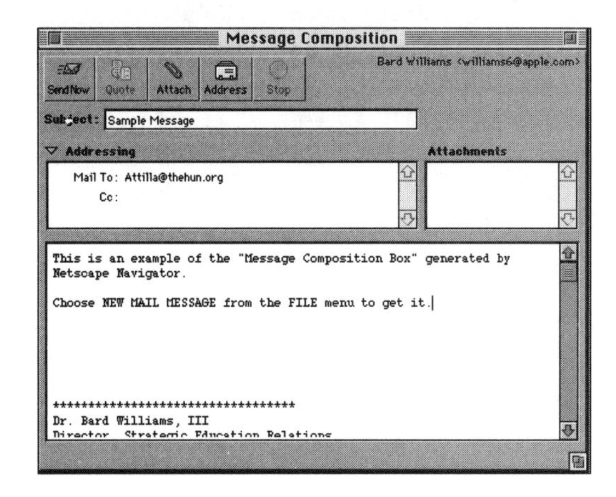

Worldwide Shopping Basket

Want to get an idea of just how useful e-mail can be in a classroom to gather information? Have your students come up with a list of ten common foods they like and create a short e-mail survey designed to compare prices. Send the survey via electronic mail to a teacher you know on the Internet and ask that teacher's students to price each item and return the results via e-mail.

Next, they'll pass the survey on to at least four other people. Ask each of those four people to e-mail the survey back to you for tabulation. With a little luck, you'll have data for a nifty activity where you discuss economics and the usefulness of the Internet for gathering information quickly. One hint: Be sure to put a limit on the number of recipients because this electronic chain letter can quickly get out of hand!

Snail mail

People who use e-mail generally refer to the Postal Service's way of delivering a postmarked letter as "snail mail." In general, no matter where you send an e-mail message — to the front office or to Zimbabwe — the message arrives much faster than a letter (usually). No stamps, no delays, no rain, sleet, or snow. It's a little hard to send your grandma's birthday present (that grand piano she's always wanted) through the Net, but who knows . . . someday it may be possible.

Chapter 11

More E-Mail Tricks

In This Chapter

- Automating Internet access
- Finding your friends on the Net
- Bouncing on the Net
- Teaching and learning Netiquette
- Getting that Internet feeling
- Running out of space

Now that you've received your bachelor's degree in electronic mail, it's time to start graduate school. This chapter can help you find your friends on the Internet, learn how to attach a file to an e-mail message, and troubleshoot undeliverable mail. You can also find a few tips on good Internet manners along the way.

President Clinton became the first U.S. President to send electronic mail via the Internet on March 2, 1993.

Automating Internet Access

After you get logged on to the Internet, you find yourself constantly stopping what you're doing, running to the computer, and signing on to get mail you're expecting. In situations like your classroom, where it's impractical to check your messages all the time, wouldn't it be nice to have a little robot friend who would grab your e-mail from all your e-mail accounts (I regularly answer five of them); sort your mail by sender, subject, or content; log off; and await your next instructions? Enter Claris E-mailer.

Claris E-mailer is a terrific tool for busy people like us. I like it so much I've included a copy of the Macintosh and Windows versions of the program on the CD for you to try. The setup is self-explanatory — a user-friendly Q & A that guides you through inputting all the information E-mailer needs to begin collecting messages from all over the planet. The program also allows you to sort and filter your mail into folders for later reference. I've named my folders "Class Projects," "Personal," "Administrivia," "Book Stuff," and "Computer Stuff." Besides a serious fixation on the word "stuff," you notice I have complete control over how I sort my messages and the categories that relate to that sort. The ability to personalize is what makes most Claris products terrific, and E-mailer is no exception.

Other tools for automating Internet access are available, including some built into online services. Take the time to explore these and see whether they fit into the way you work (and play).

Finding Your Friends on the Net

Unfortunately, there is no comprehensive white pages directory for the Internet. The easiest way to find someone's Internet e-mail address is still to let your fingers do the walking: Call your friends on the phone and ask them for their Internet addresses. Yes, having to use the phone seems like a low-tech cop-out (the phone is now low tech?), but you save yourself a lot of time!

There are a few ways to use the Internet itself to find addresses. Due to the ever-changing structure of the Net, though, these methods are unpredictable, at best. Your options include

- Obtaining a list of people that's already posted on the Internet (a list of teachers perhaps?)
- Using a UNIX command called Finger
- Accessing a knowbot via telnet
- Using Netfind, another telnet-accessible search engine
- Searching for people with a Net search engine

Requesting a teacher contact list

One way to find an address on the Internet is to request one of the many lists of e-mail addresses that are compiled by colleges and universities around the world. Using e-mail, you can request a text file that contains the names of thousands of K-12 educators and have it delivered directly to your electronic mail box. These lists are available to anyone who requests them and contain the names, e-mail addresses, locations, and short profiles of several hundred K-12 educators. The list also provides information about online project ideas. One caveat: This list contains only the names and e-mail addresses of those educators who have actually requested that their names be listed, so you certainly won't find everyone there.

To get the teacher contact list that's maintained by the Department of Education at the University of New Mexico, send your e-mail request to the following address:

```
listserv@unmvma.unm.edu
```

Leave the subject line blank or type a period there if your mail software requires something in the subject line. In the message portion of your e-mail, type the following:

```
get teacher1 contacts
get teacher2 contacts
get teacher3 contacts
get teacher4 contacts
```

Your e-mail box will receive eight to ten messages that contain the desired list. Be patient; getting the list may take a couple of days.

If you like what you see and want to add your own information to the list, send an e-mail message to this address:

```
laughon@vtvm1.cc.vt.edu
```

Fingering other users

UNIX, the operating system that forms the backbone for many parts of the Internet, has a command called Finger that enables you to request information from a host computer about someone with a name that you know. To use Finger, you must know the name of the host computer, and that piece of information is not always easy to find.

Our friend and program Eudora Light (see the CD that accompanies this book) includes an easy way for you to use the Finger command from within the program.

Here's how to search for someone by using the person's name or by using the domain name with Eudora Light:

1. **Log onto the Net and launch Eudora Light.**
2. **Choose Ph (phone book) from the Window menu.**

You see a dialog box that looks a bit like this:

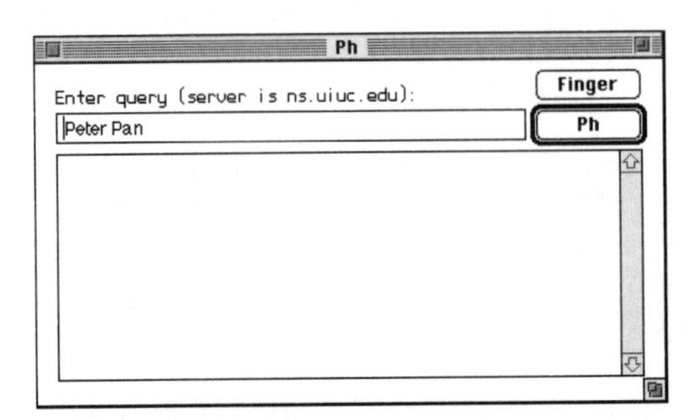

3. **Check the server name at the top of the dialog box.**

   The server name is probably set to the name of your Internet service provider's computer (your home domain). If the person you're searching for is at another site, choose Settings from the Special pull-down menu and select Hosts. You see a place to enter the name of a Finger (or Ph) server. If you decide to make a change, enter only the domain and top-domain (zone) in the blank provided (for example: `bedrock.edu`).

   Host is the term used for the computer that's serving as an Internet gateway. You can try searching your own host computer by entering your own domain name.

4. **In the User box, enter the name of the person you're looking for and click Finger.**

   Eudora (Finger) searches and then returns user names and addresses for people who are on the server that's listed at the top of the window. If you strike gold (find the person you're looking for), you see a screen like the one that follows. There you find information about the user's real name, e-mail address, the last time that person logged onto the host computer, and so on.

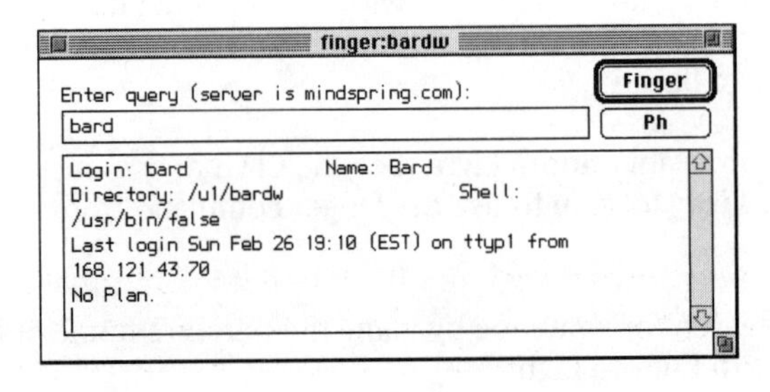

If you don't see the information about the person you want, try searching a different server (return to Step 3). You can also experiment with the Ph button, which does pretty much the same thing as Finger but returns different information.

Remember, you use Finger when you know what server the user logs onto (the domain name). Finger tells you whether that person is logged on, the person's real name, and all sorts of other information.

5. **To quit Finger, choose Quit from the Eudora File menu.**

   Note that you're still connected to the Internet until you choose Close from your PPP/SLIP control program.

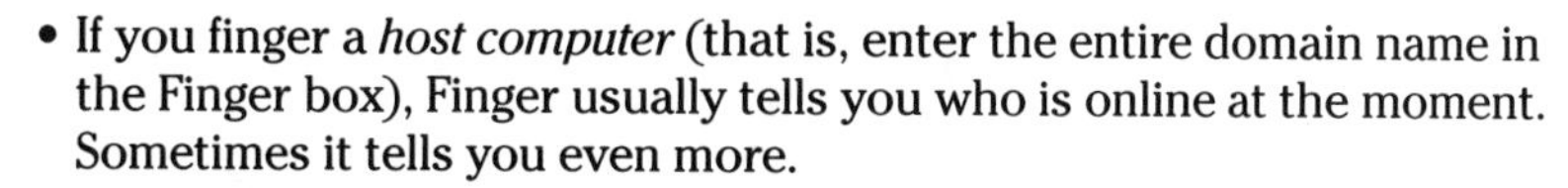

   - If you finger a *host computer* (that is, enter the entire domain name in the Finger box), Finger usually tells you who is online at the moment. Sometimes it tells you even more.

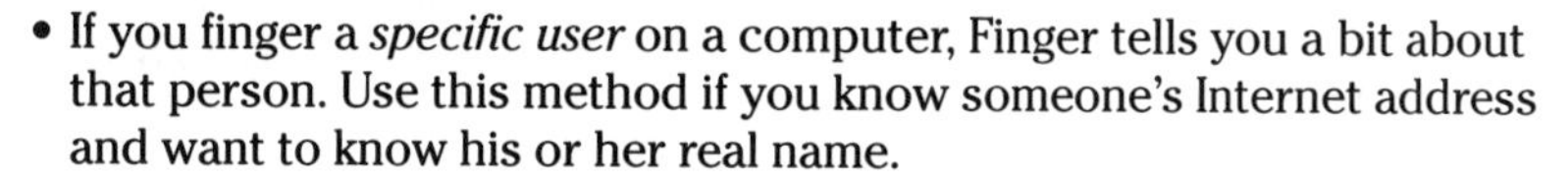

   - If you finger a *specific user* on a computer, Finger tells you a bit about that person. Use this method if you know someone's Internet address and want to know his or her real name.

Remember that you can't reach everyone through the Ph and Finger programs. Some servers don't allow invasive inquiries such as Finger at all. Just because you don't find a listing for your cousin Jenny doesn't mean that she doesn't have an Internet e-mail address. Also remember that you won't find addresses for the millions of folks who use online services such as Prodigy or America Online. To find them, you have to log onto the online service itself and use the built-in member search.

You're thinking right now that Finger is a really boring program, right? Not at all! Try entering the following users at the domains that are listed and see what comes back. I won't spoil the fun for you by telling you what you'll find.

```
jtchern@ocf.berkeley.edu
coke@cs.wisc.edu
drink@csh.rit.edu
```

In March 1996, the number of countries worldwide that were reachable by electronic mail was more than 200.

Operating a knowbot

A *knowbot* is a program that searches the Internet for information. Knowbots are experimental right now, but when they work, they work extremely well. To get to a knowbot called *KIS* (*Knowbot Information Service*), telnet to

```
info.cnri.reston.va.us 185
```

After you're connected, follow the menu prompts to conduct your search. KIS is slow — the knowbot has a lot on its mind — but it works (sometimes).

Using Netfind

Netfind is another way to locate e-mail addresses. As with its knowbot cousin, you use telnet (see Chapter 17) to gain access. Netfind systems operate on many servers, including these:

```
bruno.cs.colorado.edu
mudhoney.micro.umn.edu
ds.internic.net
```

After you arrive, log in as *netfind* and follow the prompts. Note that Netfind is useful in finding domain names, but you still have to use Finger to locate a specific user.

Let your (students') fingers do the walking . . . have students create their own directory of commonly used electronic mail addresses. If you want to get fancy, tack a world map on the wall of your classroom and use pins or stick-on dots to represent the locations of people with whom you communicate.

Finding Folks with Yahoo!

The folks at Yahoo! (`http://www.yahoo.com`) and others now provide clickable links to "people locators" like Four11 and the Internet White Pages. Use the search term "phone book" or "Internet address" for a complete list of sites. The need for locating folks on the Net continues to grow, and vendors are jumping on board with more sophisticated search engines. Commercial finder services, like Four11 (`http://www.four11.com`), now maintain databases containing millions of addresses. One caution: Beware of giving out your home address and phone number, and never, never give out a password!

Even with these new "white pages" on the Net, you won't find one comprehensive directory. You may have to check several directories to find your way around or use some of the techniques described earlier in this chapter. Watch the Netspace for more inclusive databases popping up practically every month.

Sending and Receiving Files via E-Mail

Wouldn't it be great if you could exchange lesson plans, desktop-published documents, and graphics with other people via e-mail? Yippee! The techno-deities have smiled on us and made it easy to do!

Will the real postmaster please stand?

Need to find someone's e-mail address? If you know the user's domain name, send a note to postmaster@<domain name>. Ask simply, "Does so and so have an e-mail address on this system?" Take care, though. The postmaster is probably overworked and no doubt underpaid.

The file is on the way!

Sending a file to another user via the Internet is as simple as creating an e-mail message. Eudora Light enables you to attach any file, whether it's a program, document, sound, picture, or movie, with the click of your mouse.

Follow these steps to use Eudora Light to send a file along with an e-mail message:

1. **Log onto the Internet through your Internet provider.**
2. **Launch Eudora Light.**
3. **Choose New Message from the Message menu and fill in the address and subject information.**
4. **Choose Attach Document from the Message menu.**

   You see the Open File dialog box.
5. **Choose a file to attach by double-clicking the filename in the Open File dialog box.**

   If you successfully attach a file, its name shows up on the Attachments line of the Eudora Light main mail message screen, as shown in the following figure:

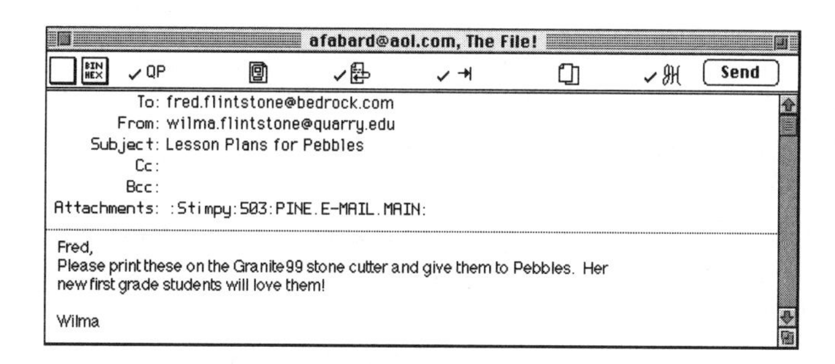

6. **After you attach the file, move to the text (message) box and type an accompanying message.**

   Telling the receiver what kind of file you're sending and how to read the document or run the program on receipt is a good idea.

7. **Click the Send button.**

   Off goes your message and the attached file.

Incoming!

Receiving a file is even easier than sending one. Eudora does all the work! Follow these steps to view a file you receive via the Internet:

1. **Log onto your Internet provider.**
2. **Launch Eudora Light.**
3. **Choose Check Mail (⌘+M or Ctrl+M) from the File pull-down menu.**

   If all goes well, you see something that looks like this:

Message status — Message priority — Sender — Time/Date — Message size (K) — Subject

In

Message status	Message priority	Sender	Time/Date	Message size (K)	Subject
		newaccounts@wired.com	2:00 AM 2/7/95 +0	7	Welcome to HotWired!
		BITNET list server at UNMUMA (1.8	6:52 AM 2/18/95 -	2	Output of your job "bardw"
		BITNET list server at UNMUMA (1.8	6:52 AM 2/18/95 -	23	File: "TEACHER3 CONTACTS" 1/9
		Netsurfer Digest	12:31 AM 3/3/95 +	7	Welcome to Netsurfer Digest
		Netsurfer Digest	12:31 AM 3/3/95 +	10	Netsurfer Digest FAQ
		Netsurfer Digest	12:31 AM 3/3/95 +	25	Your First Netsurfer Digest (HTML
R		US Dept. of Education	2:08 PM 3/4/95 -0	2	Re: Your Input Needed! New Inter
R		fred.flintstone@bedrock.com	8:33 AM 3/6/95 -0	3	Internet Book
R		Wentworth Worldwide Media	4:42 PM 3/6/95 -0	2	back issues of Classroom Connect
		Internet for Teachers	4:16 AM 3/9/95 -0	5	Cover Art Ready to Go!
•		Scott Tyson	8:23 PM 3/13/95 -	1	We're Going to Disney World!

12/82K/0K

The dot (•) means that you have an unread message. (See Chapter 10 for an explanation of other In/Out basket codes.)

4. **Double-click the line of the mail message that contains the downloadable file.**
5. **In the Save File dialog box that appears, choose the proper directory — this tells Eudora where to store the file you've received — and click Save.**

   The file is moved from your Internet host computer to your hard drive or floppy disk.

6. **If a file compression program has been used to compress the file, unstuff (uncompress) the file by using StuffIt Expander or StuffIt Lite.**

   You can tell that StuffIt has been used to compress a file because the filename ends in the `.sit` extension. StuffIt Expander is on the CD that accompanies this book.

After you've uncompressed the file, sign off (if you want) and double-click the file's icon to open the file.

Practice sending and receiving files by attaching files you e-mail to yourself. Try it; it really works!

Commercial online services also enable you to send and receive files easily. On AOL, click the Attach File icon after creating your e-mail message, choose the file you want to attach from the dialog box, and click Send Now or Send Later. Remember that attached files don't translate well *between* different commercial services; the results are unpredictable, at best.

If you want to know more about downloading files (getting files directly from another computer), check out Chapter 16.

Sorry, Wrong Number

Occasionally, your e-mail message will be *bounced* by the Internet and returned to you with a cryptic message such as `host unknown` or `connection refused`. The most common reason for a returned e-mail message is that you've incorrectly addressed it. If the return message says `user unknown` or `no such user at <domain name>`, you've entered an incorrect user name. `Host unknown` means that the destination computer can't be found at the address you've indicated. More often than not, though, your e-mail messages arrive safely. Save a phone call and just watch for those pesky bounce messages to let you know that you need to resend.

In 1995, only 35 percent of American public schools were hooked up to the Internet. In mid-1996, that figure stood at 50 percent, with many NetDay and other initiatives planned for the upcoming fall.

A Netiquette Do's and Don'ts Primer

Nothing is more annoying than rudeness. In the real world, children everywhere learn certain rules to help make life easier and kinder. Raising their hands to talk helps — when they remember. Opening doors for other people is another rule that shows that you have good manners and that you are a downright kind person. Because the Internet is relatively blind to the identity of the user and because that blindness makes rudeness very tempting at times, Net surfers adhere to a basic set of manners, too. Insiders in the Net refer to these rules as *Netiquette.*

Here are several things that you can do, or shouldn't do, before and during your visit to the Internet. Most of these suggestions apply to electronic mail, newsgroups, mailing lists, and other ways in which you and your students interact with the Internet.

Do create a custom electronic signature message for yourself or your school

It is customary in the Internet community to tag your outgoing e-mail messages with a unique signature. These user-created works of art give more information about the sender and give you an opportunity to express a bit about your personality in a word, phrase, or quotation, or even a picture created from ASCII text characters.

Here's an example of an electronic signature that may accompany Tim Buktu's e-mail messages:

```
        ****************************************
      Tim Buktu            nowhere@outtathere.com
              Dean of Men, DoRight College
                     Anywhere, USA
        ****************************************
                     "Carpe Diem,
          seize the day boys, seize the day.
             Make your lives extraordinary."
         Robin Williams, "Dead Poets Society"
        ****************************************
```

See? Electronic signatures give you and your students a nifty way of signing your e-mail messages, and you can include all those witty quotations you've always wanted to use. Use only 40 columns and no special characters so that everyone can enjoy your signature tag without reformatting their screens. You can also include such information as your school or home phone number and snailmail address. Most software, including Eudora, enables you to append your electronic signature automatically to outgoing messages.

If you're really industrious, try creating a picture by using the ASCII keyboard characters. But be prepared: This process can take hours. How many term papers are left to evaluate?

Some Net signatures are really creative. Have your students create their own Internet signature messages that reflect their own personalities. Use books of quotations or search for quotations on the Net.

You can find searchable lists of quotations and lots of other ready-reference resources by pointing your WWW browser (see Chapter 15) to

```
http://198.214.57.13/tec/reference.html
```

Don't send anything through e-mail that you wouldn't write on your classroom chalkboard

Because electronic mail is sent from your computer to someone else's computer through an Internet gateway computer, someone may catch and read your messages as they pass through. Although most universities and commercial online services have some security, nothing is completely secure. A good rule of thumb is to assume that any message that you send via the Internet is potentially readable by someone other than the intended recipient. As a result, you shouldn't send credit card information or personal information about you or your students over the Net. Better safe than sorry!

Don't flame

You're already familiar with flaming. Some people flame in the real world. Have you ever walked into the teacher's lounge at the end of the day and heard a coworker blasting an administrator for interrupting class with a message on the PA system? Ever heard the football coach launch into a bench-kicking tirade about how rotten the officiating was at last Friday's game? That's flaming.

Flaming is the term used for inflammatory messages on the Net. Basically, no matter how angry you or your students feel about what some other Internet surfer says, resist the temptation to "go off" on them, and use that energy to do something else. If you receive a flame or read one in a newsgroup, resist the temptation to reply. Replying calmly, or any other way, to a flame usually doesn't work. The people who wrote the flame have already lost their self-control and are unlikely to regain it before they read your reply. Tell your students and peers that flaming is simply an uncool thing to do.

Cryptography and the Internet

Because the Internet has major possibilities for commerce and trade, finding a way to secure data sent via the Internet is becoming the quest of many companies and organizations. Basically, you have several options for protecting your Internet account and the data you send:

- **Encryption:** Data encryption means using special software to encode messages and other data before you send them via the Internet. Encryption schemes can be as simple as a substitution cipher, like those created by the secret decoder rings that used to come in cereal boxes, or as complex as hardware (chip)-generated mathematical algorithms that require special hardware or complex software to decode. Hardware encryption is used for the most sensitive of messages sent via the Net.
- **Digital signatures:** Like the ASCII text signature you created for your e-mail address, you can create unique, and quite complex, digital signatures that attach to e-mail messages before they are sent. The idea is to give only the intended receiver the ability to authenticate your message by analyzing the incoming digital signature with a private digital *key*.
- **Firewalls:** A firewall is a network computer that is specifically configured to prevent unauthorized access to data. The information inside the firewall is available only to persons who have access privileges within a campus or organization. Data in *public* data storage areas outside the firewall is accessible to anyone on the Internet. Schools that have Internet connections should take great care to ensure that any student, personnel, or other sensitive data be placed inside a firewall. Some Internet fileservers, such as Apple's Internet Web Server, come with built-in firewall features to make it easy for you to choose what's public and what's not.
- **Password protection:** People who have your password can represent themselves as you on the Internet. Choose passwords that are difficult to guess, such as those containing random combinations of letters and numbers. Never use proper names, any word in the dictionary, your birth date, or any password that's shorter than six characters. You should also change your password often. Even though the security gurus disagree, I think it's OK to write your password down in a safe place, especially if you have a memory like mine. Safe places may include your wallet, inside the pages of a book on your bookshelf, or in a randomly selected file folder in your file cabinet (not one labeled "my password"!).

Do talk to your students about what's appropriate to send via e-mail

Some things you don't want to discuss via e-mail because they are too personal or are best said in writing (the old fashioned way) or in person. An e-mail wedding invitation is a social faux pas for sure, as would be an e-mail termination notice (gasp!) from your principal. With your students, brainstorm a list of appropriate and inappropriate uses of electronic mail to help drive this point home.

Don't type in all CAPITAL letters

Capital letters leap off the screen and get really annoying. They're the cyberspace equivalent of screaming. Of course, sometimes using all capital letters is appropriate . . . such as when you're scolding your students via e-mail about not being good network citizens. Younger students, in particular, have a tough time remembering to turn off the Caps Lock key. Do the online world a favor and have your little ones practice locking and unlocking that key several hundred times (off-line!) so they'll remember.

Emoticons: That Internet Feeling

One of the most interesting things about the Internet is the way people convey feelings and emotions.

Because face-to-face electronic chat is still somewhat of a dream for the general public, creative humans have developed their own set of letters and symbols that represent emotions, feelings, and other things that are tough to express. Those familiar with techno-speak call these symbols *emoticons* (emotional icons) or simply *smileys.*

Emoticons are lots of fun. You can read most of them by tilting your head 90 degrees left and looking at the symbol. A smile (sideways) looks like this: `:-)`

Neat, huh?

Here are a few of the basics that you see online:

`IMHO`	In my humble opinion
`ROTFL`	Rolling on the floor, laughing
`LOL`	Laughing out loud
`<grin>` or `:-)`	Happy
`<frown>` or `:-(`	Not happy
`[[]]`	A hug

Here are some wacky emoticons:

`:-P`	A raspberry (not the fruit, the thhhhh. . . .)
`?:-z`	A clueless person
`o0:-)7`	Teacher, circa 1850?
`[:-)`	Wearing a Walkman
`8:-)`	Glasses on the forehead

Ask your students to brainstorm a list of famous people who are related to a specific subject area, or share some examples from the list that follows. Challenge students to design their own emoticon for the person of their choice. Present the final product to the class and then try them out on IRC (Internet Relay Chat, which is discussed in Chapter 18) or in live conference on a commercial service, and see what happens!

Here are some famous folks, along with their emoticons, that you can use as examples:

=):-) Uncle Sam

*<:-) Santa

+0<:-) The Pope

Ready for the challenge? Start by having your students create an emoticon for these famous (or infamous) people:

- Elvis
- Abe Lincoln
- Billy the Kid
- Einstein
- Marilyn Monroe
- Themselves!

Running Out of Space

Grab the e-mail address of a teacher in another school and try this easy introductory activity. Get your students to find a favorite poem or write their own poem. (Go for the obscure; you see why later in the instructions.) Next, "despace" it — that is, remove all spaces between words and all carriage returns so the text is basically one very jumbled, crowded paragraph. Send this despaced disaster to another school and have students there "respace" the text to re-create what they think are meaningful lines and stanzas. Finally, have them return the poetry to your students. Voilà! You get as many interpretations as there are return letters. Warning: Lewis Carroll's *"Jabberwocky"* and anything by e. e. cummings will drive them nuts!

Read more about e-mail activities in Chapter 23.

Junk mail on the information superhighway

It started in your mailbox at home. Hundreds of contests, deals, and solicitations from people you don't know. Then they got your phone number and the "just-as-I-took-a-bite-of-steak" phone calls began, coming at 7 p.m. from eager-beaver college students pushing long-distance phone services or magazine subscriptions. Guess what technology the amazing marketeers have discovered now? Yup. Because my e-mail address is widely published, I get about 10-15 "junk e-mails" a week. They're usually solicitations for free Internet access (isn't that a hoot?) and aluminum siding (if they saw my home they'd know that was a lost cause). Because this random mailing to the Net can be automated, the likelihood that junk e-mail will increase is extremely high.

What can you do? Here are a few "guerrilla e-mail tips" you can try:

- Look in the header or footer of the e-mail message for a "reply to" address and send a kind but firm message requesting the removal of your name from their list (clicking the reply button on your e-mail program usually doesn't work).
- If the mailings don't cease, report the offense to your online service or Internet provider. Provide them with a copy of the message (headers and footers included) and a copy of your message asking for the mailings to cease.
- Express your discontent to the federal government. Visit the Web site at `http://www.whitehouse.gov` and click around until you find an appropriate message point.
- Use an e-mail filtering program. Claris E-Mailer and other programs offer a filter that automatically sorts your mail based on known variables (e-mail address, subject, and so on), placing "unknown" stuff in a separate folder for later reading.
- Search for a phone number in the message, then call it and threaten to send 50 third-graders to their business office with finger paints and a bad attitude.

Chapter 12
Mailing Lists-R-Us

In This Chapter

- Stalking the wild mailing list
- Joining a mailing list
- You are confirmed
- Finding a mailing list
- Stopping the mail
- Posting to a mailing list
- Policing the topics
- Surviving mail storms
- Your first subscription

If you're like most other educators, you're probably a magazine junkie. A glance at the overstuffed shelves in my home office reveals that my interests are a bit schizophrenic. I have everything from *Educational Leadership* and *National Geographic* to *Wired* and *Internet World,* with issues of *American Scholar, GQ,* and *MacUser* nestled in between. What's great about my magazine rack is that whenever I'm in the mood to browse a topic, I can find something there to explore.

A mailing list is, in many ways, like a magazine subscription. It enables you to select a topic of interest and read the thoughts and ideas of folks from around the world. What's the thing that makes mailing lists really cool? *You* can add your *own* thoughts! Your ideas can be electronically published to thousands of unsuspecting Internet users at the touch of a button. Ooooo . . . a scary and exciting thought, no?

What Is a Mailing List?

Mailing lists (a.k.a. *maillists*) are special kinds of electronic mail addresses that automatically forward topic-specific discussions to your e-mail doorstep — just like a magazine subscription does. In fact, as the next section explains, to receive mail from a list, you must first subscribe.

Mailing lists enable you and your students to talk with more than one person at a time. In essence, you're joining an online discussion. Mailing lists are sometimes referred to as *discussion groups* because they are focused on a specific topic, such as elementary education or brewing beer in Wales. You also hear mailing lists referred to as *LISTSERVs*. LISTSERVs are the most common type of mailing list.

So . . . if you find a subject that you like (for example, media or distance learning), you can subscribe to a mailing list and read what other subscribers have to say.

As of July 1996, more than 4,500 mailing lists were on the Internet, covering topics from education to jungle survival.

Joining a mailing list

To subscribe to a mailing list, all you have to do is send a message to the LISTSERV (the computer that controls, sorts, and distributes incoming messages on a particular topic). It's as easy as 1, 2, 3! (Well, maybe 1, 2, 3, 4, 5, 6?)

1. **Connect to the Internet via your information provider or online service and launch your mail program.**

   If you're connected via a SLIP or PPP connection, fire up Eudora Light, Claris E-mailer (both on the CD at the back of this book), or another mail program. If you are connected via a UNIX network, access elm, pine, or another e-mail program.

2. **Create a new mail message.**

   Compose a message to the LISTSERV computer that administers the list you're interested in. Because your subscription request is read by a big, stupid computer rather than by a bright, energetic human, you have to follow some strict rules about what you send. On AOL or another online service, select New Mail from the pull-down menu.

3. **Enter the full Internet address of the LISTSERV computer in the To box.**

   The address of the LISTSERV computer looks something like this:

   ```
   LISTSERV@bigdumbbox.edu
   ```

4. **Leave the Subject line blank.**

   Some LISTSERVers require you to enter commands in the subject box itself. Don't worry if you do it incorrectly; the receiving server usually returns a nicely worded, slightly scolding message about where and where not to type.

5. **In the Message (text) area, type the command** subscribe **and the name of the list to which you want to subscribe, followed by your *full name* (not your e-mail address).**

   Here's what a subscribe message for user Joshua James looks like:

   ```
   subscribe macintosh-l Joshua James
   ```

6. **Click the Send button to send your message and then wait for a return confirmation.**

Easy, huh? Just so you know that you've got it right, here's a glimpse at the request message Fred Flintstone sent to subscribe to a LISTSERV called `rockbreakers-l` that was running on a computer located at `bedrock.edu`

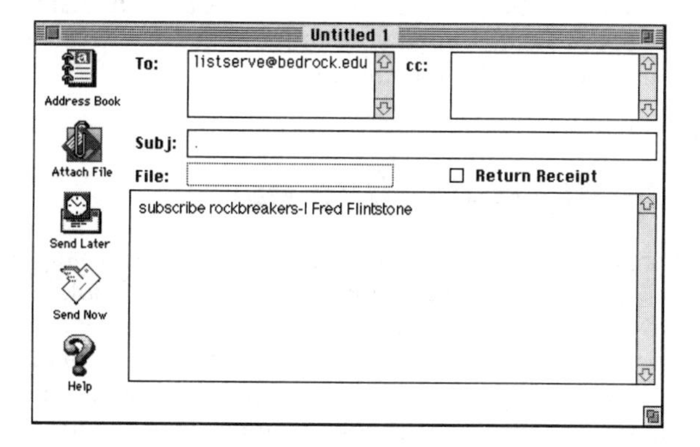

You are confirmed!

In somewhere between ten seconds and a couple of days, you receive a cryptic message from the big, dumb mainframe computer that looks something like the message that follows:

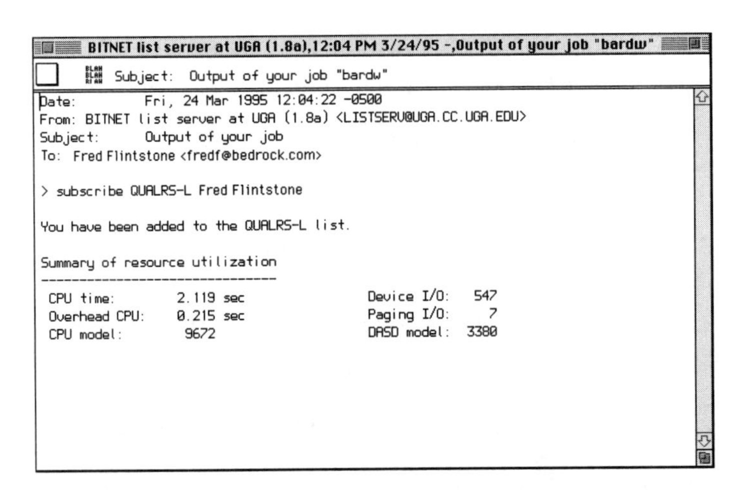

Don't you love all that techno-babble? The important thing in this message is that it tells you that you have successfully subscribed to the mailing list. Your confirmation message may also include specific information about canceling your subscription to the mailing list. It's a good idea to save this document or print it out so that when your mailbox gets overstuffed, you can stop the waterfall of e-mail from mailing lists.

Finding a mailing list

There are several ways to locate the addresses that you use to subscribe to a mailing list. The first method is to purchase a book or magazine that has a list of LISTSERV addresses. The *Directory of Electronic Journals, Newsletters, and Academic Discussion Lists,* which lists thousands of LISTSERVs and 250+ electronic journals, is available from the Association of Research Libraries (phone 202-296-2296). Of course, you can save yourself some money by starting with the dandy teacher-tested list of education-related mailing lists organized for you in Chapter 24.

Another place to obtain a list of lists is from the Internet itself. Simply use FTP (see Chapter 16), the WWW (Chapter 15), or regular e-mail to access the following addresses:

- FTP to `ftp.sura.net`
- Use Mosaic or Netscape (WWW software tools) to search Yahoo! (`www.yahoo.com`) or another Internet directory for newsgroups.
- Send an e-mail message to `listserv@bitnic.educom.com`, leave the subject line blank, and type **list global** in the message field.

Soon a list of mailing lists appears in your mailbox.

Did you notice that there are *three* ways to get the list from the Net? That's pretty typical of the Internet. Just as there is more than one way to get Archibald to do his calculus homework, there are usually different ways to get information on the Internet. The path that you choose depends on the type of Internet connection you have (an online service, SLIP/PPP, and so on) and the tools you're using (Fetch, Mosaic, Gopher, and so on). If you get stuck, try a different method. You may be surprised at what works!

In 1996, more than 20 new coffeehouses opened in U.S. cities, offering espresso, a bagel, and Internet access — à la carte.

Posting to a Mailing List

Posting to a mailing list is as simple as sending an e-mail message. It pays to have some "list smarts" before your first post, though, because after you send the e-mail, you can't take it back. Because a mailing list can potentially be distributed to *millions* of people, your little boo-boo can turn into something pretty big, pretty quickly.

Before your first post, look at the header (see Chapter 10) that accompanies your incoming mailing list messages. Notice that the sender is the *list name,* followed by the *domain name.* Remember that the domain name identifies the sending computer. If you reply to the message by using your mail software's Reply or Forward command, your reply is sent to *each* of the zillion people who get mail on the mailing list.

So . . . if you want to make a comment and you want *everyone* on the list to see it, send an e-mail reply to the address in the header. If you want to remove yourself from the list or make a comment to the list's originating human, you have to use a different address. Check your mailing list subscription confirmation or the header/footer in your incoming mail for the list owner's address.

Warning: traffic jam on the information superhighway!

As you and your students enter the information superhighway, you'll no doubt be tempted to subscribe to lots of mailing lists. Don't. A teacher friend of mine spent about 20 minutes online one night and subscribed to four popular mailing lists. By 8:00 the next morning, she had more than 200 e-mail messages. Interesting? Yes! But reading all those messages can consume your life. Choose carefully.

The posting address

The posting address is always different from the address that you use to subscribe to the mailing list. Use the `listserv@domainname` address only when you want on or off the list. Otherwise, look for an address with the letter *l* appended to it. That address is the return address for mailing to everyone on the list. For example, you may use `listserv@bozo.edu` to subscribe, even though the actual posting address of the mailing list is `cartoon-l@bozo.edu`

Stop the mail, I wanna get off!

The time will come when you no longer want to be on a mailing list to which you've subscribed. Although each LISTSERV computer requires a slightly different unsubscribe message, most unsubscribe messages look the same. The following figure shows typical instructions for unsubscribing from a mailing list:

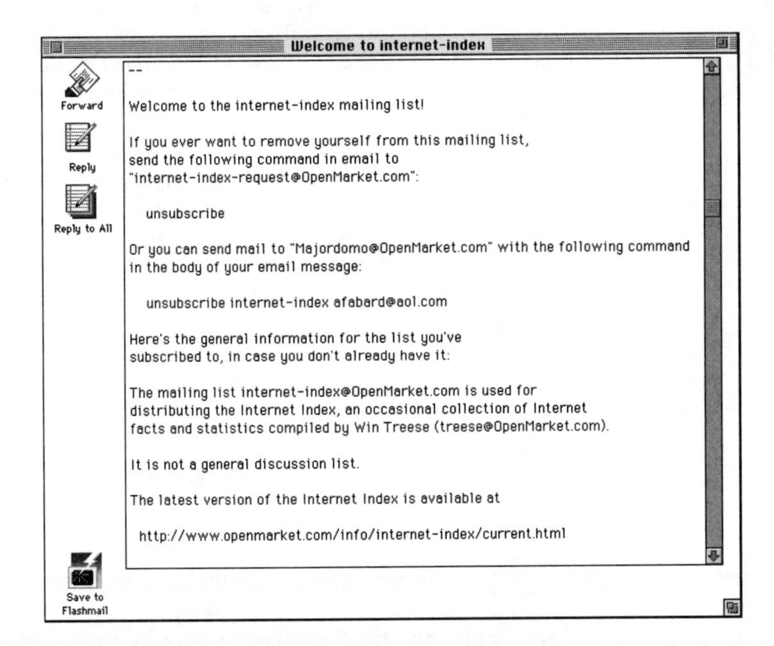

The Topic Police

Hang on a second . . . if a mailing list is open to everyone for posting, what keeps people from posting, either accidentally or purposefully, to a mailing list on the wrong topic? Enter dedicated human telecommunicators.

Mailing lists come in two flavors: *moderated* and *unmoderated.* Many mailing lists have people who regularly scan (moderate) incoming e-mail messages *before* distributing them to the world. This process ensures that the subject matter and comments are appropriate to the topic and won't curl your hair when you read them.

Unmoderated mailing lists usually have more traffic, but you also have to endure lots of false starts and inane chatter. You can tell whether the group you've subscribed to is moderated when the confirmation message returns from the LISTSERV. Encourage any student or teacher who uses your Internet account to question and verify any information on any list, especially from mailing lists that are unmoderated.

A very challenging activity for students is to have them create a list of rules about what's appropriate and what's not appropriate to post on mailing lists. The discussion brings out new ideas and, after it's over, ensures that you're all driving with the same superhighway road map.

Mail Storm

Some mailing lists deliver messages to your mailbox one at a time, as they are posted by the author. Others, called *digest mailing lists* (or just *digests*), save messages and send them in tidy bundles one or two times a week. Whichever type of list you happen to choose, know that some mailing lists are really, really busy. Thousands of college students who have lots of time on their hands begin discussions (for example, on "what's hot at the movies") that regularly produce more than 200 messages a day.

A good rule of thumb is to watch your mailbox closely for a day or two after you've subscribed and see what the traffic is like. If the information traffic jams your mailbox, find out whether a digest of messages is available. If no digest is available, consider dropping all but the most important lists to which you subscribe.

With most mailing lists, it's possible to place your subscription on "hold" when you know you'll be away from your computer and modem for a while. The commands you need to hold, or stop, e-mail from arriving are usually spelled out in the confirmation message you receive shortly after you subscribe to a mailing list.

Mailing lists are a great way to keep up on trends and issues in education and educational media. Keep a file in your classroom with a list of your favorite mailing lists and instructions for unsubscribing should the need arise. Be sure to check out Chapter 24 for a list of lists that are already teacher tested.

The average amount of time that it takes for Supreme Court decisions to become available on the Internet is eight hours.

Your First Subscription

Compose an e-mail message and subscribe to the very popular Library Media Network (Syracuse University). The LM-NET is a moderated list that offers tons of ideas and lots of information about using media and telecommunications in schools. It's a terrific first stop on your information highway mailing list tour!

Address your request to `LISTSERV@suvm.syr.edu`

In the message (text) field, type **subscribe LM-NET *<your full name>*** (not your e-mail address!) and send your message.

Remember to be sure to print out or save the confirmation message when it comes via return e-mail so you can unsubscribe when your mailbox explodes.

Chapter 13

Be a NewsGroupie

In This Chapter

- What's a newsgroup?
- What's news to you?
- Read all about it!
- NewsWatcher
- Spreadin' the news with your browser
- No-nonsense newsgroup playground rules
- Information superhighway speed bump
- Extra, Extra! Read these newsgroups!

Now that you have your students telecommunicating with Masai tribesmen and your electronic mailbox is stuffed with the contents of one or two zillion mailing lists, you've seen all there is, right? Nope!

Welcome to newsgroups, the world's biggest corkboard.

What Is a Newsgroup?

Like a mailing list (also called a LISTSERV or a discussion group), a *newsgroup* is a way to freely share information among Internet users. Newsgroups, also referred to as *Usenet newsgroups,* are like public access bulletin boards. Users float by and electronically tack messages into special message areas that are organized by topic. While users are there, they can read the hundreds of messages posted by other users.

As with unmoderated mailing lists, no one picks through the posted messages and looks for the kinds of words that you see scrawled on schoolhouse walls. The contents are often off-topic, risqué, and disorganized. The up side is that the newsgroups represent a cross-section of the planet. They're a great place to explore humanity.

Newsgroups are different from mailing lists in that the messages you read are not sent to your mailbox. Instead, they are sent to *community mailboxes,* whose home is on some huge hard drive on a server (called a *news server*) somewhere on the planet, where everyone can access them. They're chock full of messages and responses to those messages. They are organized by topic and offer a running dialog about a wide variety of subjects. The following figure gives you a glimpse at just one of the information nuggets that you might find in the newsgroup called `k12.news`

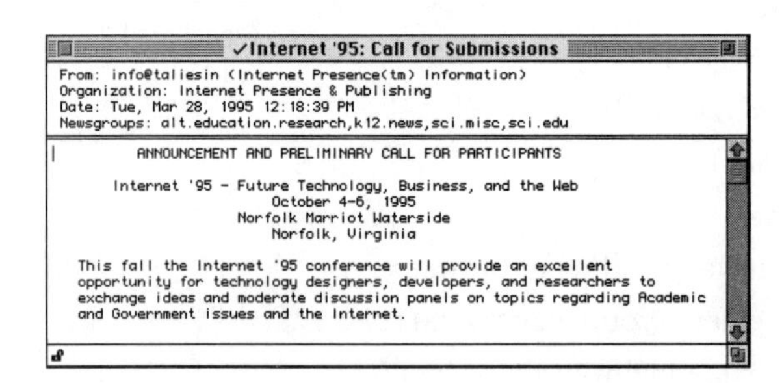
✓Internet '95: Call for Submissions

From: info@taliesin (Internet Presence(tm) Information)
Organization: Internet Presence & Publishing
Date: Tue, Mar 28, 1995 12:18:39 PM
Newsgroups: alt.education.research,k12.news,sci.misc,sci.edu

ANNOUNCEMENT AND PRELIMINARY CALL FOR PARTICIPANTS

Internet '95 - Future Technology, Business, and the Web
October 4-6, 1995
Norfolk Marriot Waterside
Norfolk, Virginia

This fall the Internet '95 conference will provide an excellent opportunity for technology designers, developers, and researchers to exchange ideas and moderate discussion panels on topics regarding Academic and Government issues and the Internet.

Finding a Newsgroup

Newsgroups are organized according to the theme of the group and the category to which it belongs. Currently, there are more than 35,000 newsgroups around the world, about 80 of them of special interest to educators.

The first three or four letters of the newsgroup name indicate the category in which the newsgroup belongs. In a newsgroup called `k12.chat.junior`, for example, you stumble on middle schoolers who are talking about what they do to their teachers each day. Need a movie review for a media class? Try `rec.arts.movies`. You and your students will never get bored; not only are there thousands of newsgroups, but hundreds more come and go each week.

Table 13-1 lists the Usenet categories you may find most useful. One category, the `k12` groups, is posted by teachers, for teachers. Each day you can find new ideas and helpful hints for everything from lesson planning to the newest strategies for fund-raising.

You'll encounter plenty more categories (prefixes) as you explore newsgroups, and new ones are added practically every day.

Table 13-1	Usenet Categories
Top-Domain Name	*Description*
`alt` (alternative)	Everything you can imagine, no matter how strange; a birthplace for many soon-to-be certified newsgroups Example: `alt.pets.rabbits`
`comp` (computers)	Discussions about the use of computers and their peripherals Example: `comp.sys.powerpc`
`k12` (education)	Discussion for teachers by teachers Example: `k12.library`
`soc` (social)	Discussions about social issues Example: `soc.college`
`news` (network news/ software)	Relates to network news and Internet software Example: `news.announce.newusers`
`rec` (recreation)	Recreation and the arts Example: `rec.music.beatles`
`sci` (science)	Research and the sciences Example: `sci.bio.microbiology`
`talk` (idle chatter)	Arguments; organized chaos Example: `talk.politics.mideast`

Read All about It

You read newsgroups by launching a newsgroup program, called a *newsreader,* or by logging on to an online service, such as America Online and CompuServe, that gives you access to Usenet newsgroups.

If you use an online service, reading newsgroups is as easy as clicking on an icon. The following figure shows what America Online's easy interface looks like. Reading, adding, and searching are all choices on the newsgroup menu (AOL Keyword: Newsgroups).

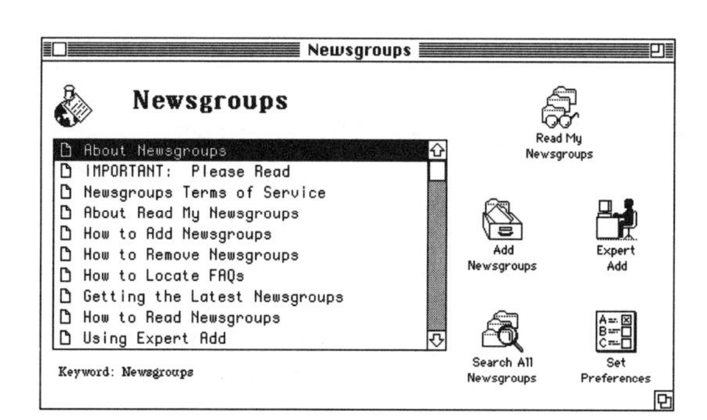

If you're using a PPP or SLIP account, the newsreaders are just about as easy. Newsreader software makes browsing for the newsgroups that you and your students need fast and efficient. The next section walks you through the process of using one of the most popular Macintosh newsreaders. Most newsreaders work in a similar manner, so you can use the steps outlined for NewsWatcher for just about any newsreader program.

NewsWatcher

From your Macintosh or PC, you can use a newsreader program to find and read newsgroups. Basically, these programs enable you to create a list of newsgroups that you want to read so you don't have to hunt for them every time you log on.

NewsWatcher is an easy-to-use and feature-rich newsreader for the Macintosh. This nifty freeware enables you to create a customized newsgroup list and easily read and post messages to Usenet newsgroups. You can get a copy of NewsWatcher via FTP (see Chapter 16 for details on using FTP) from the following address:

```
ftp.halcyon.com
```

If you use Windows, I've included a copy of Free Agent on the CD. Free Agent works much the same as NewsWatcher (described in the next section) and has a very reasonable learning curve. For Mac users, I've included Nuntius, which is also a useful — and free — Usenet newsgroup reader.

Another alternative for Windows users is Trumpet, an excellent shareware newsreader and e-mail program available via FTP from `ftp.utas.edu.au` in the directory `/pc/trumpet/wintrump/`. Trumpet also works the same way NewsWatcher does and is so fully featured that it has its own chapter in *MORE Internet For Dummies.* Check out that book, from IDG Books Worldwide, if you need more information after exploring the program on your own.

If you are using AOL or another online service, all this stuff is built in and easy as pie. Just go to the Internet forum and choose Newsgroups.

By the end of 1995, more than 25,000,000 users were accessing the Internet.

Nuzzling up to NewsWatcher or other newsreaders

Using NewsWatcher (Macintosh) to read newsgroups is pretty straightforward. Most other newsreaders, such as Free Agent and Nuntius, work pretty much the same way. (I'm just using NewsWatcher for my example because it's one of my favorites.)The first time you use NewsWatcher, though, a bit of setup is in order.

1. **Establish your connection to the Internet via your SLIP or PPP software.**
2. **Fire up NewsWatcher (or another newsreader) by double-clicking the program icon.**

   The first time your newsreader launches, it automatically searches for a news server. The news server is a computer that stores the names of Usenet newsgroups.

   If you want to change the news server, choose Preferences from the File menu in the menu bar and click the Topic box to move to the Server Addresses screen. The following figure shows what the NewsWatcher Preferences screen would look like if you were using the server `news.bedrock.com`. Your newsreader's preferences (FreeAgent, and so on) look very similar. Note that you can also set up a mail server address on this screen. NewsWatcher and other newsreaders can forward newsgroup messages to other users on the Internet in one quick step.

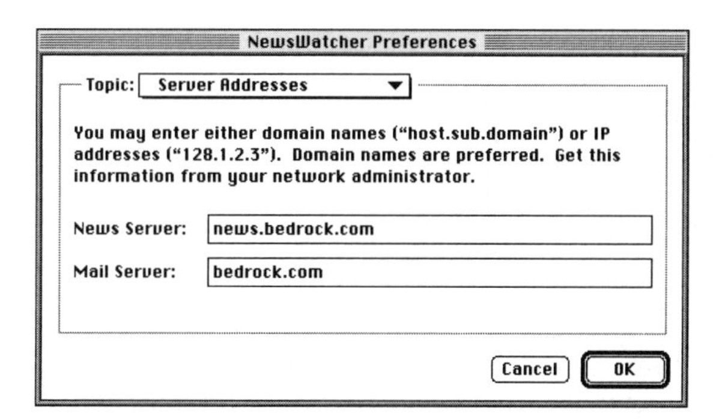

3. **The first time NewsWatcher opens, you see a window labeled "untitled," as shown in the following figure.**

   The untitled window is where you eventually see your personal list of newsgroups.

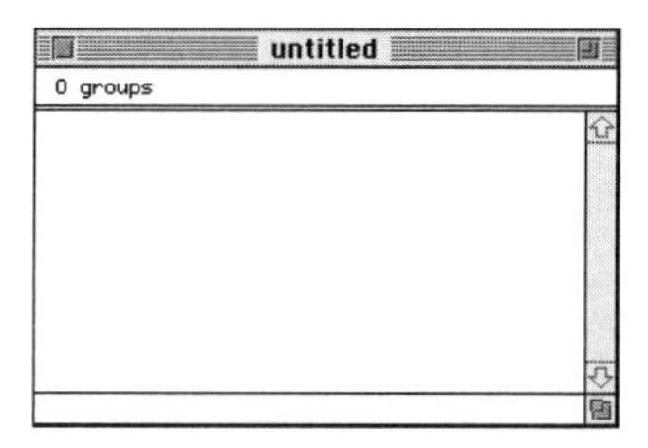

   New newsgroups are constantly being added to the Internet. On subsequent launches, you see a list of new newsgroups on startup as well.

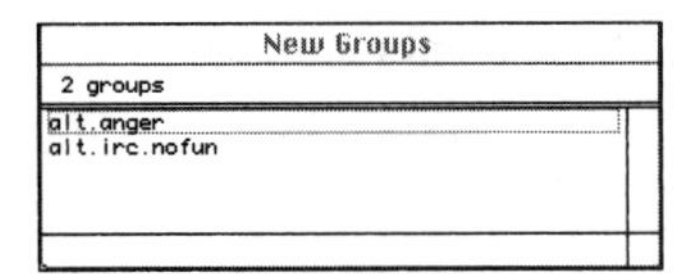

4. Next, choose Rebuild Full Group List from the Special menu.

NewsWatcher polls your news server for a list of every newsgroup on the Net and shows you the results in yet another window. Virtually all newsreader programs have a "Group List" option accessible from the menu bar.

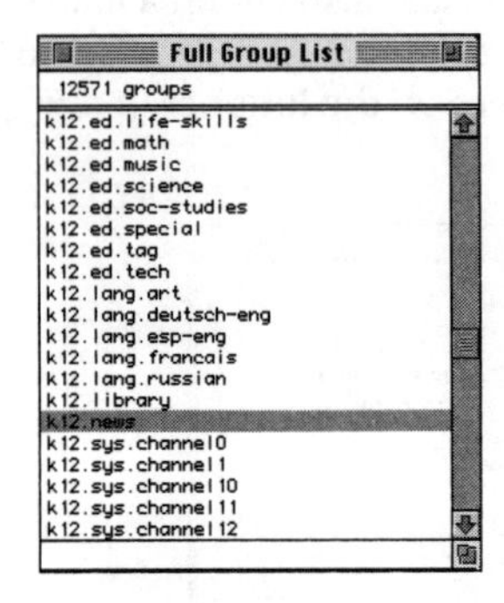

Now for the fun part! To choose a newsgroup, all you have to do is click the newsgroup name in the Full Group List window and drag the newsgroup to your untitled window.

5. Drag a couple of newsgroups over.

Voilà! Your custom list of newsgroups is born. Here's what you see:

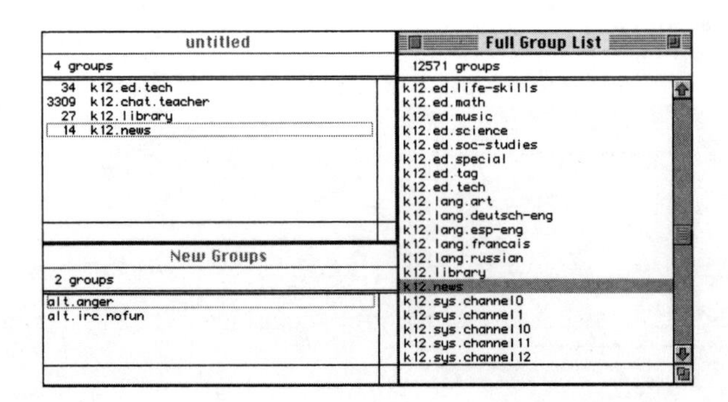

6. Choose Save (⌘+S/Ctrl+S) or Save As from the File menu on the menu bar.

7. **Name the list (choose something memorable, such as "Fred's Favorites") and click Save.**

8. **Move along to Step 3 in the instructions in the next section on reading your newsgroups or choose Quit (⌘+Q/Ctrl+Q) from the File menu.**

   Remember, quitting NewsWatcher or other newsreaders does not cut your Internet connection. You have to do that from the PPP/SLIP control panel.

Reading newsgroups with NewsWatcher or other newsreaders

After you've figured out how to gain access to the full list of thousands of newsgroups on the Net, it's time to actually look inside a category or topic and read the messages. This step's very easy — usually a couple of mouseclicks and you're in. Each step below represents a generic news reader but works specifically with NewsWatcher or Free Agent, both included on your CD.

1. **Establish your connection to the Internet through your SLIP or PPP software.**

2. **Fire up NewsWatcher Nuntius, or Free Agent by double-clicking the program icon or using the Run command from your Windows 95 Start menu.**

3. **Double-click a newsgroup to bring up a listing of all the topics in that newsgroup.**

   As the following figure shows, the topics are listed on the right, the author's name in the middle, and a number on the left. The number indicates how many replies, called *threads,* have been attached to the original post.

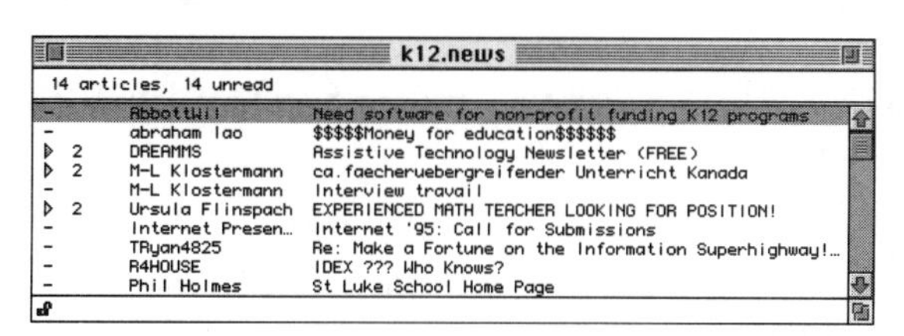

4. **Double-click the newsgroup message that you want to read.**

   Click the *triangle* to reveal additional messages in each thread as you scroll through the list.

NewsWatcher marks *newsgroups* that are new or unread with a ✓ symbol. Other newsreaders usually have a similar method of marking messages. The *articles* that you have not yet read have no symbol. In any case, all the unread items remain in your newsgroup window until you read or mark them. You can mark unread messages as read by selecting the items and pressing ⌘+M. Mark *all* messages in a newsgroup as read by choosing Select All (⌘+A) from the Edit menu and pressing ⌘+M.

As you read each message, you can reply (by posting a message, as described in the following section) or choose Save (⌘+S), Save As, or Print (⌘+P) from the File pull-down menu.

5. **When you get tired of reading, choose Quit (⌘+Q/Ctrl+Q) from the File menu.**

   Remember, quitting NewsWatcher does not cut your Internet connection. You have to do that from your PPP/SLIP control panel.

Users can post more than just text in Usenet newsgroups. You also find pictures, sounds, and movies (in binary format). Many of the `alt.binaries.pictures` groups do just that — and some of the pictures, sounds, and movies are ones that you don't want to have to explain to parents. Watch your students carefully; they'll discover them sooner or later. (See the Surf-Watch sidebar in Chapter 9 for one way to limit access to certain newsgroups.)

Post it!

The Internet community refers to those who only read and browse and don't contribute to the body of knowledge as *lurkers.* Here's how to post a message to one or more newsgroups so you don't become a lurker.

1. **Establish your connection to the Internet through your SLIP OR PPP software.**
2. **Launch NewsWatcher, Nuntius, or Free Agent by double-clicking the program icon.**
3. **Double-click the newsgroup to which you want to post.**
4. **Pull down the News menu and choose New Message. You see a box that looks like this:**

Resource for network planning?
Send
Newsgroups: k12.news
Subject:

Note that the newsgroup name appears at the top of the screen. If you want to *cross post,* that is, post the same message to several newsgroups at the same time, simply type additional newsgroup names on the Newsgroups line (the first line in the box).

5. **Enter the subject for your article in the box marked Subject. Keep it simple and to the point.**

6. **Enter your message on the line after the Subject line. Remember to be brief — your Net-peers don't like wordy messages! Check out the following figure for an example of a completed newsgroup message to be posted to the** `k12.news` **newsgroup.**

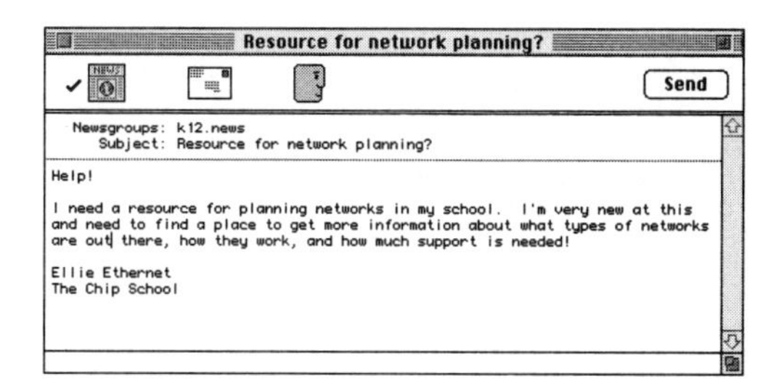

The three icons at the top of the newsgroup window indicate, from left to right:

- **Post to a newsgroup:** You see a check mark there now.
- **Send an e-mail message:** The icon looks like a letter.
- **Attach signature:** That icon looks like Rocky's profile after the big fight.

  The signature is a unique message, usually containing your name, return e-mail address, and a short message or quote. To create your own signature, go to the File menu and choose Signature from NewsWatcher Preferences. (For an example of an e-mail or newsgroup signature, see Chapter 11.)

Beginning users usually lurk for a while and post later. That's probably good, especially when they are still learning their Internet manners. Be sure to talk to your students about what's appropriate to post. (Make them memorize, word for word, the network etiquette chapter in this book!)

7. **Send your post to the newsgroup by clicking the Send button in the upper right of the screen.**

Easy, huh?

8. **Check to see whether your message was posted by choosing Check for Updated Messages from the News menu.**
9. **Don't forget to sign off by choosing Quit (⌘+Q/Ctrl+Q) from the File menu.**

   Remember, quitting NewsWatcher does not cut your Internet connection; you have to do that from your PPP/SLIP control panel.

The Internet began with only four computers that were hooked together in a research and defense network. By May 1996, more than 6,000,000 computers were hooked to the Net.

Start Spreadin' the News with Netscape Navigator

Netscape Navigator has a great newsgroup reader that's a viable alternative to using a stand-alone newsreader like NewsWatcher. You'll find it more convenient to use the Navigator reader, too.

To get your computer ready to read newsgroups using Navigator, you have to feed it a bit of information. Open the Options menu and choose Preferences. In the Preferences dialog box, select the Mail and News option (it's at the top of the dialog box). Enter the domain name your Net provider gave you for reading news, which looks something like `news.awesomenet.com`

Accessing newsgroups with Navigator

To access Usenet newsgroups with Navigator, open the Directory menu and choose Go To Newsgroups or simply click a link that has a `news:` URL (a *URL* is the address of a location on the Net). What's the difference between these two approaches? Choosing Go To Newsgroups also allows you to subscribe to new newsgroups, while clicking on a newsgroup Web link just allows you to read the newsgroup. With Navigator, you can also type a newsgroup URL (like `news:alt.education`) directly into the Location box at the top of the Navigator window.

Subscribing using Navigator

Want to subscribe to a newsgroup? (As if you don't get zillions of e-mail messages already.) Choose Go To Newsgroups from the Directory menu and you see something like the following figure. This is the electronic equivalent of a reader's service card you see in magazines.

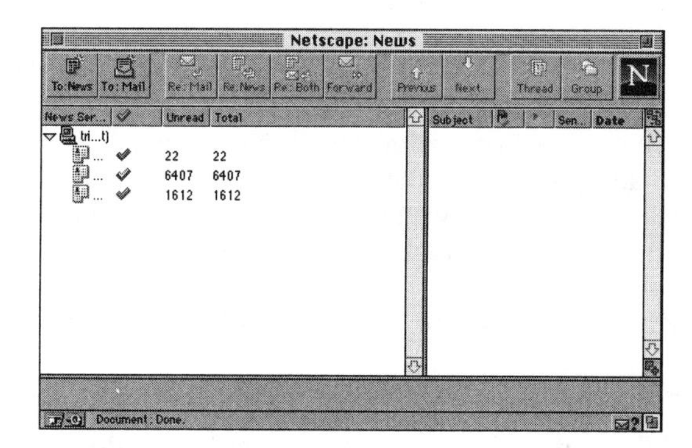

From this page you can

- Subscribe to a newsgroup by entering its name in the box and pressing the Enter/Return key.
- Unsubscribe from a newsgroup by selecting the check box to the left of a group you no longer want to read and choosing the Unsubscribe from Selected Newsgroups button.
- See a list of all newsgroups available on the Net (it's huge!). If you still insist on seeing them, select View All Newsgroups button.

Just the FAQ files, Ma'am!

Many newsgroups feature information about, or directions to, a group of downloadable files known on the Internet as FAQ files. FAQ is a TLA (three-letter acronym) that stands for frequently asked questions. Someone has taken the time to pull together all the questions that newbies ask (newbies are new Internet users) and put them in one place. In general, FAQ files are well written and very informative. Read them and have your students read them, too!

Newsgroup Playground Rules

Wash your hands before you eat.
No food in the computer room.
Don't run in the halls.
Say please and thank you.

Rules and manners are important, whether on the playground or while surfing the Internet. If you and your students mind your (newsgroup) manners, people like you better. Some advice is timeless. Because newsgroup postings often originate from packed college computer labs at midnight or from K-12 students who are trying out the newest toy while the teacher is looking the other way, the atmosphere on the Internet is pretty much one of anything goes.

In general, the newsgroup playground rules are

- Be brief, but complete and to the point.
- If you don't have something nice to say, don't say anything. (Yes, Mom was right.)
- Pay attention to the topic — don't put square pegs into round holes.
- Watch your tone of voice. Yes, it comes through even in e-mail. Sarcasm, as a rule, doesn't work because you can't see the facial expression of the sender. It usually comes off as just rudeness, and you won't get to go out and play tomorrow if you are rude.
- DoN't UsE CaPiTaL lEtTeRs WhErE tHeY dOn'T bElOnG! (It's like shouting.)
- Look for FAQ files and read them! (See the sidebar on FAQ files.)

Saving Your Job

You probably don't condone censorship. You probably believe in free speech. But let's get real. You really like your job, and your job is working with *other people's children*. You will no doubt come to realize that some things found in cyberspace aren't appropriate in most school settings.

One target of criticism is the much misunderstood `alt.` (alternative) newsgroups. These groups aren't subject to the same scrutiny as other newsgroups, and often they come and go on a daily basis. Anyone can create any topic he or she wants — any topic — no matter how crazy, lewd, or mischievous. Newsgroups represent the ideas and opinions of every person posting — whether genius or maniac. You'll find postings from every part of that spectrum in the `alt.` groups.

Some newsgroups in the `alt.` series are just plain fun, some are strange, and some might make the BOE tear up your teaching contract. A brief (and, yes, censored) glance at a small sampling from the `alt.` newsgroups listed in Table 13-2 gives you the idea.

Table 13-2 A Sampling of `alt.` Newsgroups

Newsgroup	*Topic*
`alt.fan.mst3k`	An online shrine dedicated to the "Mystery Science Theatre 3000" TV show
`alt.spam`	Celebrating a luncheon meat as a national treasure
`alt.sport.lasertag`	Indoor game where nervous children zap each other with infrared lasers
`alt.sports.baseball.atlanta-braves`	Atlanta Braves major league baseball
`alt.support.divorce`	A frank discussion about tough times
`alt.tv.beakmans-world`	The syndicated TV science/comedy show, "Beakman's World"
`alt.games.doom`	A very popular PC game that's no doubt the cause of countless wasted hours in schools and the workplace
`alt.humor.best-of-usenet`	Someone's idea of what's funniest on the Internet
`alt.society.generation-x`	Lifestyles of those born when we wish we were (maybe)
`alt.fan.heinlein`	The prolific science fiction author

(continued)

Table 13-2 *(continued)*

Newsgroup	*Topic*
alt.fashion	Everything from bell-bottoms to bustiers
alt.folklore.computers	Weird tales about possessed hardware
alt.politics.democrats	Discussion in support of the president

And you wouldn't believe some of the groups that I didn't list. Suffice it to say that the alt. groups are as varied as the humans on our planet. Be careful and don't throw the baby out with the bath water. The alt. groups are often the place where budding newsgroups first see cyberspace. Several alt. newsgroups are great sources of rumors and gossip that are so close to reality that you'll feel like a swami. Ask your Internet provider whether users can control access to alt. groups if you're concerned. Another strategy is to create a list of newsgroups, put them in a menu, and lock out changes.

Extra, Extra! Read These Newsgroups!

Hundreds of newsgroups are packed with information for educators. Log onto the Internet, launch a newsreader or Netscape Navigator, and subscribe to one of these:

- k12.chat.teacher
- k12.chat.elementary
- k12.chat.junior
- k12.chat.senior
- k12.ed.special

To help spread the word, print a few of the messages that you receive and share them with colleagues. You'll get them hooked in no time!

Usenet Anonymous

Every day, Usenet users pump upwards of 40 million characters into the system — roughly the equivalent of half the information in a large encyclopedia. You'll find that if you're not careful, you spend countless hours reading newsgroups and posting messages such as, "I'm looking for a company that makes chalk in 30 colors."

Chapter 14

Gophers and Other Net-Rodents

In This Chapter

- Cruising the Net with Gopher
- Training your Gopher
- Surfing Gopherspace
- Internet 101: TurboGopher
- Accessing Gopherspace through an online service
- Courting Veronica
- Finding your WAIS around
- Gopher college information

What does a guy on the TV series *Love Boat* have to do with the information superhighway? Well, nothing. Gopher is a program that runs on Internet servers and helps you and your students navigate through the terabytes of information that are now available on the Internet.

To access the Gopher program, you log onto an online service, such as America Online (AOL), or dial in through your Internet service provider and launch a Gopher front end program such as HGopher (Windows) or TurboGopher (Macintosh).

Choose Gopher when you are searching for information about a broad topic or when you just want to "surf the Net" until some topic catches your eye. Gopher makes navigating many types of Internet resources, such as text files, pictures, and downloadable programs, as easy as a click of your computer's mouse.

What Is Gopher?

Gopher is the name of a database and communications system that runs on Internet-connected computers that are called *Gopher servers.* Gopher can burrow as deeply as you like to help you and your students find the information you're searching for. It's really a *browsing* tool more than anything else. Not all the information you browse in Gopherspace is text — with the proper extensions to your Gopher-getting software, you also can browse pictures, sounds, movies (video), and computer programs.

Here's an example of the first screen I see when I log into the Gopher server at the University of Georgia. The folders are clickable and provide a gateway to other Internet resources.

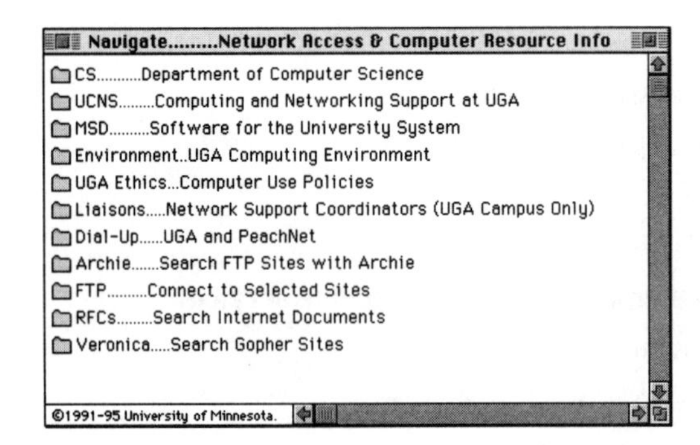

The really cool thing about a Gopher session is that the directories shown in your Gopher window may each come from a different server. As you click effortlessly from level to level, you're actually zooming from server to server, and it's practically transparent to the user. You simply "go fer it," and it's there!

In early 1996, the annual rate of growth for Gopher (database search) traffic was 1,212 percent.

What good stuff can I find with Gopher?

In addition to holding hundreds of text files, many Gopher servers include ways to access other Internet information. Here are some of the tricks Gopher can do:

- Browse and download files from popular FTP sites
- Serve as a gateway to the Archie file archive database
- Access WAIS (Wide Area Information Servers) — distributed-database systems
- Provide direct links to several types of electronic phone books
- Conduct full-text searches on many of the documents archived on local servers and on remote databases

- Access preconfigured telnet sessions for connecting to popular electronic library catalogs and information servers across the Internet
- Provide links to every other Gopher server in the world and all the unrestricted services they offer

Accessing Gopherspace

To browse Gopherspace, most people use a front end (or *client*) software such as TurboGopher (Macintosh) or HGopher (Windows) and log onto a Gopher server. These programs present the information contained on Gopher servers as a series of folders, not unlike the icon view on the desktop of your Macintosh or Windows machine. These folders, categorized according to topic, contain more menus, files, and resource information.

If you are accessing Gopher through a university UNIX network server, type **gopher** and the destination from the UNIX prompt.

Gopherspace tools

With a Macintosh or Windows PC running freeware or shareware software programs, you can be gophering in a matter of seconds. You can access Gopher through AT&T WorldNet's Netscape Navigator (included on your *Internet For Teachers* CD) or use programs that are especially designed for Gopherspace access.

To use Netscape Navigator as your Gopher-broke tool, just type the gopher URL into the Open dialog box (⌘+L/Ctrl+L) or the URL box at the top of your Navigator screen. Gopher URLs look like this:

```
gopher://gopher.tc.umn.edu.
```

On the CD, I've also included two tools, TurboGopher (for the Macintosh) and HGopher (for Windows). Using either of these programs is easy. All you do is double-click the TurboGopher or HGopher icon, and you're on your way. Gopher looks at the type of file (a program, text file, picture, or telnet session) and digs up the tool that enables you to view, transport, or access the file.

To catch your own TurboGopher, use any FTP tool (or Netscape Navigator) to ftp to `ftp.jumbo.com` and search the public folder for the Macintosh software subdirectory. A simple double-click brings TurboGopher to his new home. A new commercial version of the program, called TurboGopher VR, offers users a 3-D interface. Look for information on the Dartmouth server about this new program or to get the latest version of the TurboGopher shareware program.

Meet the Mother Gopher

Gopher gets its name from the University of Minnesota's mascot, the Golden Gopher. Gopher was born at UM to streamline the campus-wide information system. The Mother of all Gophers lives at UM, at the address `gopher.tc.umn.edu`, and is still the default Gopher search site for most Gopher programs. Gopher has been adopted by thousands of sites across the Internet. The result is a seamless network of information-packed computers that can be accessed through a single, menu-driven interface.

If you are using Windows, you can use HGopher (on the CD) or get your hands on WSGopher or Chameleon. These programs work virtually identically to TurboGopher and are easy to install. You'll find a shareware version of WSGopher, my personal nomination for best Gopher program for PCs, via FTP at `dewey.tis.intel.gov`. For the addresses of other FTP sites for Windows-compatible Gopher front ends, see Chapter 8.

For more information on using Gopher with other platforms, dash to your bookstore and grab a copy of *The Internet For Dummies* and *MORE Internet For Dummies* (published by IDG Books Worldwide, Inc.).

Internet 101: TurboGopher and other Gopher clients

TurboGopher (for the Macintosh) is a graphical front-end program from Dartmouth College (`ftp.dartmouth.edu`) that comes preconfigured with the address of the Gopher server at the University of Minnesota (the "Mother Gopher") as its *home* Gopher. Your home Gopher is the Gopher server that your TurboGopher accesses first every time you launch the program.

Don't worry, Windows users! You can fire up HGopher (also on the CD) and follow the same directions. (I think some people were looking over each other's shoulders when they created these programs!) Just think "Control key" when you see "Command key" in the following text.

Let's go gophering!

Beginning a Gopher session with TurboGopher is so easy that you can do it blindfolded (assuming that you can find your mouse with the blindfold on). Windows gopher clients work almost exactly the same way.

Before you send Gopher on its way, check to see how your TurboGopher software is configured.

1. **Double-click the TurboGopher icon to launch the program.**

   TurboGopher zips you to a home Gopher at the University of Minnesota (UM) and logs in for you. You know that the Gopher is doing his job when you see a Gopher Server window like this:

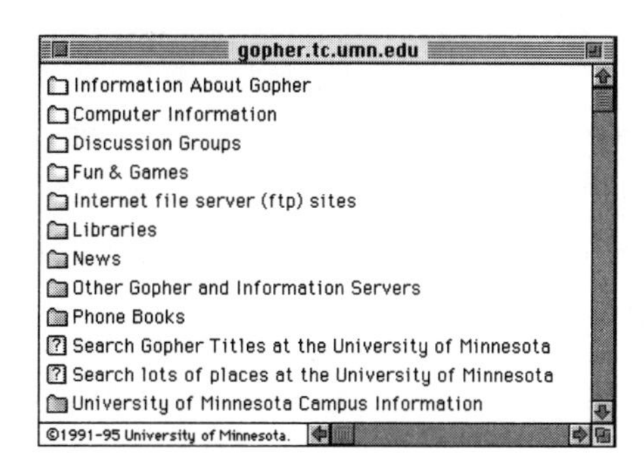

2. **Choose Preferences from the Gopher menu.**

   You see a dialog box like this:

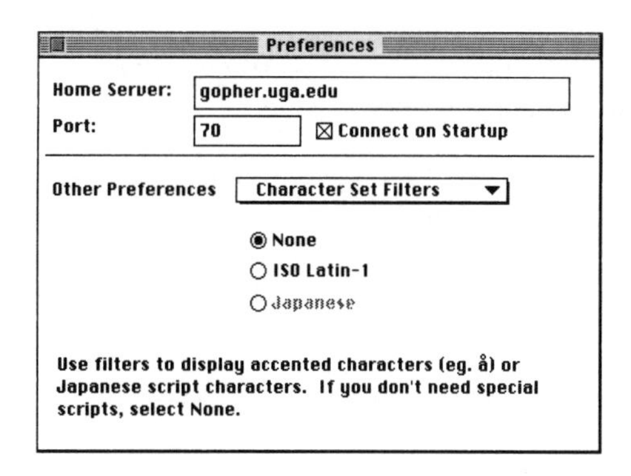

   This TurboGopher Preferences dialog box enables you to stick with the UM Mother Gopher or change to another Gopher server.

3. **Click Cancel to stick with Mother Gopher (**`gopher.tc.umn.edu`**) for now.**

   If you want to check out other Gopher servers, try entering the following addresses in the Home Server field in your TurboGopher Configuration dialog box. (Leave the port set to `70` for each site.) Happy burrowing!

`gopher.ora.com`	Good education resource
`gopher.virginia.edu`	General education and reference
`gopher.msu.edu`	Good education resource
`panda.uiowa.edu`	General education and reference
`boombox.micro.umn.edu`	Another pathway to the Mother Gopher's site
`wx.atmos.uiuc.edu`	Lots of weather maps
`gopher.eff.org`	The Electronic Frontier Foundation
`ashpool.micro.umn.edu`	Source for Supreme Court rulings
`internic.net`	A terrific directory service

Now that you've checked your Preferences, you're ready to gopher to your heart's content!

Gopher does have a few more tricks that you can find in TurboGopher by choosing Options from the Setup menu.

You'll want to check the *helper applications*. A helper application is TurboGopher's terminology for other applications that the program can launch automatically as the need arises. For example, if you retrieve a GIF file, TurboGopher checks its helper application settings and can automatically launch your GIF viewer when you open the file.

Why change helper applications? Perhaps you want to use the public domain program GIF Converter rather than JPEGView to view GIF images that Gopher tracks down. You can remap the helper application for image/GIF. Visit the Setup menu and choose Options/Helper Applications to make the changes.

The entire text of the book *Dracula* can be found at more than ten sites in Gopherspace. (I won't spoil your journey by telling you where, though.)

Getting around in Gopherspace

Using TurboGopher to navigate through Gopherspace is one of the easiest things you can do on the Internet. After TurboGopher is up and running, you simply click your way to the information you need. Gopher does the rest.

1. **Begin your TurboGopher session by making your connection to the Internet.**
2. **Launch TurboGopher by double-clicking the icon.**

After launch, TurboGopher displays information from your home Gopher.

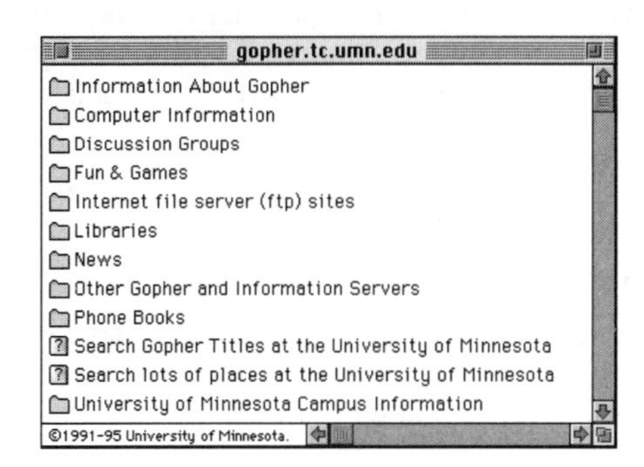

See the icons on the left? A folder icon indicates a subdirectory where more information and links to other folders are stored. A question mark (?) indicates a searchable database.

3. **Navigate through Gopherspace by clicking icons within the window.**

   As you get deeper in the menu, more windows open.

TurboGopher is smart enough to decide what kind of item you've clicked.

- If you double-click a question mark icon, you see a search prompt like this:

  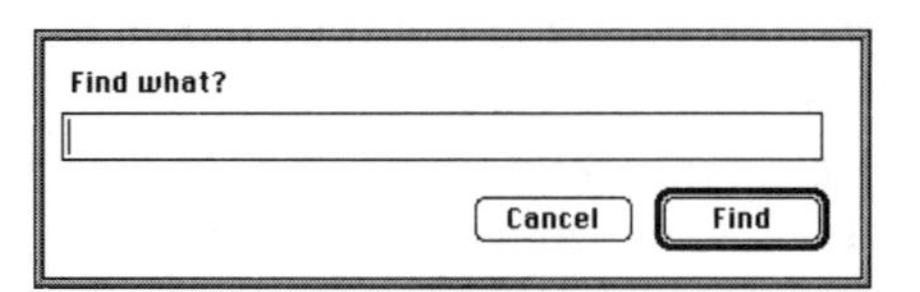

  This dialog box is your pathway to documents that contain the keyword(s) you enter.

  If you double-click a folder, the folder opens to display more choices.

- If you double-click a text file icon, the text displays on your screen, using the helper application of your choice. Set the helper application by choosing Preferences from the Gopher menu and then choosing Helper Application.
- If you double-click a disk icon, the program downloads the software to your Macintosh after asking you, as any polite Gopher should, where you want it to be stored.
- If you double-click a star icon, TurboGopher downloads a graphics file and asks whether you want to launch a helper program to display the image.

- If you double-click a terminal icon (the one that looks like a tiny computer), TurboGopher opens a telnet session by automatically launching a helper application called NCSA Telnet, another software program. (You find more information on telnet in Chapter 17.) Note that you need to have System 7 or higher to use TurboGopher to run a telnet session.
- If you double-click a phone book icon, TurboGopher takes you to a menu where you can search for another Internet user's address.

Bookmarkin' with the Gopher

TurboGopher has a feature called a *Bookmark* that provides an easy way to keep up with your favorite Gopher sites. Bookmarks enable you to save the addresses of key gopher sites to a special Bookmark window. After you bookmark a site, jumping to it is as easy as clicking your mouse.

The following steps describe how to place a Gopher site in your Bookmarks menu in TurboGopher:

1. **Double-click the TurboGopher icon to launch the program.**

   You are automatically whisked to your home Gopher.

2. **Create a new Bookmark Worksheet window by choosing New Item List from the File menu.**
3. **Click your home server window and double-click your way through the menus until you reach a site that's worthy of a spot in your Bookmark file.**
4. **Select the icon for the resource that you want to add to your Bookmark file by clicking it once.**
5. **Choose Copy (⌘+C) from the Edit menu and then Paste (⌘+V) the resource into your Bookmark Worksheet window.**

   The Announce.........Calendars, Activities, UGA Newsstand file was copied from the Home Gopher window (left) and pasted into the Bookmark Worksheet window (right) in the following figures.

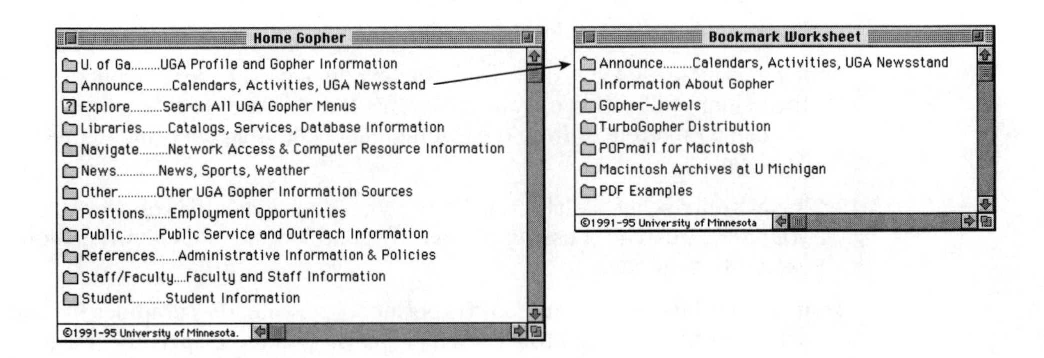

6. **After you finish cutting and pasting Gopher sites, save your Bookmark list by choosing Save (⌘+S) from the File menu.**

That's all there is to it! You can access your Bookmark list any time by choosing Bookmark Worksheet from the Gopher menu. To use a Bookmark, double-click it in the Bookmark Worksheet window, and TurboGopher does the rest.

Here are some more tips for using TurboGopher bookmarks:

- To delete a bookmark, select it by clicking its icon and then choose Cut (⌘+X) from the Gopher menu.
- You can save your Bookmark files and swap them with friends or students.
- To use a Bookmark file that someone else has created, copy the Bookmark file to your hard drive and choose Open (⌘+O) from the File menu.

Accessing Gopher through an online service

If you have America Online, CompuServe, Prodigy, or another commercial online service, you can easily put Gopher to work for you.

On America Online, click the Internet Connection icon on your sign-on menu and choose Gopher & WAIS Databases from the Internet Connection menu.

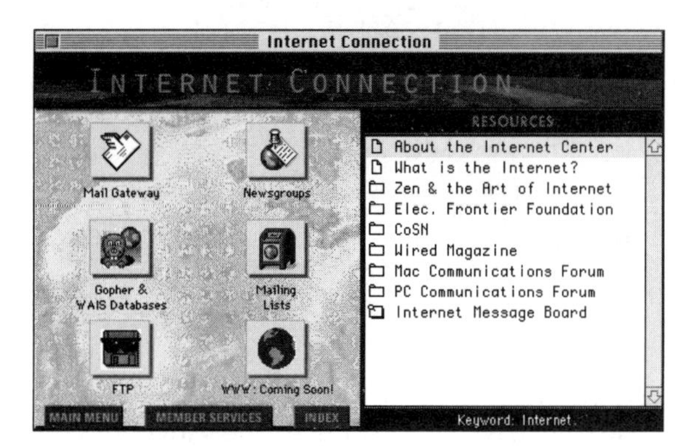

You are presented with a dialog box that contains a user-friendly menu; icons that you can use to get information about Gopher, WAIS, and the Internet; and an icon that you can use to search Gopherspace.

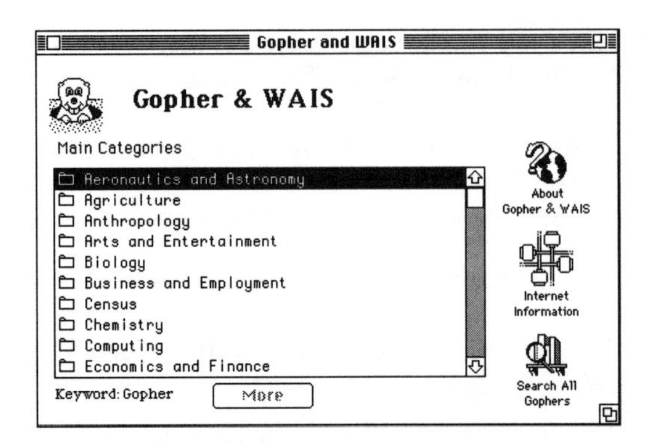

Double-click the file folders or click the icon Search All Gophers to begin your search.

Recently, AOL has incorporated Gopher and other Internet resources into the standard menus that users see in the forums. Check out the politically correct Capital Connection forum (Keyword: Politics) and you see the screen that follows:

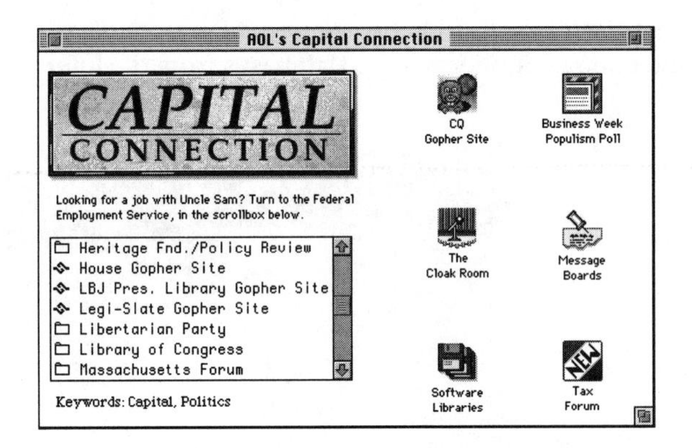

If you look in the scrolling window on the left of your AOL screen, you see that you can search the House Gopher Site with only a mouse click without leaving the Capital forum. You see the following figure if you double-click House Gopher Site:

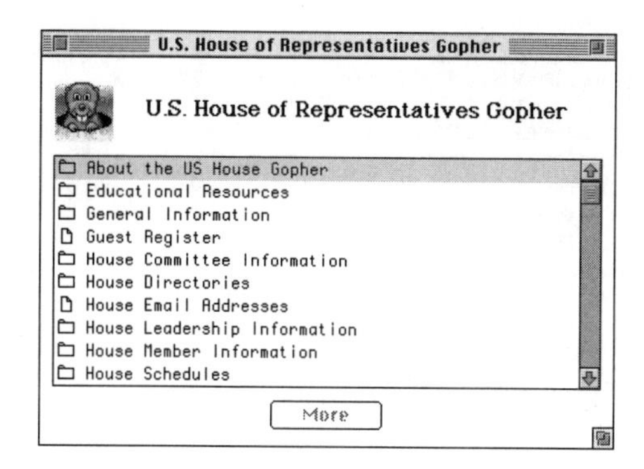

Very seamless. Mighty nice. I think this is a glimpse into a future where all Internet resources will be integrated into other regular forum areas.

Whether you use TurboGopher, HGopher or an online service such as AOL, the happy Gopher always cleans up his mess. You don't have to log in and out of servers; the Gopherware does the work for you. That way you won't make the cybergods angry. This rodent is a real worker — with manners!

Searching Gopherspace

By now you've figured out that the Internet is a huge place. You and your students could spend days hunting for a needed resource. Fortunately, Gopherspace has a wonderful tool that helps you find stuff in Gopherspace quickly.

Meet Veronica. You remember her as the girl who hangs out with Archie and Jughead, but the programmers of this search system say that Veronica is an acronym for *Very Easy Rodent-Oriented Netwide Index to Computerized Archives.* Take *that* to your next faculty meeting and see what the gang says.

Veronica is a search tool that enables you to quickly access Gopherspace and search for specific files and directories. To get to Veronica, you go through Gopher.

Using Veronica is simple. Here are the steps for a typical search.

1. **Open your Internet connection and launch TurboGopher or another Gopher-search program.**
2. **Point your Gopher to a site that offers the Veronica search engine.**

   A good place to begin is `gopher.umn.edu` (Mother Gopher's sister).
3. **Choose Veronica from the menu displayed by the Gopher server and double-click one of the question mark (?) icons to begin your search.**

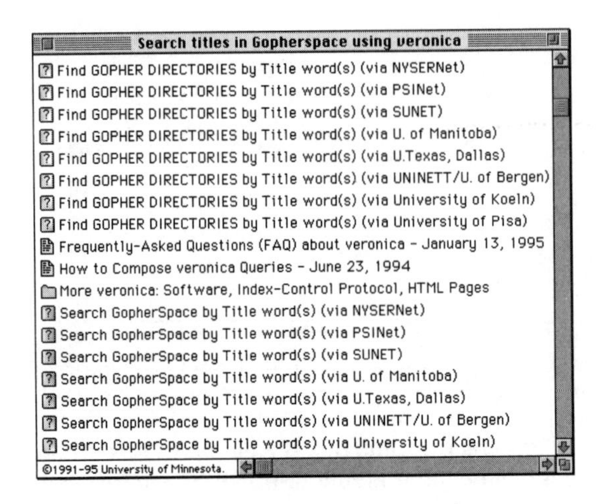

4. Enter a keyword in the Find what? dialog box and press Return/Enter.

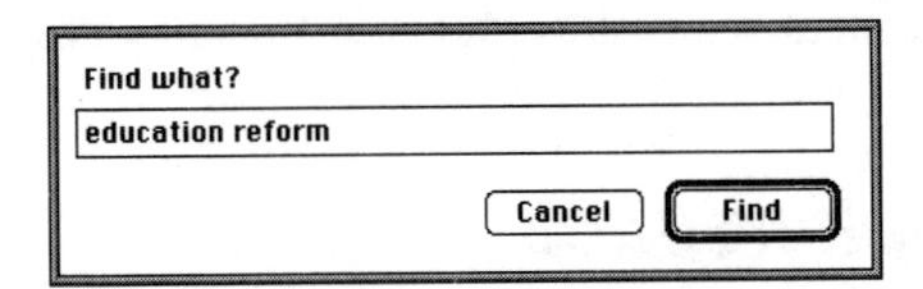

Voilà! Veronica searches the more than 6,000 Gopher servers worldwide. (That's one busy Veronica. She actually searches more than 10 million Gopher items for your keyword in a matter of seconds.)

A search for "education reform" turned up a folder full of goodies:

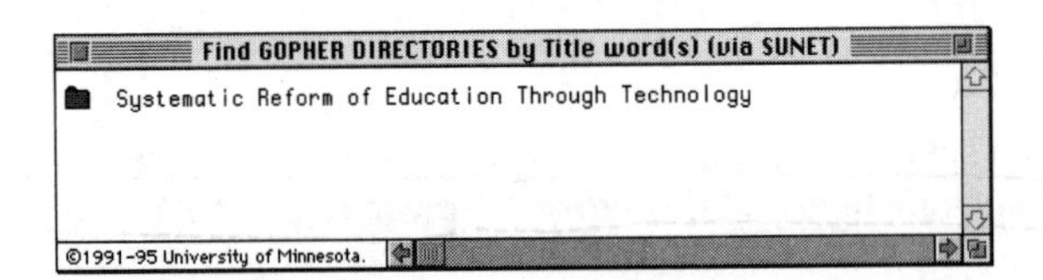

Veronica is a stickler for organization, so she returns the results of your search to a neatly arranged temporary Gopher menu that's completely browsable. This menu works like any other menu in that you can retrieve text files, programs, and pictures or start a telnet session with a click of your mouse.

Here are a few ways to keep Veronica happy:

- Veronica is a busy person. You may have to do a keyword search more than once before she's available to process your orders.
- Veronica is sometimes irritable. She tells you, via error messages, when something is wrong with your search or with the server that's running Veronica. Don't always believe what she says, though. Try again, and you often get different results.
- Veronica is secretive. You see lots of files, but she doesn't tell you where they've come from. Unless you can tell from the filename or by examining the contents of the file, you're on your own to find out which Gopher server brought forth the file.
- Veronica is redundant. She doesn't pay attention to duplicate files.
- Veronica can be slow. Be patient. Lots of folks are using the program all the time. The amount of time that you wait is directly proportionate to the number of hyperactive children in your classroom.

Veronica's honey, Archie

Just so you won't be confused, Veronica's honey, Archie, is another search engine that searches FTP sites and provides a list of sites that contain the file you're searching for. After Archie finds the location of the file, you can FTP to the site to retrieve it. Find out more about Archie in Chapter 16.

Veronica has another friend named *Jughead* (*Jonzy's Universal Gopher Hierarchy Excavation and Display*) that is another search tool for Gopherspace. You run into it at many Gopher sites. Hmmm . . . I wonder what happened to Reggie and Betty?

Analogies for techno-weenies

Veronica is to Gopherspace what Archie is to FTP.

Veronica is an index resource that locates resources in Gopherspace and saves you the trouble of clicking through a zillion menus until you stumble on the file you want.

Unlike Archie, which just tells you where the files that you want can be found, Gopher actually gets the information that you want and brings it to your computer screen.

WAIS to Make Your Life Easier

It turns out that Gopher has a cousin. The Wide Area Information Servers (WAIS) network is a group of freeware, shareware, and commercial software programs that help users find and retrieve information on the Internet. WAIS was developed by Thinking Machines, Apple Computer, Dow Jones, and KPMG Peat Marwick. WAIS is like Gopher in that you can use it to retrieve information in the form of text, pictures, sound, and even movies.

WAIS is a *client-server system.* That means that you run a WAIS *client* (a fancy name for software on your own home or school computer) that works with a WAIS *server* (a fancy way to say that a big computer with WAIS software on board is in a basement somewhere). You simply ask for documents by entering keywords, and the server does the rest.

Here's an example of what WAIS access looks like through TurboGopher:

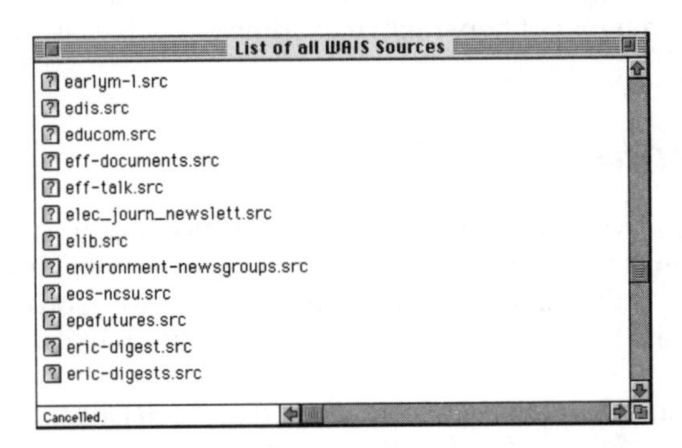

Clicking the question mark icon next to `educom.src` and searching for the terms *education* and *Internet* yielded the following list of documents:

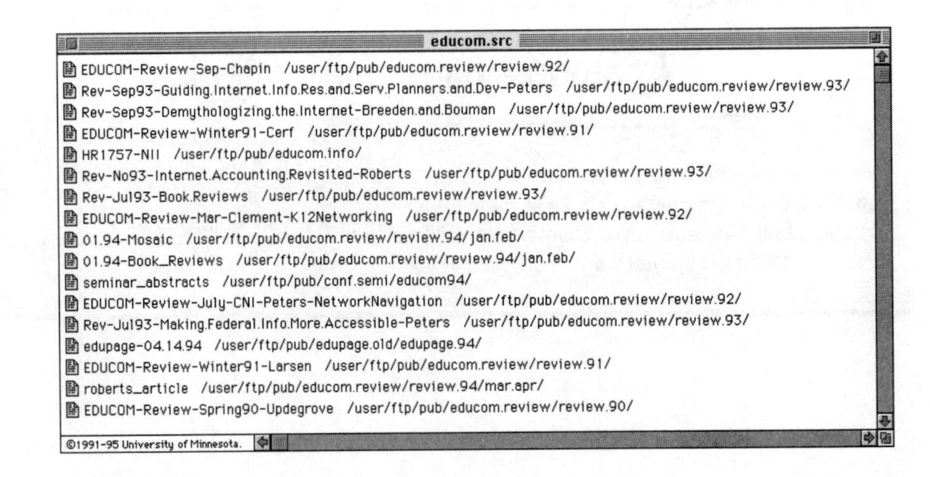

The icons to the left of each item indicate that the item is a document (text file). Double-clicking the icons or document names automatically displays the document to your screen. From that point, you may save, print, or just read and cancel (click the close box in the upper-left corner of the active window).

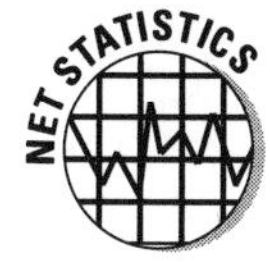

As of mid-1996, more than 1,500 WAIS servers were on the Internet, offering adventurous surfers the opportunity to explore topics ranging from recipes and movies to bibliographies, educational research reports, and newsgroup archives.

Finding your WAIS (software)

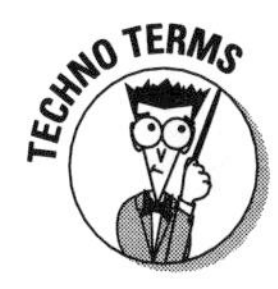

There's more than one way to skin the WAIS cat. Like other Internet resources, WAIS gives you choices. You can either access a WAIS server (called a WAIS station) through Gopher (as in the example presented earlier in this chapter) or download WAIS software for your computer that automatically dials into a WAIS server for you.

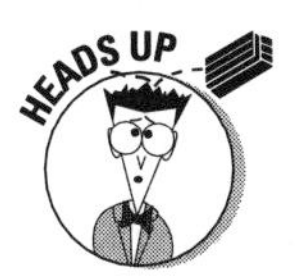

TurboGopher or HGopher is all you need to access WAIS through Gopher. If you require "WAIS only" software, which has more WAIS-specific searching features than TurboGopher and HGopher have, download the file (via FTP as Chapter 16 describes) from one of the many WAIS servers on the Internet.

Like many other Internet tools, WAIS software comes in both a free (freeware) version and a commercial version. The support and development of WAIS freeware has been taken over by CNIDR (Clearinghouse for Networked Information Discovery and Retrieval). To help reduce confusion, current CNIDR releases are called *freeWAIS.* (Visit CNIDR's WWW site for more information about the history and structure of WAIS: `http://cnidr.org/welcome.html`)

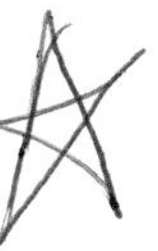

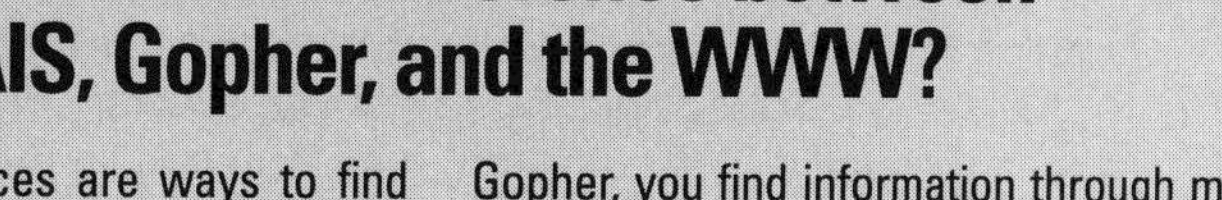

Wait, what's the difference between WAIS, Gopher, and the WWW?

All three Internet resources are ways to find information. However, you use very different methods to find information on each of them. In Gopher, you find information through menus; in WAIS, you do a keyword search; and in WWW, you use text and graphics.

The other way to search WAIS servers is to telnet to a WAIStation server. This method is the one to use if you don't have WAIS software on your computer or a WAIS client program on your local network. (For more information on how to telnet, check out Chapter 17.) Telnet to `quake.think.com` (the home of WAIS) and log in as `wais`. If that's busy, try one of the WAIStation servers in the following list:

- `telnet sunsite.unc.edu`
- `telnet aol.com` (Log in as `guest` or `wais`)

This method gets you a text-based interface that will do in a pinch, but it's not for the faint of heart.

More ways to get information about WAIS

WAIS is a very powerful search engine, and it probably deserves much more space in this already chock-full-'o-tips book. Here are a few resources you can check to find out more:

- **Subscribe to a newsgroup:** `comp.infosystems.wais`. The guys who wrote WAIS, and other experts on using both WAIS and other resources on the Internet, hang out there.
- **Surf the Web:** CNIDR offers great up-to-the-minute information via its WWW server at `http://kudzu.cnidr.org/`
- **Subscribe to a mailing list about WAIS:** Send an e-mail request for the WAIS discussion list to `wais-discussion-request@think.com`. This list is a digest (it comes in bundles), and it is moderated (screened for off-topic content).
- **Get a cool video from the U.S. Geological Survey entitled "Wide Area Information Servers (WAIS)":** Find out how at its Web site: `http://billings.nlm.nih.gov/current_news.dir/wais_tapes.html`

If Gopher and WAIS got in a fight on the playground, Gopher would stomp WAIS into the ground. Both Gopher and WAIS retrieve documents, regardless of where in the world they're stored, but Gopher is a much better browser.

Gopher Information about Colleges

Students everywhere are thinking about their future — whether it's 20 minutes from now when P.E. begins or 6 months from now when they'll choose a college or vocational school. Gopherspace is a great place to find information about colleges. Everything from courses offered to a faculty list is there if you know how to find it.

WAIS software sources

Here's a quick listing of some popular WAIS software for your Macintosh or PC. Use Fetch (Macintosh) or another FTP program to scoot through the Internet and retrieve the programs at the addresses in the list.

Mac WAIS software

- WAIStation: A Macintosh interface client based on MacTCP. FTP to

  `sunsite.unc.edu/pub/wais/clients/macintosh/`

- AppleSearch: AppleSearch is Apple's client/server information retrieval system. It enables users to search large text documents and other kinds of files for topics of interest. AppleSearch runs on a Macintosh server and provides an easy way for network users of Macintosh or Windows to access WAIS and other search engines. AppleSearch users don't have to have direct Internet access to use Internet resources. They can go through the server from their desktop computer or portable computer without being directly connected to the Internet themselves. This gateway approach enables the file-server administrator to make decisions about which WAIS sources are available to network users. For more information, use your WWW browser to visit `http://www.apple.com`

WAIS for Windows and OS/2

- WinWAIS: The USGS (U.S. Geological Survey) version of WAIS for Windows. Works with SLIP, ODI, and CRYNWR drivers. FTP to

  `usgs.gov/software/`

- OS/2 WAIS: A WAIS program that's OS/2 compatible. FTP to

  `ftp-os2.nmsu.edu/os2/`

Have your students use TurboGopher to find a site that offers a Gopher search tool such as Veronica. Search the Net for "college." Just so you know what's possible, here's the beginning of a list I found when using Veronica to search the Internet.

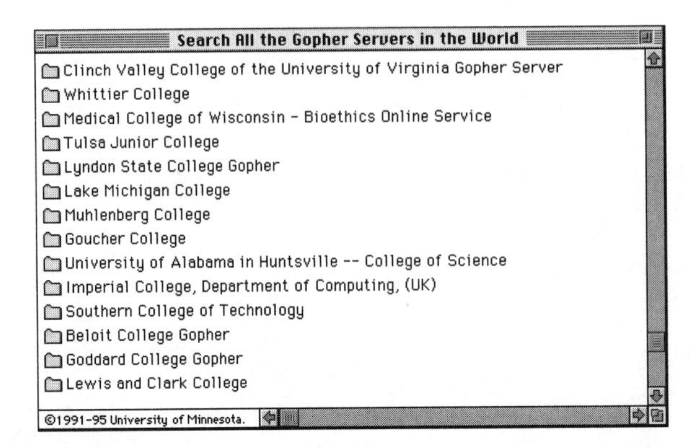

You'll be surprised by what is on that list and what is not on it. (You might say that this activity separates colleges that are "technology aware" from those that are not.) Ask students to compile the resulting information and share it with the rest of the class. Who says Gopher isn't smart? He's going to all those colleges!

Chapter 15

Jumping into the World Wide Web (WWW)

In This Chapter

- What is the Web?
- Web nuts and bolts
- How do I jump on the Web?
- Meet URL
- Internet 101: Netscape Navigator
- Great places for a first visit
- Germs-r-us

Ladies and gentlemen, please return your seat backs and tray tables to their upright position. We're about to take off on a journey you won't forget. The World Wide Web (WWW) is somewhere between a visit to the library and a roller-coaster ride at Disney World.

The *WWW,* most often referred to as simply the Web, has all the things your students (and you) love — dazzling in-your-face graphics, access to sound files, a slick graphical interface, and thousands of places to visit — many linked to databases, file libraries, and interactive online chats.

The Web is by far the neatest thing on the Internet, and more and more schools and businesses are jumping on the bandwagon. Public schools are creating Web pages that contain information about projects. Universities offer Web-tours of their campuses and information about everything from campus organizations to what's on the menu at the cafeteria. Government agencies and nonprofit organizations feature access to huge databases of information and thousands of retrievable files. Companies such as Apple, Microsoft, Levi Strauss, IDG, and Coca-Cola are all sporting fancy new Web pages. And there are plenty more examples of how this new medium is fueling the excitement about the Internet.

So . . . fasten your seat belt and get ready for the ride of your life!

What Is the Web?

Welcome to the World Wide Web. The Web is the place where the emphasis shifts from *what* information is available to *how* it is available. The Web is an Internet resource that is built on a computer language called *hypertext markup language* (*HTML*), a HyperCard-like language that gives even the novice user the ability to create a graphical jumping-off point called a *Web page*. You access a Web page by using a computer program called a Web *browser* and click on *links* (pictures or words) on the screen to jump to other Web pages. Each page has a different theme, with graphics, sound, movies, documents, and more.

A good Web browser program, such as Netscape Navigator, is the Swiss Army knife of the Internet world. It slices, it dices, it does just about anything. In fact, the Web browser will probably be your primary tool in searching for information on the Internet.

Using the Web and a good browser program gives you and your students easy access to

- Documents available on the Internet
- Files containing programs, pictures, movies, and sounds from an FTP site (host computers containing files you can copy)
- Usenet newsgroups (which are like bulletin boards where you can post and read messages on specific topics)
- WAIS searches (database searches)
- Computers accessible through telnet (logging into other people's computers)
- Hypertext (click-and-go) documents
- Java applets and other multimedia browser enhancements
- And much more

Web nuts and bolts

The Web was developed and introduced to the world in 1992 at CERN, the European Laboratory for Particle Physics. The object was to build an easy-to-use, distributed, hypermedia system. CERN accomplished its task and more.

The concepts used in designing the Web have even earlier roots — all the way back to 1960 when a guy named Ted Nelson came up with the idea of *hypertext,* a way to link documents that are stored on different computers. The *hypertext* concept is familiar to people who use HyperCard and HyperStudio on the Macintosh and to folks who use the LinkWay application in Windows. (See the sidebar entitled "Getting hyper" for more information on hyper-stuff.)

Getting hyper

The Web offers users an adventure in hypermedia, fueled by hypertext and hyperlinks. It's a truly hyper place that's perfect for hyper students (and teachers).

Hypermedia is a term used to describe the union of hypertext and multimedia. The term *hypertext*, coined by Ted Nelson, describes text that, when selected with the click of a mouse, zips the user to another source of related information. For example, clicking on the hyper-linked word "projects" in the sentence, "NASA offers many online projects to students," might whisk you away to another site (residing on another computer halfway across the globe) that offers a list of specific projects and information about how to participate.

Multimedia refers to the union of different data types, such as text, graphics, sound, and sometimes movies. Hypermedia connects these data types together. With hypermedia, highlighted and linked text, called *hyperlinks* (or just *links*), enables a user to move between data in a nonlinear manner. You're just as likely to hear a sound when clicking on a hyperlinked word while browsing a hypermedia file, for example, as you are to view a picture.

The language that Web programs use to create hyperlinks is called *HyperText Transfer Protocol* (HTTP). HTTP enables users to create their own Web page and post it to the Internet and ensures that the file is readable by Web browsers. When you enter a Web address, you enter the following text before the Web address:

```
http://
```

The prefix tips off the Internet that the URL (Uniform Resource Locator — an Internet resource address) you're looking for is a Web address and not a Gopher or FTP site. So, in the address, `http://www.aol.blue.com`, the `http://` tells you and the Net that the site you seek is on the Web.

To help you remember to add the prefix, I've appended the `http://` prefix to Web addresses in this chapter. Other places in the book, however, may omit the prefix. Be sure to type the prefix before all of the Web addresses, or your browser will get confused.

How do I jump on the Web?

It's possible to access the Web through a text-only browser if your connection to the Net won't let you display graphics; or you can use one of the many browsers that offer slick, graphical interfaces that make browsing easy.

If you're connecting through an online service or through a commercial Internet provider, you've got it made. Or you can use a graphical browser such as Mosaic, Internet Explorer, or Netscape Navigator (which is on the CD that comes with this book). If you have a PC that is running Windows, you can also try WebSurfer, which is part of a program called Internet Chameleon from NetManage. Browsers read documents, called *Web pages,* that provide information or are jumping-off points for other information resources. The browser finds the Web pages by using an address called a *URL* (pronounced U-R-L).

Meet URL

URL stands for *Uniform Resource Locator.* A URL lists the exact location (address) of virtually any Internet resource, such as a file, hypertext page, or newsgroup.

URLs look like this:

A Web page	`http://www.apple.com/education/`
A picture file	`ftp://fabercollege.edu/graphics/flounder.gif.sit`
A newsgroup	`news://news.lists`
A Gopher site	`gopher://gopher.tc.umn.com`
A telnet session	`telnet://ibm.com`

The first part of the URL, the junk before the colon, tells the browser what method to use to access the file. The part of the URL that's after the colon indicates the address of a host computer.

WWW without SLIP or PPP?

Some very creative programmers have come up with a prescription for all those frustrated Net surfers with text-only access programs that "emulate" SLIP and PPP connections.

The Internet Adapter (TIA) for the Macintosh is a software program that converts a shell account into a "pseudo-SLIP" account the same way that an electrical adapter converts a two-pronged outlet into a three-pronged outlet. This handy tool enables shell account users, who previously could view the Web only by using Lynx or other text-only programs, to use graphical browsers like Netscape Navigator and Mosaic. Get your copy of TIA at

```
http://marketplace.com/tia/
   tiahome.html
```

For Mac and Windows users, a program called SlipKnot also offers users without a SLIP or PPP connection a chance to browse the Web through a graphical interface. It's slow and not nearly as good as Netscape Navigator or Mosaic, but it'll do in a pinch. SlipKnot is available via FTP from

```
ftp.wentworth.com
```

(If you need a refresher on what SLIP and PPP are, refer to Chapter 5.)

Internet service providers are not overjoyed by the emergence of The Internet Adapter and SlipKnot because they traditionally make more money (and charge more) for SLIP and PPP accounts than they do for shell accounts. Service providers probably have nothing to worry about, though, because the SLIP and PPP accounts have a speed advantage, and "work-arounds" almost never work as well as the real thing.

The average cost for four minutes of surfing time at one of San Francisco's Internet-friendly coffeehouses is 25¢. (The espresso is $2.00.)

Netscape Navigator

Netscape Navigator is the granddaughter of *Mosaic,* a freeware program that enables users to browse the World Wide Web. Netscape Navigator provides users of Macintosh and Windows with a fast, easy-to-use interface that makes zipping around the Web easy. It's feature-rich, provides access to the Web, Gopher, and FTP resources, and — here's the best news — it's *free* for educators!

So, what are we waiting for . . . let's go!

Fetching your free copy of Netscape Navigator

First things first. It's time to grab your free copy of Netscape Navigator. It's on the CD that accompanies this book, so getting it is just a matter of popping in the CD and copying the file to your computer's hard drive.

Just in case your CD gets eaten by the dog or you want to update your copy with the latest release, here are a few instructions about how to get Navigator from the Internet. Follow these simple steps and you'll be surfing in no time! The directions below are more or less generic, regardless of whether you use a Mac or a PC running Windows, and work the same way for HyperFTP (Mac) and wsFTP (Windows), which are both on the CD. They also work for Fetch (my personal favorite), a Mac shareware program available at `www.jumbo.com`

1. **Establish your connection to the Internet.**

   If you're using a Macintosh, connect to the Internet by choosing MacPPP, MacSLIP, or InterSLIP from your control panel menu.

   If your PC is running Windows, double-click your browser, FTP application, or WinSLIP icon.

2. **Launch your FTP application by double-clicking its icon on your hard drive.**

   (If you have not yet installed HyperFTP or wsFTP from the CD, double-click the installer provided with the disc to install the appropriate application on your computer's hard drive.)

A window appears, and another window, labeled something like Open Connection, also appears. The default (built-in) host address is probably your service provider or the home of the earliest FTP programs, Dartmouth College.

3. **Enter the following address in the box marked Host (or something similar) and click OK:**

```
ftp.mcom.com
```

   Your FTP program searches for the host computer with the name *mcom.com* and displays the root "/" directory.

4. **Search the scrolling list of directories (folders) until you see Netscape Navigator and double-click the folder to reveal the programs and other subdirectories inside.**

   Look for the version of Netscape Navigator for Macintosh, Windows, or Windows 95. If more than one version exists, check the date column to the right and choose the one that's most recent. Be on the lookout for a directory called `/pub` (the open directory most system administrators use to store their public domain files).

5. **After you find the version of Netscape Navigator you want, double-click the filename or highlight the file with a single click and click the Get File (or similarly-named) button.**

   The folks at Netscape also provide documentation for the program, as well as licensing information in the form of downloadable files. The free use of Navigator by educational organizations is explained in these documents.

6. **Verify the filename in the Save dialog box that appears and click Save.**

   Zoom! Netscape Navigator is copied from the host computer. It's a large program, so don't be surprised if the download takes about eight minutes at 28.8 Kbps.

7. **Exit your FTP program.**

8. **Next, terminate your Internet connection. (Click Close on your MacPPP/SLIP control panel or exit WinSock.)**

That's it! Now a recent version of Netscape Navigator is safe and sound on your hard drive (whether it's from the CD or from the Net), and you're ready to begin to do some Web surfing! You use these same steps, by the way, to update your software as new versions become available.

Connecting to the World Wide Web via Netscape Navigator

You've retrieved your copy of Netscape Navigator by using your FTP program, and now you're ready to fire up the program and get surfing! Netscape Navigator is the leader in browser interfaces for a very good reason — it's very easy to use and very powerful. Using the program is as simple as starting the program and entering a URL (an Internet address). Here's how:

1. **Connect to the Internet by choosing MacPPP, MacSLIP, or InterSLIP from your control panel menu and then double-click the Navigator icon to launch the program.**

   Windows users can double-click Netscape Navigator or enable your Internet connection through WinSock or WinSLIP.

   Navigator automatically logs you onto Netscape's home page.

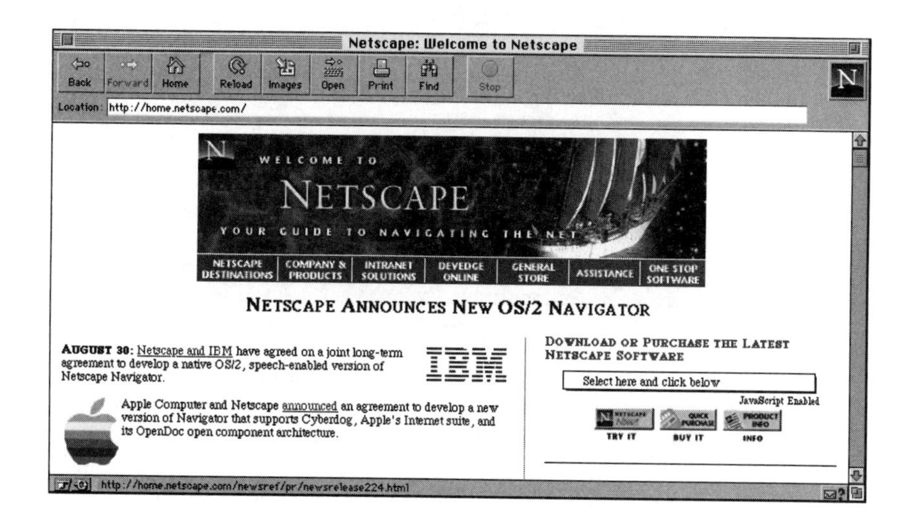

As you move your mouse over some of the words and pictures on the home page (they're blue or purple if you have a color monitor), the mouse pointer turns into a pointing hand. Clicking on these words or pictures takes you to another Web page. Clicking the word *weather,* for example, zips you to a server somewhere on the planet that has weather information.

2. **Need a cool place to start? Try Web 66. Click the Open button (⌘+L/Ctrl+L) at the top of the screen and type this URL (address):**

```
http://Web66.coled.umn.edu/
```

When you click OK, you are whisked away to the University of Minnesota's College of Education site. Easy, huh?

Here's what you see when your browser reaches Web 66:

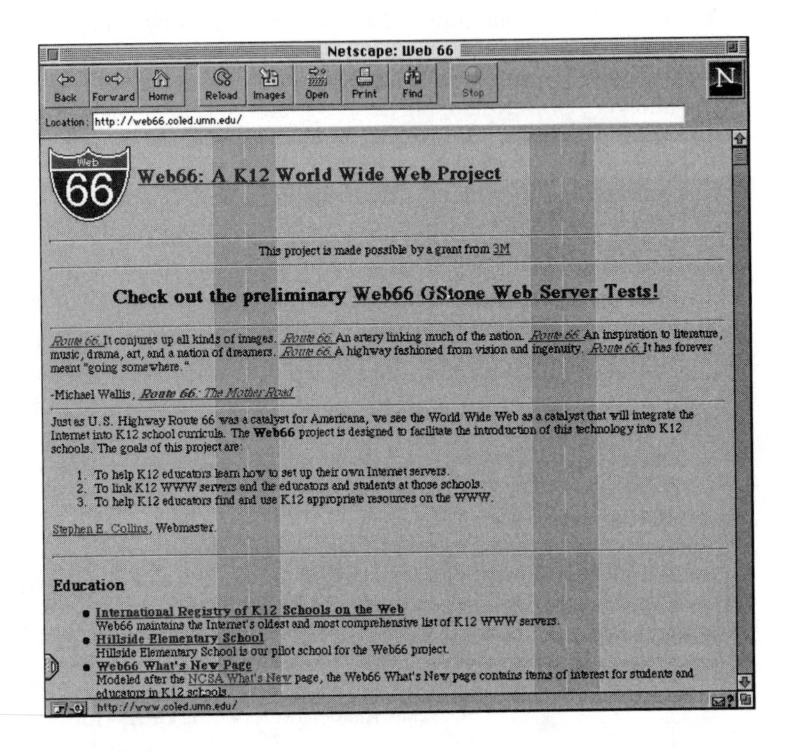

You'll want to spend the next few minutes clicking and browsing. Notice that the button bar at the top of the Netscape Navigator window has buttons for Back (⌘-[or Ctrl+[, which returns you to the last Web site), Home (which returns you to Netscape's home page), and Stop (⌘+./Ctrl+X, which cancels your request and tries another Web site).

Don't get excited if you encounter a `404 not found` error or a `Connection refused by host` error. It just means that the Web site is busy, has moved, or that your URL wasn't typed correctly. Retype the URL or try again later.

Occasionally, your browser fails to load pictures correctly, and then it displays a "broken icon" graphic. Click the Reload button at the top of the screen, and Netscape Navigator refreshes the graphics on your screen.

3. **When you finish surfing, exit Netscape by choosing Quit from the File menu.**

   Remember that you've just quit the browser, *not* the Net itself. You can launch Eudora Light and get your mail, do other Internet tasks, or return to your PPP or SLIP control panel to terminate your connection.

The Web provides several pages that are lists of other sites or that contain a searchable database of Web addresses. Here are a couple of jumping-off points on the Net. From these sites you can get virtually anywhere. Use the Open button and try each of these URLs:

```
http://www.yahoo.com
http://www.netsurf.com/nsd/index.html
http://www.well.com
```

Happy surfin'!

Saving the cool stuff

Your first time on the Web, you're likely to go bananas, surfing from page to page and marveling at all the great information and cool graphics you see. Forgetting where you've been is very easy. Luckily, Netscape Navigator has an easy way to remember where you've been. It's called a Bookmark.

Setting a Bookmark is easy. Simply get to the Web page that you want to save and choose Add Bookmark from the Bookmark pull-down menu. The items are added to the list in the order that you enter them.

Your Bookmark list is now available, and you can "resurf" a Web page, Gopher address, or FTP site by choosing that location directly from Navigator's Bookmark menu. No more messy URLs!

You can add, delete, and reorganize your Bookmarks by choosing View Bookmarks from the Bookmark pull-down menu. (See the Bookmark menu that follows.) Don't look now, but you'll have a hundred or so Web sites in your Bookmark before you know it, so a bit of organization goes a long way.

Bookmarks Options Directory Help
Add Bookmark ⌘D
View Bookmarks... ⌘B
•• Fun Stuff ••
•• Education ••
•• Computers ••
•• Search Sites & Starting Points ••
•• Reference ••

The White House has its own Web site. Hear Socks (President Bill Clinton's cat) at the following address:

```
http://www.whitehouse.gov
```

Navigating the tangled Web

Finding things in the Web can be a bit tough. Thousands of Web pages are out there, with more being added every day, so it's tough for any one place to have a full listing of what's on the Net.

Luckily, after you are on the Web, you can do keyword searches by using one of the Web's many search engines. One of the best Web search engines is WebCrawler, which searches for documents whose title *or content* match your keyword. WebCrawler's URL is

```
http://www.webcrawler.com
```

Using WebCrawler is easy; simply enter the search term and click Search. You see the following screen:

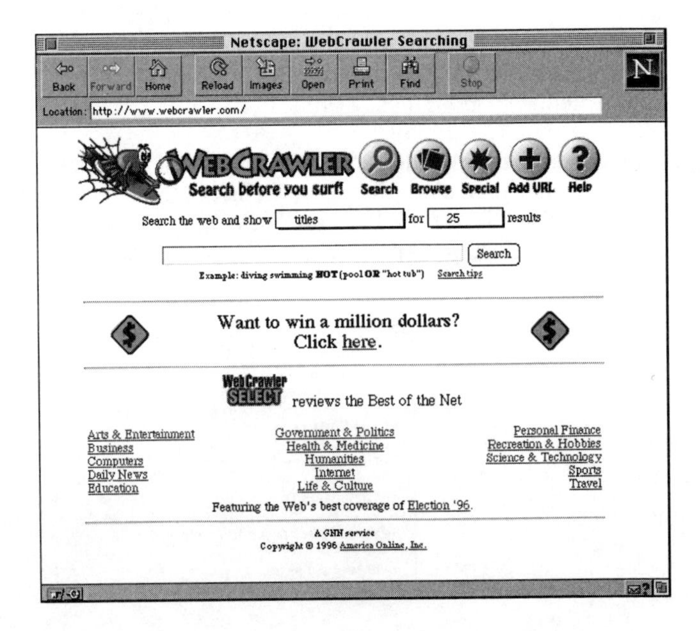

Another Web search engine that you probably will want to check out is the World Wide Web Worm (WWWW). The Worm's URL is

```
http://wwww.cs.colorado.edu/wwww
```

Mr. Worm is not quite as efficient as WebCrawler, but it works in a pinch.

You or your students can easily create your own home page. If you're connected to the Internet via a SLIP or PPP account and your information provider has room on the server, you're well on your way. Your school's home page might include

- Links to other schools' home pages
- Links to favorite reference resources (including Gopher sites)
- Links to home pages created by your students
- A picture of your school
- Information about your school and the surrounding community

To learn how to create your own home page, visit Web 66 at the following URL:

```
http://Web66.coled.umn.edu
```

There you find complete instructions. With a standard word processor and a few special commands, you're in business.

If you want to see a really neat education-related Web site, try this one:

```
http://gagme.wwa.com/~boba/kids.html
```

If you'd like to check out more home pages that other schools have created, you can find links to them at the preceding site as well.

Need another resource for information about creating a home page? Try

```
http://www.netscape.com
```

How not to get caught in the Web

Here are some points to ponder that can save you loads of time and a few gray hairs:

- If images are coming in too slowly, deselect Auto Load Images from the Options menu. This gives you a text-only interface. When you reach a page you'd like to examine more closely, click the Reload button to show the Web page's graphics.

The Web goes 3-D

What's the next level in Web exploration? The Web goes 3-D! A software program called WebSpace is the first commercially available three-dimensional viewer for the World Wide Web. The program, which runs on Power Macintosh, Windows, and UNIX platforms, works along with popular Web browsers. With the WebSpace viewer the possibilities are amazing. The programmers, Silicon Graphics, claim that users can

- Fly through 3-D worlds, exploring event venues, cities, libraries, museums, tourist resorts, and imaginary places
- Inspect 3-D models of products in online catalogs
- Visualize information such as stock market trends in 3-D

The new technology also creates a new standard called VRML (Virtual Reality Modeling Language), an open, platform-independent file format for 3-D graphics on the Internet. Similar in concept to the core Web text standard HyperText Markup Language (HTML), VRML encodes computer-generated graphics into a compact format for transportation over the network. As with HTML, a user can view the contents of a file — in this case, an interactive 3-D graphics file — as well as navigate to other VRML "worlds" or HTML pages. In addition, VRML is infinitely scalable so that as users navigate through virtual worlds and approach objects, greater levels of detail emerge.

This new technology has some very exciting possibilities for education. The days of electronic field trips in 3-D are not far away!

For more information on VRML and WebSpace, point your Web browser to `http://www.sgi.com/Products/WebFORCE/WebSpace`

- If at first you don't succeed . . . sometimes the third time's the charm. Web pages can be very busy.
- Remember that you can copy, print, or save the text and graphics that are displayed on any Web page.
- Want to write your own Web page? ClarisWorks has a neat HTML (Hypertext Markup Language) translator available for download on most online services or from the Claris Web site at `www.claris.com`

Netscape Navigator also enables you to capture the HTML code from any other Web page. It's a great way to learn, but no cheating, please!

Great places for a first visit

All dressed up and no place to go? Try these great educational Web links for your first surfing outing. Choose the Netscape Navigator Open button and type the following URLs exactly as you see them. Be sure to mind your capital letters.

Playing roulette

If you and your students feel like living dangerously, you can dive into a very nifty Web site called URouLette.

The University of Kansas delivers a new way to travel the World Wide Web. Basically, you click a graphic of a roulette wheel and get shuffled away to a Web site that's chosen from a random list.

As in real life, sometimes you go bust when you get zipped off to a server that died or a URL that no longer exists. More often than not, you end up someplace surprising. There's no telling what you'll see next, but be warned — it's downright addicting.

No wagering, please.

The URL for the URouLette wheel is

```
http://www.uroulette.com:8000/
```

- Visit the K-12 Outpost and explore a great collection of K-12 Web links.

  ```
  http://k12.cnidr.org
  ```

- Apple Computer's home page that's just for educators

  ```
  http://www.education.apple.com
  ```

- A great weather map

  ```
  http://www.mit.edu:8001/usa.html
  ```

- You won't believe what you get when you go here. See the Iguana *real* time (a picture taken every minute or so) or find out about traffic on San Francisco's Bay Bridge. Some really outrageous stuff!

  ```
  http://www.yahoo.com/Computers_and_Internet/Internet/
         Entertainment/Interesting_Devices_Connected_to_
         the_Net/
  ```

Germs-r-us

A Science Activity: Visit the Center for Disease Control and Prevention's Internet sites and find out about the latest nasty diseases that are creeping into the human population. From Brazilian fever to cat-scratch disease, you'll find pathogens everywhere.

There are three ways to reach the CDC. It maintains a Web site at

```
http://www.cdc.gov
```

and an FTP server at

```
ftp.cdc.gov
```

or you can subscribe to its mailing list by sending the message `subscribe EID-TOC` to the following address:

```
lists-@list.cdc.gov/
```

Chapter 16

I Want My FTP!

In This Chapter

- Getting files for (almost) nothing
- Working with FTP
- FTP: the basics
- FTP and online services
- FTP with your Web browser
- Finding files on the Internet: Meet Archie!
- Squeezing files
- Capturing the flag

A student and I once spent a full hour searching our school's media center for a picture of a tapir. The report had long since been written into a well-planned HyperStudio stack featuring everything any human could want to know about the strange creature. Everything, that is, except a decent picture. None of the pictures in our school media center or on our online service were appropriate for the stack. We found a tapir peeking around a tree and a tapir peeking out of the swamp. But no tapirs eating. No tapirs smiling for the camera.

(For those of you who, like me, think of a candle [taper] when you hear the word *tapir,* a tapir looks like a cross between a pig, an elephant, and a miniature rhino. It hangs out in swamps and is nocturnal. It has a short trunk that it swings out of the way when it eats, instead of using the trunk to pick up food the way an elephant does. It weighs more than 500 pounds at full maturity. If all this is too much to believe, visit one in South America — or at the zoo.)

Well, FTP came to the rescue. The student, while I wasn't looking, of course, logged onto the Internet, found a graphics library online that had lots of pictures of strange creatures, and downloaded (transferred the file from the host computer to our classroom Macintosh's hard drive) a most magnificent "two-shot" of a mom and baby tapir. Not something for a Christmas card, mind you, but perfect for the report.

Moral of the story: If you can find a picture of a tapir on the Internet, you can find almost anything.

Files for Almost Nothin'

FTP stands for *File Transfer Protocol.* FTP is, technically, a protocol (set of rules) for data transfer. It allows files (programs, pictures, sounds, movies, and so on) to be exchanged between different kinds of computers, without regard to how the computers are connected or what operating system they are running. Through FTP, you can transfer files from a host computer to your computer's floppy or hard disk drive.

To understand what people mean when they talk about FTP, you have to get out your parts-of-speech manual. You use FTP, the noun, when you refer to the actual File Transfer Protocol, as in "That file is available via FTP from Microsoft." When you describe the process of sending or receiving files on the Internet, you use FTP as a verb, as in "You ftp that file from Harvard's server."

The Internet provides access to zillions of files. Whether your students are searching for a picture of the White House or a sound file of Martin Luther King's "I Have a Dream" speech, you can probably find it through FTP.

FTP is sometimes referred to as *anonymous FTP* because the host computers don't require the user to have an account to log in and access information. Anonymous FTP sites allow anyone to enter publicly accessible directories, so you and your students can (anonymously and legally!) sneak in and access the files.

What can I do with FTP?

Using FTP is a little like going to a flea market. You can find nearly anything there you can imagine, but not all of it is high-quality stuff. As you browse the Internet, you and your students will develop lists of favorite FTP sites and the resources found there. Luckily, there are plenty of files to browse.

Hundreds of systems connected to the Internet have file libraries, also called *archives,* that are open to the public. Much of what's in these libraries is free or low-cost computer programs for all types of personal computers.

Here are a few samples of what you can download by using FTP:

- A QuickTime movie of JFK's inaugural address
- The sound of a dog barking
- A program that strips unnecessary carriage returns from a text document
- A picture of a tapir!

FTP: The basics

Regardless of what type of computer you're using, the process of using FTP is similar. The speed of your file transfer varies, of course, based on the speed of your Internet connection.

A typical FTP session consists of these seven steps:

1. **Launch your FTP software (Fetch, Netscape Navigator, wsFTP, Minuet, and so on).**
2. **Tell your software the address of the computer you're seeking.**
3. **Tell the FTP server who you are (usually *anonymous*).**
4. **Enter the password when prompted.**

   Most of the time, entering a password is optional for public sites. It's common Net courtesy to enter your entire e-mail address instead of just leaving things blank.
5. **Browse the directories for files you want.**
6. **Get the files you want.**
7. **Log off (usually by typing QUIT, EXIT, or BYE).**

After you log off the server, you can open the files you've downloaded by using a word processor for a text file, a graphics program for a picture, or a multimedia tool for a QuickTime or other digital movie.

Jumping firewalls

Got those asbestos britches ready? Time to learn about firewalls! *Firewall* is the term used for hardware or software that protects one or more computers with Internet connections from access by external computers connected to the Internet. The firewall digs an impassable moat around networked computers within the firewall, shielding them from computers outside the firewall. The computers within the firewall are a secure subnet with internal access capabilities and shared resources not available to the computers on the outside.

Often, a single machine atop the firewall is allowed access to both internal and external computers. Because the computer atop the firewall is directly interacting with the Internet, strict security measures against unwanted access from external computers are required.

A firewall is commonly used to protect information such as a network's e-mail and data files within a physical building or organization site. A firewall reduces the risk of intrusion by unauthorized people from the Internet. However, the same security measures can limit or require special software for those inside the firewall who want to access information on the outside. A firewall can be configured using proxies (or SOCKS) to designate access to information from each side of the firewall.

FTP on online services

Accessing files through FTP on most online services is pretty straightforward. Usually, you just need to get to the right place and click a couple of icons. On America Online (AOL), you access FTP and other Internet resources from the Internet Connection area.

To begin your FTP session on America Online, follow these steps:

1. **Sign on to AOL.**
2. **Use Keyword: Internet (⌘+K) or click the Internet Connection button on AOL's main menu.**
3. **Choose FTP from the Internet Connection menu.**

   (The icon looks like a floppy disk with sunglasses. Is that a bright idea, or what?)

   You're in the right place if your screen looks like this:

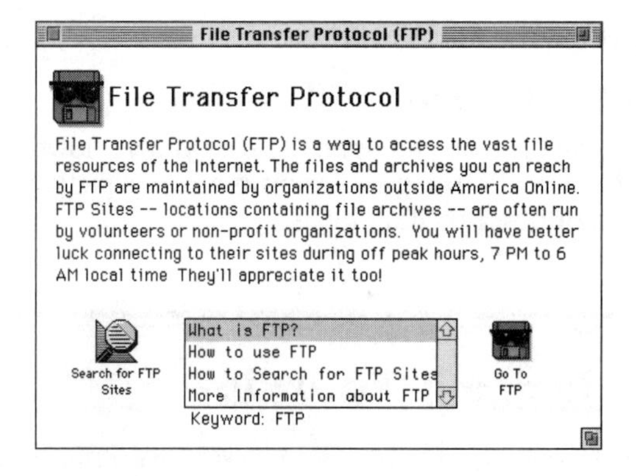

   Note that the scrolling window offers users more information about FTP and instructions about how to use the service. The icon labeled Search for FTP Sites enables you to conduct a keyword search for specific sites that offer public files via the Internet.

   You can also reach this screen by using Keyword: FTP.

4. **Click the Go To FTP icon (more sunglasses).**

   You are transported to AOL's Favorite Site listing.

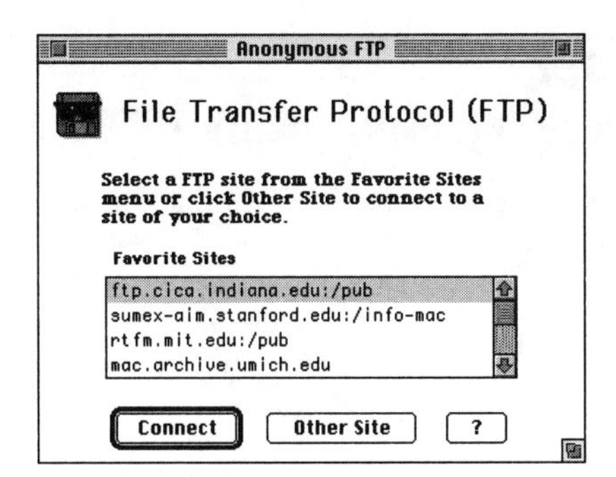

5. **Choose one of the FTP sites from the scrolling window by double-clicking the site's name.**

   Try clicking `sumex-aim.stanford.edu:/info-mac` first.

   Clicking the Other Site button at the bottom of the FTP screen enables you to enter your own FTP address.

   Watch as AOL logs onto the FTP server at Stanford University and displays a list of available files and subdirectories (folders) for you to search, as shown in the following figure:

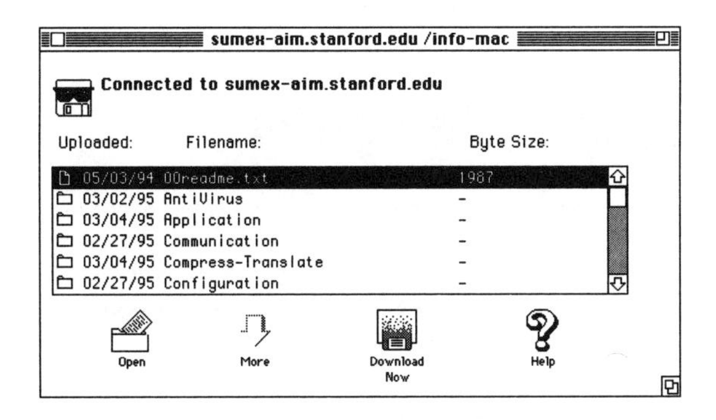

6. **After you find a file that you want to retrieve, click the Download Now icon.**

   AOL presents you with a Save dialog box, and, after you've told your Mac where to save the file, downloads (copies) the file from the Stanford (host) computer to your (client) computer.

7. **After you finish the download, click the close boxes on the open windows to work your way back to AOL's main menu, or sign off by choosing Quit (⌘+Q) from the File menu.**

Are Internet programs really free?

Well, some are; some aren't. You can sort the files on the Net into three categories: public domain software, freeware, and shareware.

- Public domain programs and files carry no copyright and have no limits on redistribution, modification, or sale.
- Freeware programs and files are free for you to use and give away, but not to sell or modify. The author retains the copyright.
- Shareware programs and files allow you to road-test programs for a short evaluation period and then either pay the author a small fee or erase the program from your computer. The author retains all copyrights; although you can give shareware programs to your friends, all shareware information must accompany the program, and they have to pay the author, too.

You can set a good example for your students by always paying shareware fees and by discussing the issue of intellectual property rights with them. Most of the programs that come with this book are programs that wouldn't be available if there weren't lots of honest computer users, like you, out there.

After you log off, AOL automatically decompresses the file with its built-in StuffIt Expander program. You can then double-click the resulting file, program, graphic, movie, or sound to launch the program.

FTP via Netscape Navigator

You've got two categories of tools to choose from when you consider how to send and receive software programs via the Internet: Use an FTP program like HyperFTP or wsFTP (included on your *Internet For Teachers* CD) or use that all-in-one wondertool, your Web browser. What follows are simple directions for using Netscape Navigator as your FTP client.

To send or receive a file via FTP using Netscape Navigator:

1. **Log on to the Internet (through your PPP or SLIP connection).**
2. **Double-click the Netscape Navigator icon to launch your Web browser.**
3. **Click the Open button (⌘+L/Ctrl+L) and type in a URL that begins with *ftp* (short for file transfer protocol).**

   Need a starting point? Try `ftp://ftp.dartmouth.edu`

   When you're connected to the FTP site, you can navigate directories, view files (including HTML and image files), download software, and upload software.

Netscape Navigator lets you access FTP servers in the same way you access World Wide Web (HTTP) servers. The biggest difference is that the FTP directory and content pages have minimal formatting. When possible, Navigator shows the type, size, date, and a short description of each file in a directory. A directory is presented as a list of clickable links, with each link often preceded by a small icon indicating another directory or a file. Clicking on a directory link displays a subdirectory. Typically, at the top of a subdirectory is a link that displays the parent (top-most) directory. Here's what an FTP site looks like when accessed using Navigator:

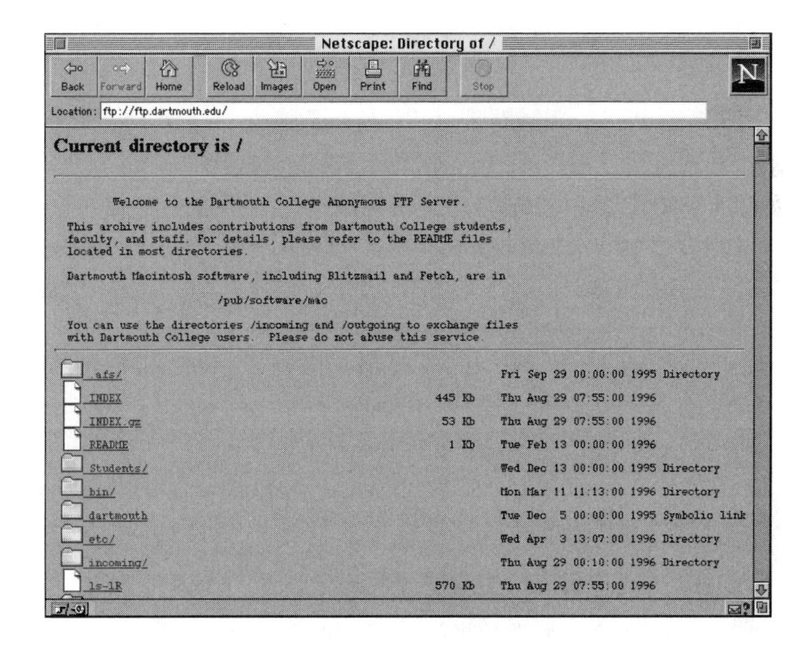

4. **Click on any binary file or program and it automatically downloads the software to a folder (designated in the Netscape Navigator General | Helpers panel — look under the Preferences item on the menu bar) on your computer.**

   After downloading, Netscape Navigator automatically looks for a suitable helper application to launch the file. (For information on Helper Applications, see Chapter 15.) If the necessary helper application is not available, a dialog box asks whether you want to save or discard the downloaded software.

   Note that not all files are downloaded using FTP. By using the pop-up menu or by clicking on a link with the Shift key held down (use the Option key on a Macintosh), you reveal the dialog box for saving a Web (HTTP) page, an image file, or other file type (such as a program) to disk.

If uploading is your goal, choose the File | Upload File menu item (or upload by dragging and dropping files from the desktop to the Netscape Navigator browser). In the resulting dialog box, select the file on your hard disk that you want to upload. Most servers require write access (permission) to the FTP server to upload files.

5. **When you've finished the download/upload process, simply Quit (⌘+Q/ Ctrl+Q) Netscape Navigator or type in a `www` or another `ftp` URL.**

UNIX and FTP

If you're using FTP from a UNIX prompt, do one of the following:

- Type **ftp** and press Enter.
- Type **ftp open <domain name of site>.** (See Chapter 10 if you need an explanation of ***domain name.***)

Then you get the fun of using UNIX commands to navigate. Here are the most commonly used UNIX FTP commands:

Command	***Function***
`ls`	File directory (sometimes `dir` works, too).
`cd`	Change directory.
`get <filename>`	Retrieve a file.
`binary`	Use this, entered on a line by itself, before `get <filename>` for binary/graphics.
`bye` or `exit`	End the FTP session.

Here's what a sample UNIX session looks like. The left column shows what a user may type; the right one explains each command:

`ftp`	Begins FTP and returns `ftp: prompt`
`ftp open apple.com`	Name of site.
`cd Mac`	Change directory.
`binary`	A transmission control command.
`get tapir.gif .bin.hqx`	A picture. (See the `.gif` and `.bin`?)
`exit`	Bail out!

Because FTP requires a large amount of computing resources, both on your system and on the remote system that you are accessing, it's best to schedule long FTP sessions during nonworking hours (usually 6 p.m. to 6 a.m. local time). You'll find that the speed of file transfer is faster "after hours," and you get fewer `server not available` messages.

This time constraint sometimes puts a cramp in using FTP in your classroom, but you can usually squeeze a short session in without getting a busy message. Get in and out quickly during regular business hours, and everyone is happy.

Finding Files on the Internet: Meet Archie!

Archie is an Internet search resource that runs on selected Internet host computers. Archie gets its name from *archive* because it looks through hundreds of different FTP sites and tells you where the files that you want are located.

If you want to find an updated copy of Eudora Light, for example, you can go to an Archie server and search for Keyword: Eudora. In a couple of seconds — poof — you see a list of sites that have the program. Is that great or what?

To be more correct, Archie is actually a bunch of servers. Each server is responsible for keeping track of file locations in several different FTP sites. About once a month, all the Archie servers talk to each other and combine their information into a huge, global database.

Archie keeps up with more than 1,500 anonymous FTP sites that contain more than 50 gigabytes (60,000,000,000 bytes) of information.

Want to find Archie? You have four choices, but the third and fourth ones are a pain.

- Run an Archie client (program) on your computer that contacts an Archie server on the Internet. (There are several such programs. One is a shareware Macintosh program called Anarchie. You can get another Archie program that's called just plain Archie by using FTP to get to `sumex-aim.stanford.edu`)
- Use TurboGopher or HGopher (see Chapter 14) to search the Archie database.
- Establish a telnet connection directly to an Archie server (for example, `telnet archie.unl.edu`)
- Send an e-mail letter directly to an Archie server.

One of the all-time best lists of stuff on the Internet comes from Net-wizard Scott Yanoff. "Special Internet Connections" is a list of resources that includes Online Public Access Catalogs (OPACS), IRC (Internet Relay Chat) lines, Campus Wide Information Systems, and other reference resources. The URL for this list changes all the time (it's a moving target), so the best way to find it is to visit `http://www.yahoo.com` (or another search engine) and search for *Yarnoff.*

Another cool resource is the "SURAnet Guide to Selected Internet Resources." Ftp to `ftp.sura.net`, go to the directory `/pub/nic`, and get the file called `infoguide.1-93.txt`

But what if you want to find song lyrics? A verse from the Bible? Ftp to `ocf.berkeley.edu` and look in the directory `/pub/Library`. This site at Berkeley offers quite a few resources.

Want a list of telnet servers? Ftp to `pilot.njin.net`, check out `/pub/`, and look for the file that contains the word `list`. The filename may change when the list is updated.

If it's software you want, try using FTP to get to `sumex-aim.stanford.edu`. You'll find loads of stuff for Macintosh and Apple II computers and for Windows. Ftp to `nau.edu` and check the directory `/pub/` for lots of pictures and sounds.

One more, I can't resist . . . ftp to `oak.oakland.edu` for tutorials on the Internet and Internet utility programs.

ExSqueeze Me?

Some programs and files, especially pictures, take quite a while to download. Things could be worse. Most files are squeezed (compressed) by using data compression software before storage on the host computer. The good news is that downloading a compressed file takes less time. The bad news — and it's really not that bad — is that you have to uncompress the file before you can view it, run it, or read it.

Most of the files on the Internet look a little different from the files on your hard drive. They have lots of extra letters attached. Some of the letters indicate the *file type,* and some cue the user about how the file was *compressed* (packed) before sending.

Here's an example:

```
outcomes.txt.hqx
```

Watch that computer virus!

Unlike the files you download from an online service, files from the Internet have probably not been screened for computer viruses. That means you have to screen them yourself.

Stop what you're doing right now and do two things:

- Establish a school policy on screening downloaded files for viruses.
- Visit an online service, search the Net, or go to a local computer store and purchase a virus protection and screening program. (Some great freeware, shareware, and commercial virus protection programs are out there.)

If you work in a school, you've probably already had to deal with infected computers. It's not fun. Now you have to worry about files coming into the school from *all over the planet* instead of just all over your community. Never fear, though, the virus scanning programs work very well. Just be proactive.

In this example, `.txt` indicates that the file is a *text file,* readable by most any word processor. The extension (suffix) `.hqx` shows that the file is in *BinHex format.* BinHex is a special cross-platform format that allows files to be accessed by almost any computer, regardless of the hardware or software installed. You'll also see the extension `.bin` that indicates a binary file. Binary files are often (but not always) picture files.

Most Macintosh files are compressed by using a program called StuffIt. When the files are compressed, the author (or the program) appends the letters `.sit` to the end to let you know what kind of compression was used. Here's an example of the way you write the name of a file that was compressed by using StuffIt:

```
roadrunner.gif.sit
```

After downloading the file, Macintosh users can unpack it by using a program such as StuffIt Expander, which is freeware on the *Internet For Teachers* CD, or the commercial fully-featured program StuffIt Deluxe. DOS users can use PKUNZIP, and Windows users can use WinZip, which is also on the CD.

Literally hundreds of compression formats are out there. Here are the extensions (suffixes) for a few of them:

Extension	*Type of Format*
`.zip`	A file created by PKZIP or WinZip
`.shar`	UNIX, shell archive
`.arj`	A DOS compression scheme; created by ARJ

Extension	*Type of Format*
`.z`	A file compressed by UNIX
`.tar`	Another UNIX compression routine
`.sit`	A Macintosh file created by StuffIt
`.shk`	Apple II format; created by Shrinkit

Sometimes folks get really crafty and use more than one compression scheme on a file. In general, StuffIt and WinZip can handle those, though.

More than 1,200 users downloaded a sound file containing samplings from a new release from the band Aerosmith on the first day it was posted.

Capturing the Flag

One of the most interesting things you can do is search for pictures online. Rest assured, I won't ask you to search for anything as obscure as a tapir `<grin>`.

Here's a challenge for your students. Think of a new country, one that may not be on the maps in your social studies or geography textbooks. Have your students use Netscape, Fetch, or telnet to ftp to a site that offers a picture of the flag of that country (look for `GIF` or `JPEG`). I think you'll find most any country; I found Serbia without any problem.

Download the flag and paste it into your favorite word processor. Have students write a short paragraph about their experience with "capturing the flag."

Chapter 17

Using Other People's Computers: Telnet

In This Chapter

- What is telnet?
- Working with telnet
- Internet 101: NCSA Telnet
- Searching (for) ERIC

In the movie *War Games,* actor Matthew Broderick's character logged in to a military computer from his bedroom, typed `Global Thermonuclear War`, and accidentally sent bombers scrambling and military officials racing around trying to figure out who was controlling their computer. Although this example may seem a little "Hollywood," it's technically possible. Your screen becomes a window into someone else's computer network. In most cases, the concept of computing via remote control is now commonplace. Telnet enables users to log in to computers from a remote site and appear, to the host computer, to be issuing commands from right down the hall.

When you log in to a computer via telnet, you have to deal with an interactive, command line interface. No graphics, just plain text. Welcome to the world of *dumb terminals.*

Although your students are not likely to launch any bombers, they can control other people's computers in more productive ways to, for example, find a book in the public library or register for classes at the local college.

So, telnet is all about using OPCs (other people's computers). By the way, if your students see the computer message `Would you like to play a game?` from a mainframe buried deep in a Colorado hillside, have them answer `no` and save the military a lot of grief.

What Is Telnet?

Telnet is a remote login program that enables you and your students to access a network remotely (either by phone or through a local area or wide area network). By running a telnet program on your computer after you are logged in to the Internet, you can have your Macintosh or PC simulate a dumb terminal and take advantage of information resources at the host site.

You type commands on your keyboard that telnet relays from your computer terminal to your local Internet service provider and then from your provider to the remote computer that you have accessed. If you have a fast Internet connection, using telnet is just like being there.

Because telnet is like being there, the performance of the computer system for those people who are there is affected by your access. The bottom line, then, is that you should telnet only when:

- You've been given your own username and password to gain access to a specific computer for a specific task (such as registering for a college course).
- You need resources that you can't retrieve any other way.

In 1996, U.S. Internet host computers represented 64 percent of the computers connected to the Internet. The next closest countries in number of host computers were Germany and the United Kingdom, logging in at 5 percent each.

What Can I Do with Telnet?

Gaining access to other people's computer systems can net some very productive results. Among other things, you can do the following:

- Access huge databases to do research.
- Use resources in libraries around the world.
- Register for classes.
- Fill out forms to request information and supplies.
- Gain easy entry into the world of Gophers and the World Wide Web.

You hear the word *telnet* used both as a noun, as in "I will use telnet to access the database," and as a verb, as in "Please telnet to our server to register your software." Regardless of the part of speech, telnet can be a powerful tool in your Internet toolbox.

Telnet basics

All telnet sessions, regardless of the type of access to the Internet or what type of computer you have, work in the same way. Here's the short list of the simple seven steps:

1. Sign onto the Internet.
2. Launch your telnet program.
3. Enter the telnet address.

   Telnet addresses, like other Internet addresses, can be either text, such as `glis.cr.usgs.gov`, or numbers, such as `152.61.192.54`. The numbers, often referred to as a *dotted quad,* are just another way to identify a host computer. Every computer logged onto the Internet directly or through a SLIP or PPP connection is identified by a unique dotted quad.
4. Write down important information, such as how to log off and what the escape character is (in case you get stuck or your "terminal" freezes).
5. Enter a username and password.
6. Type commands or choose numbers from text-based menus to complete your task.
7. Exit or log off the host computer.

Internet 101: NCSA Telnet

Personal computer users can easily log in to a remote computer by using telnet software such as the programs available from the National Center for Supercomputing Applications. NCSA Telnet (Macintosh) and NCSA WinTel (Windows) are shareware programs designed especially for accessing telnet sites with your computer. More good news: Both programs are on the CD that comes with this book. (For the newest version of either program, use FTP to go to `ftp.ncsa.uiuc.edu` and check the `/pub` directory.)

Windows users can also use telnet client software such as Trumpet Telnet (available via FTP from `ftp.trumpet.com.au` in the directory `/ftp/pub/beta`) or Chameleon (`ftp.halcyon.com` in the directory `/pub/slip/chameleon`), which works just about the same way as NCSA Telnet.

Getting ready for your first telnet session? For your first logon, you zip over to St. Louis to a Washington University library system called World Window. It's a great jumping-off point for other places on the Net. Note that NCSA Telnet and WinTel work the same way. If you're using a Windows PC, just substitute the control key for the command key in the directions that follow:

1. **Establish your connection to the Internet.**
2. **Double-click the NCSA Telnet icon to launch the program.**
3. **Choose Open Connection (⌘+O) from the File menu. You see the screen shown in the following figure.**

Host/Session Name: locis.loc.gov
Window Name
FTP session (⌘F)
Authenticate (⌘A)
Encrypt (⌘E)
Cancel
Connect

The last address that you visited is in the Host/Session name box when the screen appears.

4. **In the box for the Host/Session name, enter the domain name of the host computer that you want to visit.**

   (For this example, use `library.wustl.edu`)

   Leave the Window Name box blank. You can use it later to name active windows in case you want to get fancy and begin more than one telnet session at a time.

5. **Click OK.**

   Telnet establishes a connection to Washington University's World Window, and you see something like this:

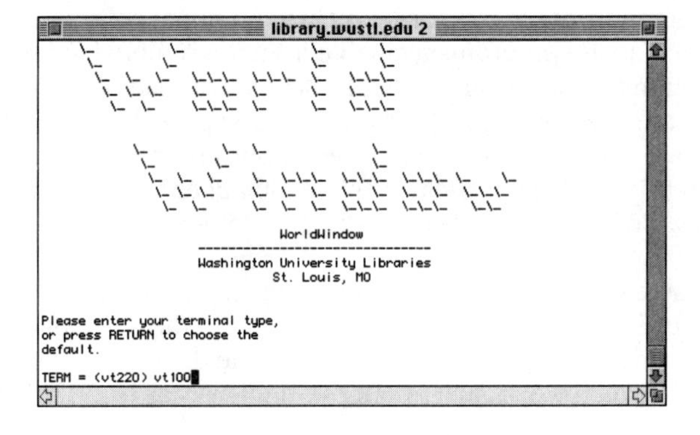

Some computers (like the one accessed in this example) require that you identify your terminal type.

6. **Resist the temptation to say, "I'm not terminal yet!" and type** vt100.

7. **Press the Return or Enter key when you are asked for a username and password.**

   Finally, you make it to the WorldWindow main menu! Check out all your choices:

Being anonymous

The way you log in to a telnet session may vary, but usually logging in with *anonymous* as the username and your e-mail address as the password does the trick.

Here's a sample of how to be anonymous with a UNIX-based connection (the user types what is shown in boldface and replaces the information in the brackets with the real stuff):

telnet

telnet> **open <domain name>**

login: **anonymous**

pswrd: **<your e-mail address>**

A menu with available resources and further instructions is displayed. You type **exit** to end your session.

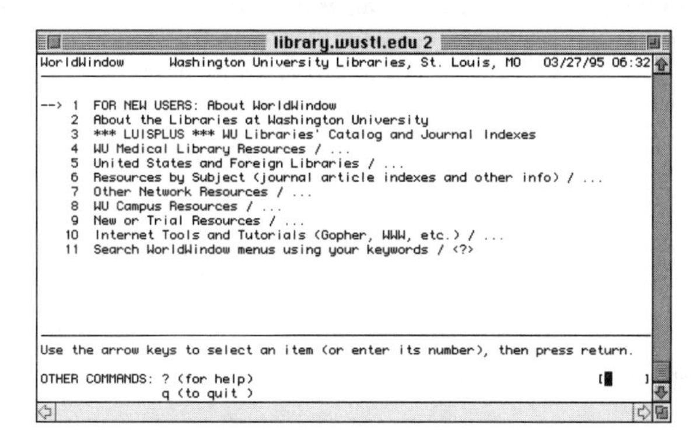

8. **Use keyboard commands to navigate through the choices.**

   Note that on this system, typing a lowercase *u* takes you back a page, and you can use number keys and the arrow keys as an alternative way of selecting items from the World Window menu.

9. **When you are finished, type** q **to quit and then close your connection.**

In mid-1996, the number of Web servers on the Net was approximately 252,600.

Great Telnet Spots

There are hundreds of telnet spots to visit. Here are some of the ones that are easy to navigate and hold lots of surprises. Find more educational sites in Chapter 28.

- Use telnet to get to `pac.carl.org` and log in as PAC for a great source of library resources, including magazines and books.

- Use telnet to get to `unc.edu` for a great "laUNChpad" to other sites. (Type **launch** at the login prompt.) This one's worth the trip! You can find everything from Supreme Court decisions to curriculum guides.

Show your students how to telnet to LaunchPad and download a Supreme Court decision. If you've never seen the text of a decision, reading the decision is a technical writing interpretation challenge that you and your students will never forget.

Go Ask ERIC

Several sites offer telnet access to the ERIC education database. Syracuse University offers five years' worth of ERIC database information on its SUINFO computer. Users can search by author, title, descriptor word, abstract, and more. (This method of accessing ERIC databases is *much* more convenient and much less expen-sive than driving to your local university, don't you think? Use all the money you save to buy more *The Internet For Teachers,* 2nd Edition, books for your friends!)

Follow these steps to access ERIC via the Syracuse host computer:

1. **Sign on to the Internet through your online service, your Internet service provider, or your university dial-up account.**
2. **Launch NCSA Telnet, WinTel, or another telnet client program.**
3. **Enter the following address in the box labeled Host:**

   ```
   sklib.usask.ca
   ```

4. **When asked for a login name, type** eric **(lowercase).**
5. **Read the screen for further information.**

   Use ERIC to search for articles in educational journals and research publications. Try searching Keyword: Internet and see just how hot this topic is today.

What color is your terminal?

When you telnet, often the computer on the other end of the line (the host computer) asks you what type of terminal you're using. If you enter the wrong type of terminal, you may not be able to see what is displayed on your screen, or you may get unpredictable results when you enter information from your keyboard. Virtually all systems support vt100 and vt102 terminal types. If you're accessing telnet from a Macintosh or most DOS/Windows machines, always choose vt100. If you make your connection to telnet using telecommunications software, be sure to set your terminal preferences to the same terminal type you're telling your telnet site to use.

Chapter 18

IRC Techno-Talk Shows

In This Chapter

- Chatting on the Internet
- Chatting via online services
- Internet 101: IRCle
- Finding a place to chat
- Stalking MOOs and MUDs
- A meeting of the minds

Internet Relay Chat (IRC) is the Internet's answer to a fire drill. Think of hundreds of people, many of them bored college students with idle time in a computer lab, chatting live across the wires on any topics you can imagine.

IRC offers real-time conferencing that's similar to conference chats on online services. IRC is not very pretty, but it can be very powerful as a collaborative tool. In a classroom, IRC can help break down classroom walls to connect students with peers and experts around the world. IRC can also be a part of the solution to the problem of extending learning to your community. Read on to find out more about extending your reach with IRC.

IRC: Chatter at 28.8

IRC is a software-dependent method of holding live online conversations with people around the world. It kind of reminds me of a global CB radio network that you access via computer. A free-for-all place where people speak their minds to whoever will listen, IRC is organized into *channels* that are based on topics.

Basically, after you log onto the Internet and join a chat (channel), you type something on your computer, and all the other people tuned into your channel can see it instantly. At any one time, hundreds of channels are buzzing with chatter. You can either join one of them or create your own.

After you learn how chats operate, you can make your chats private or by invitation only, and you can assign yourself a nickname.

If you and your students want to study humanity, IRC is a great way to begin. It's raw, uncensored, mile-a-minute dialog, and spelling doesn't count! As with any free-form medium, you are likely to see things that will curl your hair. I recommend using IRC very cautiously with your students and only with a specific purpose in mind. The best use of IRC may be to begin your own chat and invite other classes from across the country to participate. Use newsgroup or mailing list postings to invite them (see Chapters 12 and 13).

Live Chat via an Online Service

If you've chosen to surf the Internet via a commercial online service such as America Online (AOL), you can converse live online in electronic conference rooms. The interface makes chatting easy and fun. The online hosts keep order and facilitate discussions. AOL also allows voting, comments, and even rolling dice.

To "go live" on America Online, log on and choose an electronic conference room. (Find conference rooms on AOL by clicking the "people" icon in the toolbar.) The Schoolroom, located in the Electronic Schoolhouse (Keyword: ESH), is a great place for teachers to get together. It's kind of a teacher's lounge in cyberspace.

The number shown below People in (top center) tells you that 19 people are attending the chat. The screennames of the last five users who entered the room are shown next to People in. Icons on the top left of the chat screen enable users to see information about others in the room, check other available electronic chat rooms, get help, and configure the software to block access to certain other areas on AOL (a handy feature for educators). Users send messages by typing in the box at the bottom and clicking the Send button.

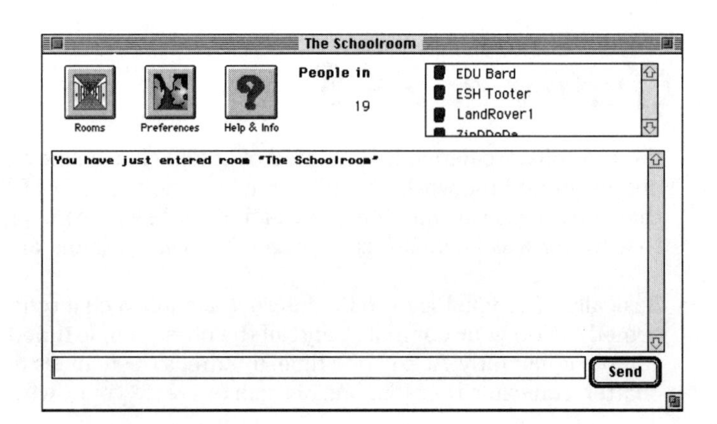

Chatting electronically via an online service is much simpler than using IRC, but it also costs more because you are paying by the minute instead of at a flat rate.

Join educators in AOL's Schoolroom for weekly electronic chats on education-related topics such as the Internet and critical thinking. Check the schedule in the Electronic Schoolhouse for more information. (Don't be surprised if you see me pop in from time to time.)

In 1995, Internet service providers reported cumulative earnings of more than $300 million. By the year 2000, that number is expected to reach more than $5 billion.

Internet 101: IRCle

If you are connected to the Internet via an Internet service provider, you can chat *live* by using a software application that supports IRC. You can access IRC from your own computer by using telnet to connect with another computer that is running an IRC client or by using software such as IRCle, Talk, mIRC (Windows), or Homer (Macintosh). A copy of IRCle for the Macintosh and mIRC for Windows is on your *Internet For Teachers* CD. To download an updated copy of IRCle, go to `http://www.xs4all.nl/~ircle/`. WSIRC, a PC shareware client that offers an alternative to mIRC, can be snagged via FTP from `cs-ftp.bu.edu` in the directory `/irc/clients/pc/windows`. IRC II is another Windows client available from `ftp.cica.indiana.edu` in the directory `/pub/pc/win3`. (For more information on FTP, see Chapter 16.)

Here's how IRCle (Mac) works. (Windows users note that mIRC works pretty much the same way — look for the Windows exceptions following.)

1. **Make your connection to the Internet.**
2. **Double-click the IRCle icon to launch the program.**

   A dialog box appears, asking for information about the IRC server that you want to contact.

   Windows users: Use your Program Manager or Start button to run mIRC.
3. **Type** irc.colorado.edu **(an IRC server in Colorado; others are listed later in this chapter).**

   (Leave the Port box alone; it always reads `6667` for Internet Relay Chat.)
4. **In the Nickname box, enter a name by which you'll be known during the chat and then press Tab to get to the next box.**

   The name that you use is kind of like a CB handle.

5. **In the Mail address box, enter your own e-mail address in the format** `e-mailaddress@domain` **(for example,** `Flintstone@bedrock.com`**) and then press Tab to get to the next box.**

   Almost ready ! So far, your IRC setup box should look like the following:

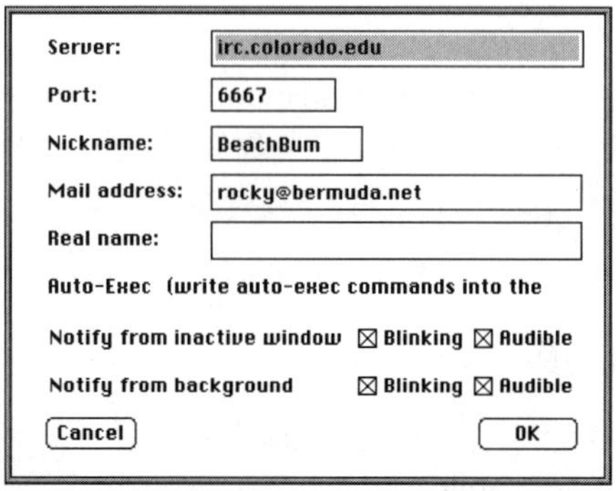

   Server: irc.colorado.edu
   Port: 6667
   Nickname: BeachBum
   Mail address: rocky@bermuda.net
   Real name:
   Auto-Exec (write auto-exec commands into the
   Notify from inactive window ☒ Blinking ☒ Audible
   Notify from background ☒ Blinking ☒ Audible
   Cancel OK

6. **Enter your real name in the box.**

   This name is the one that people see when they use the UNIX command `\who`

7. **Click OK, and you're in!**

   The IRC command box appears along the bottom of your screen. You type all your commands and the text you want to send in this box. In the following figure, you see what I'd type in the command box to join the channel (chat) called "education."

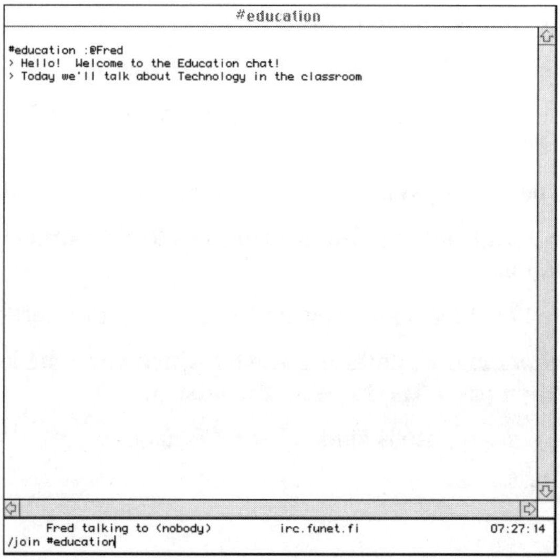

   #education
   #education :@Fred
   > Hello! Welcome to the Education chat!
   > Today we'll talk about Technology in the classroom
   Fred talking to (nobody) irc.funet.fi 07:27:14
   /join #education

8. **To get a listing of what channels (chats) are already under way, type the UNIX command** /list **in the command box and press Return. (For mIRC users, just click the List Channel icon, the icon sixth from the left on the toolbar.)**

   A complete list of currently running chat rooms appears. (It may be a *long* list.) Note that these rooms could have been created by any user anywhere on the globe. Neat, huh?

   ```
   *** Channel  Users  Description
   *** #schools        School CA$H
   *** #oboes   1      My favorite instrument!
   *** #irp     1
   *** #zoosrus 1
   *** #wonderkids     2       The MacMillan School Online
   *** #comix   4
   *** #macintosh      3
   *** #barney  1      Dedicated to bashing a purple creature
   ```

   Snip! I just spared you the other 111 chats that were listed.

   Just like other places on the wild Internet frontier, some chat channels have names that'll curl your hair and make you nervous. As with any Internet session, *supervision* is the key when you are working with students.

9. **To enter a room, choose Join from the Commands pull-down menu or type** /join #channelname **in the command box.**

   The UNIX command `/join` appears in the command box.

10. **Enter a room name, preceded by a pound sign (#), and press Return to enter your room of choice.**

   For example, you use the command `/join #windows` to enter the room called *windows* from the listing. (If you enter a name that's not on the list of currently running chat rooms, you create a new room.)

   All IRC commands begin with a forward slash (/). The slash tells the computer that you are about to enter a command, rather than a message.

   A window opens with the room name on the title bar. You're in! (A second window opens behind the current window, showing the status of your connection and lots of other information for techno-brains.) Now all you have to do is invite someone else to join in or begin typing in the command box. As you type and press Return or Enter, your text is distributed so that everyone in your room can see it.

   Here's a sample of an Education chat that I participated in recently. Note that the names of all the participants are at the top of the chat and that each person's name automatically appears next to comments he or she makes. You also see system commands, such as `***Signoff` or `***Entered`, indicating someone leaving or entering your channel.

```
On IRC via server jello.qabc.uq.oz.au :University of Queensland, Australia
idle for 130 seconds
Topic is: #Education :Yippee!
#Education :Bard Boppo Pug Demi Gradu Gavel TFool MacS Acne Fred
Teacher Kidz Banshee Scotter @Master
Mode is +tn

*** Candice [Trustee@iquest.net] has joined #Education

Boppo changed the mode on #Education to "+o Boppo"

<Bard> What kind of multimedia do you use in your school?
<Pug> Mostly CD-ROM and some videodisc.
<Scotter> HyperStudio is great for videodisc stuff.
<TFool> really, Scotter?  Is it easy?
*** Signoff: Gavel
*** Signoff: Kidz
<Pug> It's so easy my third graders are making multimedia so much I had
to buy a 1 GB hard drive!
```

For more information about using IRC, check the newsgroup `alt.irc` or FTP at `cs.bu.edu` in the `/irc/support` directory.

If you join a very busy channel, the chat window is quickly filled with messages. Each message starts with a person's IRC nickname, followed by the message.

IRC chat seems awfully confusing at first, kind of like homeroom on the first day of school. Just be patient and read as much of the text as you can. When your students are online, typing speed becomes a factor. Be sure to warn other users if the typist is a bit slow.

11. **To quit your IRC session, click the close box on the open windows and choose Quit (⌘+Q) from the File menu.**

    Remember that quitting IRCle doesn't mean that you've severed your Internet connection. You have to visit your control panel (MacPPP/MacSLIP/InterSLIP) to do that.

The error message `TCP Connection status open failed` means that the server is busy. Just wait a minute and try again or choose another IRC server.

When you are connected to an IRC server, try some of the following commands:

Command: `/JOIN #channel`
What it does: Joins the specified channel.
Example: `/join #irchelp`

This command takes you to the `#irchelp` channel. When on a channel, anything you type can be seen by all the users on that channel. The `#irchelp` channel is very useful, so say hello and then ask any questions you want. If the channel you specified doesn't exist, a channel with that name is created for you.

Command: `/PART #channel`
What it does: Leaves a channel.
Example: `/part #irchelp`

Command: `/LIST [#string] [-MIN #] [-MAX #]`
What it does: Lists currently available channels.

You can also tell mIRC to show only channels with a minimum and a maximum number of people. If you specify a # string, mIRC only lists channels with that string in their title.

Example: `/list`
Example: `/list -min 5 -max 20`
Example: `/list #love`

Command: `/ME message`
What it does: Tells the current channel or query about what you are doing.

Command: `/MSG nickname message`
What it does: Sends a private message to this user without opening a query window.

Command: `/QUERY nickname message`
What it does: Opens a query window to this user and sends him or her a private message.

Command: `/WHOIS nickname`
What it does: Shows information about someone.

Command: `/NICK nickname`
What it does: Changes your nickname to whatever you like.

Command: `/QUIT [reason]`
What it does: This command disconnects you from IRC and gives the optional message as the reason for your departure (this message only appears to people who are on the same channels as you).
Example: `/quit That's all folks!`

Command: `/AWAY [away message]`
What it does: Leaves a message explaining that you are not currently paying attention to IRC. Whenever someone sends you a MSG or does a WHOIS on you, they automatically see whatever message you set. Using AWAY with no parameters marks you as no longer being away.
Example: `/away off to get something to eat, back in a moment!`

Command: `/TOPIC #channel newtopic`
What it does: Changes the topic for the channel. (***Note:*** You must be a channel operator to use this command.)
Example: `/topic #friendly Oh what a beautiful day!`

Command: `/INVITE nickname #channel`
What it does: Invites another user to a channel.

Finding a Place to Chat

For the fastest connection, choose the IRC server that's geographically closest to you. Enter one of these addresses in IRCle's Server box:

Address	***Location of Server***
`csa.bu.edu`	Massachusetts
`csz.bu.edu`	Massachusetts
`irc.colorado.edu`	Colorado
`irc.uiuc.edu`	Illinois
`ug.cs.dal.ca`	Nova Scotia
`irc.funet.fi`	Finland
`cismhp.univ-lyon1.fr`	France
`disuns2.epfl.ch`	Switzerland
`jello.qabc.uq.oz.au`	Australia
`sokrates.informatik.uni-kl.de`	Germany

You can find systems that are running IRC by telnetting to one of the following addresses:

`sci.dixie.edu`
Login: `anonymous` or `guest`

Or check the Usenet newsgroup `alt.irc` for more recent information.

For UNIX users

IRC currently links host systems in 20 countries, from Australia to Hong Kong to Israel. Unfortunately, it's like telnet — either your site has it or it doesn't.

If your host has IRC access, just type **irc** at the UNIX prompt and press Return or Enter. You get something like this:

```
*** Connecting to port 6667 of
    server irc-2.mit.edu

*** Welcome to the IRC, fred
    flintstone

*** Your host is urc-2.mit.edu,
    running version 2.7.1e+4

*** If you have not already done
    so, please read the new user
    information

*** with +/HELP NEWUSER

*** This server was created Sat
    Jun 22 1993 at 11:27:02 EDT

*** There are 454 users on 221
    servers

*** There are 137 channels.
```

You are now in channel 0, the *null channel.* From here, you can use UNIX commands such as `/join#channel` and `/who #channel`, as well as the UNIX commands explained previously.

For more information about IRC, jump on the Net and visit

New*IRC*Users page	`http://www.neosoft.com/~biscuits/niu.html`
Internet Chat	`http://www.azstarnet.com/~emdee/irc.html`
IRC FAQs:	
IRC FAQ	`http://www.kei.com/irc.html`
IRC Info	`http://www2.undernet.org:8080/~cs93jtl/IRC.html`
IRC Hints	`http://mistral.enst.fr/~pioch/IRC/hints.html`
IRC Networks:	
Undernet	`http://www.undernet.org/`
Dalnet	`http://www.dal.net/`
IRC for Kids	`http://www.kidlink.org/IRC/`
More Networks	`http://uptown.turnpike.net/L/Larry14/irc.html`
IRC Servers:	
EFNet IRC Servers	`http://www.sisna.com/users/danib/irclist.html`

Undernet IRC Servers	http://http2.brunel.ac.uk:8080/~cs93jtl/servers.html
Dalnet IRC Servers	http://www.xmission.com/~dragon/dalnet/server.html
Dalnet IRC Servers	http://www.bazza.com/sj/irc/servers.html
IRC Channels:	
IRC Channels	http://www.funet.fi/~irc/channels.html
Yahoo's list	http://www.yahoo.com/Computers_and_Internet/Internet/Chatting/IRC/Channels/
Popular Channels	http://light.lightlink.com/irc/channels.html
Technical IRC documents:	
IRC RFC	http://ds.internic.net/rfc/rfc1459.txt
DCC Documents	http://www2.undernet.org:8080/~cs93jtl/irc_dcc.txt
CTCP Documents	http://www2.undernet.org:8080/~cs93jtl/irc_ctcp.txt
Undernet Development	http://www.wildstar.net/ircd-dev/
IRC3	http://www.the-project.org/

A Bit about MOOs and MUDs

Now for something "udderly" silly. A special hybrid of Internet chat was invented by research scientists and has a name only a cow could love. Some of these really serious scientists are trying to make MOOs a regular resource for Internet users. Someday, you may see a greater use for this interesting Internet resource in your classroom. For now, though, it's just a lot of bull.

What's a MOO?

A MOO is basically an Internet game, but it can also be used as a powerful tool for collaboration and information exchange.

MOO stands for *MUD, Object-Oriented. MUD* is an acronym for *Multi-User Dimension* (or sometimes *Multi-User Dungeon*). Yep, you guessed it; MUDs are a derivative of the dungeon games played by college students and others as a brain-rest (or brain-drain?). A MOO is a dungeon-like, text-based game in which online players move around an imaginary environment. Text on the screen describes each scene, and users issue commands such as "go north," "take shield," or "look rock."

Why should teachers care about a computer game whose name sounds like a cow? Because MOOs are multiuser, players can interact with each other. Imagine immersing students in a MOO environment in which they explore a Sherlock Holmes mystery or an African rain forest. MOOs may turn out to be the exploration tool of choice. And they are much cheaper than a plane ticket.

Biologists and other scientists are experimenting with MOOs and MUDs as a possible collaborative research environment.

Playing in the MUD

The acronym MUD originally referred to a game written in 1979 by Roy Trubshaw of Essex University in Great Britain. MUD enables users to participate in an online adventure in which players work to earn points by moving between a few interconnected locations (rooms) and making creative decisions in response to challenges set forth by a set of complicated and slightly strange computer programs. The object of the game is to overcome obstacles, many of them randomized, and to earn enough points to rate a "wizard" status. The Internet game first became popular in Great Britain and with researchers who needed a break from their brain-intense activities. Other games, such as JANET, MIST, LAND, and MUD-2 appeared. The original MUD is commercially available on CompuServe under the name "British Legends."

So what does MUD have to do with education? With the rise in popularity of simulation games such as the Maxis SIM series and the introduction of inexpensive Internet connections, the opportunity to create a multiuser educational game is definitely there. Within a few years, for example, some crafty programmer may crank out a MUD that enables users to explore a rain forest virtually. Users would run into all the perils that a rain forest holds and see all the beautiful sights along the way. Guess we could call it a multiuser school environment — MUSE.

You can access MOOs and MUDs via telnet. Check Usenet newsgroups for popular MOO and MUD addresses.

A Meeting of the Minds

For your first foray into the world of online chat, I suggest using a commercial service. It's easier to access than IRC and, by and large, online services offer more control over who wanders into your chat and whether they abide by the rules of the information superhighway. This activity works for any kind of electronic chat, whether you choose IRC or an online service.

Send an e-mail message to two or three of your teacher friends across the country and invite them to an online chat or IRC chat on a topic relating to education or technology. (How about the Internet?) During your chat, share ideas, talk about issues, and think about how you can use this medium with your students.

Some helpful hints for your electronic discussion:

- Arrange for a dress rehearsal beforehand if you intend to invite administrators or other visitors.
- Be sure to pay attention to time zones so that everyone shows up at the right time.

- "Log" or "trap" the incoming text for later reference. (Both IRCle and real-time conferencing on commercial services enable the user to capture the text of a real-time session and save the resulting conversation to a text file for later use. This is referred to in Internet-speak as *logging* or *trapping* text.)

Chapter 19

New Net Tools and New Issues

In This Chapter

- What's an intranet?
- What is HTML?
- New issues, new challenges
- New tools

The technologies and tools surrounding the Internet are changing faster than we can edit these books. I just can't resist the opportunity to give you a glimpse into what's new on the Net (probably what's not-quite-new-anymore by the time you read this book) and some prognostications about some of the new issues raised by all this fast-moving technology.

The vocabulary (jargon) of the Internet continues to expand with the introduction of new spins on networking (intranet) and new tools for transmitting and receiving multimedia on the Net (VRML, Shockwave, Java, and RealAudio, for example).

The material that follows was conceived during a conversation I had with a 16-year-old computer whiz after a meeting to plan this year's *Macworld* convention. You'd have to meet this kid to believe he's 16; he's helping me configure a Net server, add JavaScript to my Web page, and figure out a way to add full-motion video to a Web page at a local school. Lest you think this kid is spending all his time exercising his fingers on the keyboard, he's also on the state gymnastics team and can throw a baseball so far I'd have to have a telescope to follow it.

Sigh. Just another reminder of how far behind we feel sometimes. Don't worry, though; I've condensed our conversation down to a few points that may help keep *you* on the cutting edge.

What's an Intranet?

Just when you thought you'd mastered techno-speak, here's yet another word to ponder — *intranet.* An intranet is really nothing more than an internal network, a LAN or WAN, that uses Internet tools like browsers and e-mail programs to organize, present, and archive information. *Intranet* is becoming a word you hear a great deal as more and more schools become "wired." Some schools are using Netscape Navigator and mail programs like First Class as the main communication and storage tools on their file servers. Teachers post everything from the lunch menu to afterschool activities to classroom rolls using a Web-page format. What makes the idea of an intranet so cool is that you use the exact same tools when you search for information or access resources outside your school — on the Internet.

All you need to set up an intranet, then, is a couple of computers; some way to connect them; some software tools, such as a browser, an e-mail program, and a word processor or Web-page-making tool; and some knowledge of HTML. Uh oh, a four letter word! Sorry.

What Is HTML?

Like any other innovation, the Internet carries its own load of jargon that delights and confuses. *HTML* is an acronym that you see everywhere these days because it's the name for a simple scripting language (HyperText Markup Language) that's used to make all those fancy Web pages you visit. Working in HTML is much easier than programming in languages such as BASIC and Pascal, because most commands are in "plain English" and the structure is pretty straightforward. HTML was derived from SGML (Standardized General Markup Language — eek, another chunk of jargon!) as a way for developers to quickly create Web pages that can be accessed by a variety of different computers.

In Chapter 22 of this book, you discover that learning HTML code isn't the only way you can build your own Web page. For an up-close-and-personal understanding, however, you need to jump to *The World Wide Web For Teachers,* written by yours truly and also published by IDG Books Worldwide, Inc. You'll find zillions of Web sites to emulate and a whole bunch of strategies for working with your students to produce for the World Wide Web.

New Issues, New Challenges

If I were a betting person (as if educators had any money to bet), I'd wager that within the next five years, the bickering about whether to use Windows NT, Windows 95, or Macintosh OS will cease. It's certainly possible that HTML, Java, and other Internet tools will become the foundation for the operating systems of tomorrow. You'll still need those driver thingies and special programs to get your computer going, of course, but most of the overhead stuffed into today's bulging operating systems may be handled by programs that come from the Internet. Here are three reasons I think this prediction will come true:

- The Internet is a better place to store information than your hard drive. Just how large do you think they can build these drives before it doesn't make any practical sense? It's kind of like a school bus that seats 250 kids. It's very convenient, but it's way too hard to find Johnny or Sue quickly, and you can forget about navigating the thing around town. Why not use the vast "cyberspace" accessed by the Net? You'll need your local hard disk only for storing documents and such that you create from resources out there on the Net.
- Data types are changing faster than your PTA's focus. We used to deal with text and pictures (graphics). Now we have QuickTime movies, QuickTime VR, VRML (Virtual Reality Markup Language), JavaScript, and much more. Making easy, compact tools for reading these data types, rather than going through a 15-disk upgrade every time a new data type comes along, makes better sense.
- Your desktop machine may become obsolete. Instead, you may navigate the Net using something dubbed an *information appliance*. It may sit on your TV or your desk, or you may wear it on your wrist. It accesses the Net spectacularly, but it doesn't do Windows. Information appliances are already being developed, like Bandai's Pippin@World cable box that brings Internet, Audio CD, and CD-based programs to your television, leaving the PC sitting in the corner wondering what Pippin will do next.

So is it time to throw all those computers in the trash and start over? Nope. Apple's OpenDoc, for example, with its CyberDog Internet integration tool, makes lots of sense. It's basically an open operating system that accepts little programs that do very specific tasks. You sit down, open a "workspace," and simply assemble the little tools you need to do your work. Some of these come from the Net, some from your hard drive, and some from your local network. The best news of all is that these tools can be added to your current Mac OS now, most for free, with no need to go back to the beginning and roll the techno-dice again. Microsoft is jumping on the bandwagon with something called ActiveX, too, but it remains to be seen whether anyone will develop components for it.

Jumbo time

One of the neatest prospects about the Net is the availability of thousands, perhaps tens of thousands, of programs created by folks who spend way too much time with their computers. (I can say that because I'm one of 'em.) The product of their intense concentration is often a wonderful shareware program that they choose to post to the Internet.

You can go wandering around the Net, getting lost and bumping into a lot of stuff you don't care to see, searching for these great shareware programs, or you can log on to the Jumbo site.

Jumbo is the mother-of-all shareware sites on the Internet. The site provides access to zillions of programs, organized into neat, searchable categories.

Jumbo's categories include:

Business Applications

Corporate Sites

Desktop Publishing and Graphic Design

Education

Games

Hobbies and Home

Internet and Communications

Java

Kids

Multimedia

PDA's

Programming and Development

Science

Utilities

Windows 95

The site gets the "teacher approved" rating not only because Jumbo has done the Net world a great service, but because the folks who work at Jumbo are so enthusiastic and meticulous — kind of like those precocious students in your 5th period class who are so brilliant it's almost scary.

Visit them at `http://www.jumbo.com` You won't be sorry you did! (Remember to use a virus detection program on any shareware or software you download from the Net!)

So, don't give your Macintosh away or pitch your Windows PC out the window. Watch for a "transition period," when technologies like OpenDoc that can run on your desktop machine ease the move from bulky memory-hogging programs to "compartmentalized" or specialized mini-applications. Kind of like trying to step off a moving train, no? You can't jump off — so you may as well stay for the ride. Just keep your arms and heads inside the windows.

Addressing Tough Internet Challenges

Go and look in the mirror. Right now. Look at yourself and decide whether you're one of those people who sits around worrying about how the Internet may lead to the inevitable degradation of human values or, perhaps more apocalyptic, the extinction of the human race. Or do you see a bigger picture and realize how the Internet, used most effectively, can bring the world closer together and keep all of us Cro-Magnons from reinventing the wheel every day or so? Some people can find lots of negatives to point out about the Net these days. Sure, some issues challenge all of us, but do these concerns really make sense? Here are a few I've heard. What do you think? (You're obviously an open-minded, wonderful person, because you so kindly bought this book.)

Too-tough URLs

The other day I was driving down the Massachusetts Turnpike (where the Bard tolls) and spied a large billboard for a popular brand of blue jeans. Terrific billboard, by the way, except for one thing . . . down below the very distracting picture was a URL that looked something like this: `http://www.jeans.com/~blue/pictures/catalog/`. . . I didn't get the rest. After all, I was doing 65 miles per hour (give or take 10), and I couldn't do the Exorcist maneuver (the 360-degree head-twist) without hitting the car in front of me. Did this manufacturer really expect folks to pull off the highway and copy this Web address down? Sigh.

Everyone's got a Web page — it's the new status symbol. Some companies are smarter than others, though, selecting URLs that are short and sweet, like `www.apple.com` or `www.ibm.com` or `www.classconnect.org`. These I can remember. Some folks think URLs are too complex, but that's what bookmark programs are for! Complex, sure, but watch for graphics and bookmark programs to shield you from those URLs someday soon.

Telephonus interruptus

Sometimes the phone just hangs up. You know: You're in the middle of a huge demonstration for a gym full of students, and just as you click a link, the line drops, leaving you making pheasant and doggie shapes with your hands in front of the overhead projector screen. Phone lines, especially those old phone lines run to schools back in 1920, are not very dependable. Luckily, help is on the way. RBOCS (regional bell operating systems) are working hard to upgrade the phone system. Also, dedicated lines, like high speed T-1 or T-3 lines, are always "on," so you don't have to hold your breath as you wait for the modem to connect anymore. Whew!

Porno pandemonium

Yep. You can find plenty of stuff on the Web that you may consider pornography. The hitch is that some people don't consider naughty what you consider naughty. Some folks even like the stuff. The challenge is that there's a huge "beware of unacceptable content in your classroom" between free speech and what kids may jump into while mining the Internet from your classroom. What do you do if Sarah finds an underwear-clad Marky Mark while she's supposed to be looking for a current map of Bosnia? Read the chapter on Internet responsibility one more time. If you're really worried, you can dig up acceptable use policies, hardware, and software solutions, and get more information from sites on the Net. (Search Yahoo! or your favorite search site for keywords: **acceptable use** or **filter**.) You can also watch Sarah more closely and make sure she feels some time pressure to get what she was after. No time for surfing for porno. Nothing is as effective as watchful eyes (the four every educator has — two in the back, of course).

High tech or high touch?

Lots of people think that with the many opportunities for entertainment and education on the Net, we'll all retreat into our homes and end up seeing folks only via our computers. Gone will be the "high touch" — the intimacy, the feeling of being near someone, and the occasional pat-on-the-back, so rare but welcome. Hmmm. I'm really not sure about this one. I know I can't stand to write for more than about four hours at a time or I get really nuts. I gotta see and be with other people. Alvin Toffler, author of *Future Shock, The Third Wave,* and a few other brain-busters, believes a balance is needed between high technology tools and opportunities to do what humans do by nature — namely, have occasional physical contact. I think Alvin's got a point, don't you? Okay. Put the book down and go find somebody to hug.

Gender-centric

Statistics show that most of the people on the Net these days are male. The number is more than a majority — it's a regular landslide. Why? Probably because surfing the Net and sending e-mail is what many in the mostly-male world of computers and technology do most of the day when they're supposed to be working. Inevitably, this situation must change. When activities like stock tickers, real estate transactions, home control, and bill payment via computer become a regular fixture, everyone, male and female, will *have* to log on. Some of the best and brightest Web page designers I know happen to be female, by the way. They seem to have both the technical expertise *and* the sense of what looks great on a screen.

One-way street

The Net is kind of passive these days. Most of what people do is click from link to link. But some new technologies, like NetPhone, Shockwave, and others (see Chapter 22) are changing that. Look for the Net to get extremely interactive as it continues to grow up. Already you can watch movies, hear speeches, or talk on the phone via the Net. The Internet's just begun to crawl these days. If you're like me, you can't wait to see it walk!

Lost in the mall

A student once described the Internet as a "shopping mall without directories." A common criticism of the Net is that it is difficult to navigate. Simply too much information is out there.

Just as mall managers have taken to constructing easy-to-use maps and kiosks, complete with the all-important "you are here" dot, Internet guardians are coming up with new and easy ways to navigate the Net. Apple Research, for example, has a program called Project X that guides the user through a 3-dimensional view of a Web site. You simply "float" to the document, ftp site, or Web page you'd like to view, double-click the label — *poof.* The directions are sent to your Web browser, and you're there! (Snag Project X free from Apple at `http://www.atg.apple.com`)

The Windows folks aren't asleep, either. They've pushed the envelope with a large number of bookmark managers and high-performance Web browsers like the one hiding in The Microsoft Network. Soon you'll have no excuse to get lost. Now, where did I put my car keys?

Surfboard

Grab your sunglasses and your beach towel and get ready for a terrific tool to help you organize all those bookmarks you've accrued surfing the Net. *Surfboard* is a terrific Internet accessory from Abbott Systems (`http://www.abbottsys.com`). Find it on the CD at the back of this book. You're gonna flip when you see this thing.

The program uses the familiar setup of a TV remote control. Instead of channel buttons, you've got category buttons. To bookmark URLs, you just click a plus sign, and *zip* — the URL is in your master list. Drag the bookmark you created onto one of several user-configurable main menu items (your *saved channels*), and you've got a super-easy organization system. You can create and name multiple lists, too. After you've stored a bookmark, just choose from the master list (something you can hide or reveal at your whim) or the pop-up menus that appear when you click on a category list, and *zoom* — Surfboard transfers the URL to your Netscape Navigator or Microsoft Internet Explorer browser. You're on your way!

The best part about Surfboard? You can't lose this remote control!

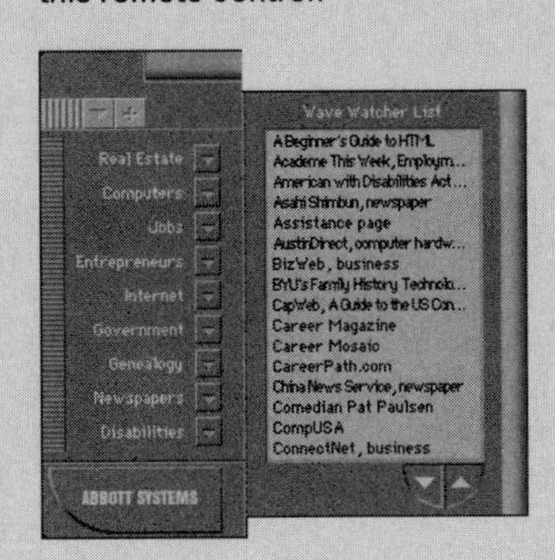

Warp Ten on the Info Highway

If you think the rate at which new information is being posted on the Net is incredibly fast, wait until you get a glimpse at the speed with which new tools are being developed. Practically every week, three or four new mini- programs, called "plug-ins," that work with your Web browser are thrown out to the world, creating new opportunities and fueling lots of ideas on the Internet.

What follows is a short-and-sweet summary of what some of the emerging tools are and what they're for. For a closer look at these tools, rush out to your bookstore and grab one of the . . .*For Dummies* books immediately (like *Java For Dummies*), before these books are left behind by the rush to create newer and better tools.

What's Java?

Used to be Java was what you had with cream and sugar. Nowadays, Java represents an Object Oriented Programming (OOP) language similar to C++ used to create stand-alone applications that can incorporated into a Web page.

JavaScript, a decendent of Java developed by Netscape Communications and Sun Microsystems, is a scripting language (like HyperTalk or dBASE). It's easier to use because it has more built-in functionality, easier syntax, and is somewhat forgiving. JavaScript can make text appear to dance (animation), create an automated form that works like an up-to-the-minute stock ticker, or any number of very interesting multimedia enhancements for a Web page. The Java world also includes small programs called *applets* (which are automatically downloaded to your computer) to control your Web browser and make great things happen on the screen — everything from smart information agents (that retrieve information at the click of an on-screen icon) to interactive games.

For an overview of Java and lots of great examples, visit Sun's site at `http://java.sun.com`

Here's an excerpt of some Java code that makes text jump around on your screen. It's only an excerpt, however, and it won't work if you try to type it in.

```
[lots of Java mumbo-jumbo here]
if (seed > 100) {
    seed–;
    var cmd="scrollit(" + seed + ")";
    timerTwo=window.setTimeout(cmd,100);
}
else if (seed <= 100 && seed > 0) {
    for (c=0 ; c < seed ; c++) {
        out+=" ";
    }
    out+=msg;
    seed–;
    var cmd="scrollit(" + seed + ")";
         window.status=out;
    timerTwo=window.setTimeout(cmd,100);
}
[more Java mumbo-jumbo follows]
```

Some folks are concerned that the way Java works can allow unwanted programs, messages, or viruses to be downloaded into your computer or that it allows for unscrupulous users to access information from your computer or network. Several large companies have encouraged employees to disable Java on their Web browsers (check your Preferences menus) until Java gets more secure. I think the Java issue is a bit overblown, so don't freak out and de-Java your computer just yet. Just beware, especially if your school's network isn't separated (physically or by a software firewall) from the network you use to access the Internet. You make the call on this one!

Java has a lot more to offer and is really similar to the Pascal and C++ programming that some chipheads love to do. However, lots of teachers are learning the easier JavaScript with their students, and together they're creating some amazing projects.

Getting shocked

Shockwave is a terrific innovation, from the folks at Macromedia, that enables anyone to add animated graphics, sound, and multimedia to Web sites. *Shocked* sites offer interactivity, such as moving from screen to screen, zooming, and panning, as well as presentation-quality slideshows that you can use to wow your audiences.

For educators, Shockwave may be just the ticket to bring auto-instructional learning to the Net. It also offers an opportunity to provide real-time presentations related to key curriculum areas on your school's *intranet.* (Look back to the first of this chapter if you haven't master the jargon yet.)

To create these Net-wonders, you use Macromedia's Macromind Director (available at an educator's discount, by the way). To view your amazing creations, however, all you need is the Netscape Navigator plug-in called Shockwave (a *plug-in* is a software program that goes in your Netscape plug-in folder and adds functionality to the browser). Find information about both of these tools at `http://www.macromedia.com/`

Audio-R-Us

One of the early challenges of the Internet was to find a way to transmit sound so that folks with all kinds of computers and all kinds of speakers could hear and understand it. Enter tools like StreamWorks and RealAudio. Both tools allow the transmission of sounds, now in CD quality, from a remote location on the Net to your computer. Both these tools also allow *streaming audio* (audio that begins almost immediately, without waiting for a large sound file to completely download first) and creates a very usable, almost perfect, method for transmitting large sound files.

Find out more about StreamWorks at `http://www.xingtech.com`

Get the scoop on my favorite, RealAudio, at `http://www.realaudio.com`

Motion on the Net

Now you can watch movies on the Internet. Jeesh . . . there goes another twenty hours a week! We've come a long way from filmstrips in the classroom, no?

With powerful tools like Apple Computer's QuickTime (available for Macintosh and Windows computers)and QuickTime VR (virtual reality-like movies), you can now use your Web browser like a movie projector. Of course, the faster the connection, the better your picture. Using today's 28.8 modems is a little like yesterday's TVs with *rabbit ears*. Fast network connections are smooth as silk. Grab info about QuickTime at `http://www.apple.com` and QuickTime VR at `http://qtvr.quicktime.apple.com`

Another tool for Windows and Windows 95 users is called VDOLive. It offers full control of video files transmitted on the Net. Explore VDOLive at `http://www.vdo.net`

Phone home

The telephone companies are not smiling these days. In fact, they're madder than wet hens. First, the cable TV people stepped on their feet by offering Internet access through your TV (through set-top boxes like Pippin, `http://www.bandai.com/`), and now some crafty lads and lasses have created a program that allows you to make the equivalent of a long-distance phone call on the Internet — for free. (Can't you just see the phone folks quivering now?) I'll go out on a limb, though, and declare that the folks at Ma Bell will either figure out how to optimize this technology (and charge for it) or figure out how to use your telephone to get cable TV. They're very creative and don't sit still when it comes to innovation.

I've included several telephony programs on the *Internet For Teachers* CD for Macintosh and Windows users, along with documentation to get you started. You can get more information about telephone software (sorry, Ma) at `http://www.netphone.com`

Conferencing

Somebody really creative finally figured out how to allow users to see and be seen (and heard) on the Net. Using a small video camera and a Net program called CU-SeeMe (it's on the CD accompanying this book), you and your students can interview scientists across the globe in real-time. Sure, everyone looks like Max Headroom because the connection isn't quite fast enough, but you can see an emerging technology that's going to improve quickly.

Apple's also figured out a way to leverage their QuickTime technology to create QuickTime conferencing. It's quick, it's easy, and it has a dandy *whiteboard* for collaborating and sharing documents.

Find out more about CU-SeeMe videoconferencing via Net at `http://www.cuseeme.com` and Apple's QuickTime video conferencing at `http://www.apple.com`

Part IV

The Net Meets the Classroom

The 5th Wave By Rich Tennant

"NOW, THAT WOULD SHOW HOW IMPORTANT IT IS TO DISTINGUISH 'FERTILIZING PRACTICES' FROM 'FERTILITY PRACTICES' WHEN DOWNLOADING A VIDEO FILE FROM THE INTERNET."

In this part . . .

In this part, you can discover some specific ways to use the Internet to enrich and enhance what goes on in your classroom. Find out strategies for learning the Internet and for teaching its use to others. Discover how your role will change as you move from "sage on stage" to "guide on the side." New in this 2nd edition is a glimpse of what happens when you move students from being consumers of Net information to producers by using a handy home page creation tool included on your CD.

Chapter 20

CyberTeachers, CyberLearners

In This Chapter

- Planning an online experience
- Managing time, materials, and kids
- Teaching (yourself) about the Net
- Special-needs students and the Net
- Evaluation and the Net

Get ready for *that feeling*. You know *that feeling*, the one you get when something exciting is going on in your classroom, the students are enthusiastic and on-task, and the lesson plan that you spent three hours writing is working. You and the students have achieved the mystical state of being on an educational roll and are rocketing toward a meaningful educational experience.

With a little planning and a smattering of good luck from the technology gremlins, educational expeditions via the Internet can be among the most rewarding and motivating activities you'll ever experience.

Planning an Online Experience

How many thousands of lesson plans have you written? You know the drill: objectives, materials, procedures, evaluation, and so on. Planning an online experience isn't all that different, although you need to consider some things that can make the difference between a great lesson and a technological disaster.

I want your first (and every) experience of using the Net with students to be a positive one, so I'm gonna share those deep dark planning secrets that I've gleaned from peeking around classrooms and watching my mentors teach. Shut the curtains, lock the doors — here are Bard's 12 Steps to Planning and Implementing Successful Internet Projects (and pardon me for sometimes stating the obvious):

- Think about your goals for the lesson. What do you want to accomplish? What outcomes would constitute *learning* for this lesson?
- Consider whether the Internet is the best way to accomplish your goals. Sometimes, using paper and pencil, a protractor, a workbook, garden tools, a test tube, and other more, uh, *traditional* media makes more sense. The Internet is like any other classroom resource: there's a right way and a wrong way to use it, and a right time and a wrong time, too. Let the curriculum drive the use of technology, and not the other way around.
- Identify and analyze the Internet resources that your students may use. Do they need access to e-mail? FTP? Tools for downloading, unpacking, and decoding files? What are the pitfalls they may encounter?
- Check your hardware and software, including your telephone connections, before class begins. Murphy is alive and well and living in a modem near you.
- List the steps necessary for success. Follow the KISS rule and establish a step-by-step procedure if that's the way your particular group learns best. The Internet is *huge.* Your students can, and probably will, get lost there more than once. The more specific you are at the beginning, the better your students will become at navigating on their own.
- Set parameters for time. You need to consider not only how long completing the project may take, but also how much lead time you need to give your fellow teachers or collaborators on the Net. If you're planning an online writing project, for example, think about how long students may need to wait for a reply. Things happen, and sometimes delays can be excruciating. Guess what, your kids will be as anxious as you are.
- Build in opportunities for feedback. When are students on target, and when are they just surfing aimlessly around the Net? How will you let them know where they stand?
- Think about the final product. What should the final report, document, or outcome look like? What constitutes success? How will you grade it: rubrics, an analysis of printed documents, evaluating reflective writing in journals?
- Identify how and when students should, can, or must use their fellow students, teachers, parents, and so on as resources.
- Think about your role. How closely do you need to supervise the students? Should you answer questions?
- Try it yourself. As a beginning teacher, I once showed my middle schoolers a science film without previewing it. The film, entitled something such as "Man, the Incredible Machine," featured an opening shot where a camera panned a young woman's body from the top of her head to the tip of her toes. I saw my life, and my teaching contract, flash before my eyes well

before the camera reached the toes. (Thankfully, the film skipped the parts that would've been the end of teacher Bard.) I vowed never to make that mistake again. The potential for chaos/disaster/bizarre stuff is just as high on the Internet. Try the project yourself *first.*

- Make time to look back and debrief. You'll find that there's more than one way to accomplish nearly every task in the Internet. Leave it to the students to startle you with new ways to link information and to locate new resources you'd never imagined.

How to cite electronic media

After your students find information on the Net, how do they properly give the author credit when they use material? Here's a set of standards modeled on the 1994 APA guidelines:

- **Electronic mail messages:**

  Author (year, month day). Subject of message [sender's e-mail address], [Online]. Available e-mail: receiver's e-mail address.

  For example:

  Templeton, P.K. (1995, June 5). Project Deadline [templeton@ed.com], [Online]. Available e-mail: phikap@aol.com.

- **Articles available via mailing lists:**

  Root, C. (1994). ESL and learning disabilities: A guide for the ESL practitioner. TESL-EJ 1. Available e-mail: LISTSERV@CMSA.BERKELEY.EDU. Message: GET TESLEJ01 A-4 TESLEJ-L F=Mail.

- **FTP or telnet:**

  Kehoe, B.P. (1992). Zen and the Art of the Internet (2nd Ed.), [Online]. Available FTP (Telnet): quake.think.com. Directory: pub/etext/1992. File: Zen10.text.

- **Computer programs:**

  Sandford, J.A. & Browne, R.J. (1985). Captain's log: Cognitive Training System (Version 1.0), [Computer program]. Indianapolis: Psychological Software Services, Inc.

- **Online databases:**

  The educational directory. [Online]. (1992). Available: Knowledge Index File: The Educational Directory (EDUC6).

These guidelines are available via an e-mail message to `LISTSERV@CMSA.BERKELEY.EDU` with the message `GET TESLEJ-L APAGUIDE TESLEJ-L F=MAIL` (leave the Subject line blank).

Students Online: Managing Time, Materials, and Students

Okay. Let me guess. You have one computer and 30 kids. You're teaching in a room the size of a closet, and if you can't complete your lesson in 50 minutes, the fifth period teacher will put out a contract on you.

Never fear. There *is* hope for Internet activities in your classroom! The good news is that if you plan well, activities involving research and the exploration of the Internet can be easily segmented into bite-sized (period-sized) pieces.

Here are ten tips for managing time, materials, and students:

- If you're doing a live (real-time) project, don't forget to think about time zones and the cultural differences of the groups with which you're communicating. The information superhighway covers all times zones — now was that two hours' or three hours' difference?

  In case you and your students get time-confused, point your Web browser to `gopher.uidaho.edu:70/1/news_time_weather` for the current time and weather anywhere on the planet!

- Plan to supplement your Internet activities with a variety of print, video, and computer software resources. The information superhighway is rich with resources, but it's only one tool!
- Think about using a contract or acceptable use policy (AUP). (See Chapter 9 for some tips for creating a contract for your school.) Surfing can be hazardous to your health.
- Always have a backup plan. If you haven't given the proper oblations to the techno-gods, you could end up as road kill on the information superhighway. Your hard drive will explode, or the phone company will choose to service the school's phone lines in the middle of your class. (A teacher friend of mine refers to the backup plan as an "escape route.")
- Be sure that students have some kind of directions (a road map) before they travel the information superhighway.
- Make sure that students obey the road signs on the highway: Be nice. Don't go where you're not supposed to go or where the resources that you need aren't located.
- Stop periodically and ask students what they've accomplished. Are they surfing aimlessly? Are they drowning? Or are they shooting the Internet waves like a pro?
- Every classroom has a supersurfer or two. Be prepared with enrichment activities or have students create their own.

- Think about using a timer to encourage kids to focus on the activity at hand and not to stop at every roadside diner.
- Remind students to *think* before they telnet, Gopher, FTP, e-mail, or Web-surf. What is the right tool for the information superhighway journey of the day?

The yearly cost of dial-up access to the Internet in Great Britain is £1850.

Special Needs Students and the Internet

A wonderful teacher named Dr. Elizabeth Garrett gave me a virtual slap on the face one day — a wake-up call that every educator should one day experience. She invited me to visit our school district's special needs center. Before that day, I thought of the special needs center as the place where they keep "those kids" that we couldn't handle. I knew that severely handicapped kids were there, along with those placed there because we weren't able to meet their needs in a regular classroom. As I walked up to the door of the building, I really didn't know what to expect.

Beyond pen-pals . . .

E-mail can be a very powerful tool in your classroom. The first thing you probably think of is simply finding an electronic pen-pal for your students. That's nice, and can be interesting, but I've found, particularly with K–8 students, that the quality of pen-pal writing often degrades to something such as the following excerpt from a fifth grader's pen-pal writing:

> How old are you? What do you look like? Which is your favorite Teenage Mutant Ninja Turtle?

Wouldn't you rather have this excerpt from a fifth grader's essay on "A Special Person in My Life"?

> My grandmother is the nicest person I know. She cares about me, about my mom, and about my puppy, Joker. I like the way her cheeks turn red when she laughs. That always happens when we play together on the porch. She always takes time for me. She must have been a great mommy.

As you think about using the Internet with your students, you'll discover many projects that focus on higher-order thinking skills, like analysis and evaluation. A teacher in New York developed a writing project that featured autobiographies of the "everyday person on the street." She exchanged them with teachers at other schools and together, they created a "Profile of America." A media specialist from Canada built a database of children's book reviews collected from students all over the world via e-mail. The final product was posted to a Web site that features children's literature and other resources. (`www.ucalgary.ca/~dkbrown/index.html`)

Sigh. I had a nice grandma, too. Think about moving your students *beyond* pen-pals.

What I saw changed the way I look at education, at students, and at myself. I saw some of the most attentive, caring professionals coaching some of the brightest-eyed, most energetic kids you can imagine. I saw what happens when they have access to technology. I saw computers with adaptive aids change the *quality of life* for those kids. Without access to the technology, many of these kids simply could not communicate, or create, or explore, or have fun. And then I saw one of them type "I love you" to his mom on a keypad with a foot-long pointer clenched between his teeth.

That did it.

If I had a zillion dollars in the bank, I would make sure that each and every student around the planet had a computer and the adaptive aids necessary for teaching and learning.

The bottom line is that it's important to consider students with special needs when thinking about using the Internet in your classroom. Here are a few suggestions from the experts for using the computer to access the Net with special needs kids:

- Set your browser for larger font sizes for visually impaired students
- Investigate alternative devices (switches, sip & puff devices, wands) to substitute for the mouse
- Explore screen-readers (like the Ultimate Reader) that can read the text from a Web page or any other source
- Think about low-tech help, like placing non-skid materials under keyboards and mousepads, using monitors that swivel and tilt, and using built-in adaptive aids, like the Mac's built-in Easy Access and CloseView (similar programs are available for purchase for your Windows machine)
- Plan for extra time for students with special needs to use the computer; think of pairing them with understanding, patient partners
- Explore using Braille output for printout of information from the Net
- Use At Ease or another powerful tool to automate the process of logging onto the Net

Thanks, Liz Garrett, for that cyberslap. It worked. There will forever be a special place in my heart for the teachers of students with special needs and their equally special students.

Staff Development and the Internet

The Internet learning curve is a bit steep, but you can overcome it easily. The best way to learn is to ask someone who's already an Internet surfer to show you the way. And guess what, these mentors don't even have to be in the same country as you are! They can be anywhere in cyberspace. You can use telecommunications such as e-mail, LISTSERVs, and so on to communicate. Someone recently called this relationship *telementoring*. I think that's a nifty way of saying, "Find a mentor and have that person teach you about the Net."

I like to think of Internet tools as "stumbleware." One of the best things about the Internet is that you very often stumble onto resources or ideas that you'd never dreamed of finding. The best way to learn about the Net is just to dive right in and try it. An easy introduction through a commercial online service is a great way to begin.

During your first visits, focus on *one* tool or *one* type of information. Think about how you can make your next visit more productive as you explore. As with any technology, the more you use it, the better you become. Happy surfing!

Evaluation and the Internet

How do you evaluate students on Internet projects? The answer depends on your goal. Think about whether the goal of your lesson is to do one or more of the following:

- Teach something *about* the Internet
- Teach how to *use* the Internet
- Teach something by *using information gained from* the Internet

Regardless of whether you're focusing on the Internet, the process of using the Internet, or the way the resulting information is used, you can use the same techniques of evaluation that you use for other classroom projects. Checklists, rubrics, peer-evaluation, pen-and-paper exams — they all work just fine.

Okay, teachers, this one is for you. Launch your WWW browser and get to the Wentworth Communications Web site (`http://www.wentworth.com/wentworth`). There you find lots of sample articles, hyperlinks to valuable education sites on the WWW, and even some home page links to schools on the Internet. The Wentworth folks publish what I believe to be the best monthly education resource for Net-surfers, *Classroom Connect* magazine. To get on the *Classroom Connect* mailing list, send e-mail to `crc-request@wentworth.com` and type **subscribe** in the body of the message.

Leave the subject of your message blank. You also can visit their FTP site for some great educational software and documents (`ftp.wentworth.com`).

In early 1996, more than 20 new PBS affiliates established Web sites.

Role over?

Carolyn sat quietly at the computer, hunting-and-pecking away for at least an hour. Every once in a while, you'd hear a strange noise or the sound of a video tape being rewound. Once, Carolyn came over to the group of students I was helping with a science lab and asked, "Do you like programs that read to you or ones that you just read yourself?" I told her that I liked both, particularly if the things I was learning were new or complicated.

Another 20 minutes later, Carolyn called me over to see her finished product. In the next few minutes, she introduced me to the "Creatures of the Georgia Coast," one at a time. I saw sea gulls, starfish, even a turtle — each with a stunning photo and voice narration. Some even had rudimentary animation and background music. Her last frame read, "Carolyn Baxter, Age 12." Okay. I admit it. I was totally humbled. Not only was I amazed at Carolyn's ability to synthesize information, but Carolyn had no formal training in the program she'd used — Roger Wagner's HyperStudio.

It has been a few years since I saw Carolyn's project and realized that the use of technology was dramatically changing my role in the classroom. I also realized that the students' role is changing too.

The good news is that after you realize that your role is changing, a whole new world of possibilities is open for you. The Internet simply provides another avenue for you to explore. Perhaps technology, in general, and the Internet, specifically, can help more students move toward a higher-level learning goals.

How is the role of the student changing as technology becomes an easily available tool? Think about these roles . . .

The Student Was/Is	***The Student Can Be (and Some Already Are!)***
A passive listener ("Today we heard about climate.")	An active learner ("Today I used the Internet to study climate photos of our state.")
A doer of teacher-prepared tasks ("Read page 23 and do questions 1 to 44.")	A teacher of others ("Can anyone explain how to telnet to NASA to access the payload list?")
A slave to the curriculum ("If it's March, it better be Chapter 2.")	A researcher student, who works toward a goal at his or her own pace ("I'd like to finish by Friday.")
An examiner of the textbook ("It has nice pictures.")	A knowledge navigator ("I found information in 21 places, but the best one was. . . .")

By now you're probably thinking "Uh oh, we're not in Kansas anymore." You're right. Many of you have already changed the way you teach as you incorporate technology into the curriculum. Think about these roles. . . .

The Teacher Was/Is	***The Teacher's Role Is Becoming More of***
A deliverer of information, a sage on stage	A coach; a guide on the side
A teacher of the textbook	A teacher whose lessons are driven by reality and up-to-date information resources
A coordinator of group work	An information manager
A dictator in a controlled democracy	A knowledge navigator
An educational island	A member of a learning team (technology coordinator, media specialist, teachers, administrators, parents, and students)

In July of 1996, there were more than 3,000 Internet service providers worldwide.

Chapter 21

CyberJourneys: Learning Expeditions into the Net

In This Chapter

- A day in the life . . . (K-5)
- Spaced out (6-8)
- The great scavenger hunt (9-12)
- Fighting for a cause (college and up)
- Cyberplanning for the teacher
- Spinning your own Web

Here they are — teacher-tested and ready for your classroom — a few starter ideas for you and your students. When I sent a request over the Internet for ideas, I got more than 120 replies in less than two weeks. I've sifted through them and chosen a few that I think you'll like. Planning Internet journeys takes a bit of practice, but the payoff is huge.

Each journey begins with a short description and ends with a *starting point,* an address or tip that will help you and your students begin in the fast lane of the information superhighway. Even though the ideas are presented by grade level, you can adapt most of them for use with any student, from kindergartners to adults. Happy motoring!

Don't forget to spend some time talking with students about citing electronic resources. For a standard format, see the sidebar in Chapter 20.

A 1995 report entitled "School Facilities: America's Schools Not Designed or Equipped for 21st Century" (GAO) reveals that only 52 percent of K-12 schools have telephones located in instructional areas.

A CyberJourney for K–5

Here's an activity that's perfect for younger students' first excursion into the Internet. It comes from Frances Kinsey, an elementary teacher from Topeka. It's based on the popular *keypals* project, where students from various places around the world write to each other about a topic that's predetermined by the teachers on the project team.

Enjoy "A Day in the Life . . ."

Remember when you'd come in from school and your parents would ask, "What did you do in school today?" I'd usually shrug and give the obligatory "Nothin'" response. Here's a chance for your students to find out what other people do, both at school and in the workplace.

Ask students to conduct short interviews, either in person or via e-mail, of other students, parents, teachers, or community members and put together a short story describing "A Day in the Life of . . ." It can be a list, a short paragraph, or even a picture. Before they begin, be sure to help students generate a few "who, what, when, where, why, and how" questions and also discuss how to ask questions.

Subscribe to newsgroups (such as `k12.chat.elementary`) or write to your teacher friends on the Internet and set up an exchange. Send the stories via e-mail to another school for response and comment.

As an extra bonus after a couple of exchanges, try linking the two classes via real-time chat by using IRC (Internet Relay Chat) or by using the conference room of an online service. (America Online's Electronic Schoolhouse is a great place for this activity.)

Starting Point: Subscribe to the newsgroup `k12.elementary` or visit project libraries on online services. (Check the Electronic Schoolhouse, Keyword: ESH, on America Online.)

In a survey conducted in late 1994, more than 90 percent of school principals believed that Internet access would be an important school goal within two years.

Here's a great K–5 Web site you won't want to miss. It can be a good resource for this activity. Point your browser to Uncle Bob's Kids Page at `gagme.wwa.com/~boba/kids.html`

A CyberJourney for 6–8

Bob Chris, a wizard from a private school in Atlanta, offers this out-of-this-world activity that he uses with his eighth-grade earth science students. It has students locating information, downloading graphics, and surfing the World Wide Web (WWW) to find information about the scope of the U.S. space program.

Get ready for "Spaced Out."

Have students make believe they are reporters for a major newspaper or magazine. Their assignment editor has just received word that funding may be cut for the U.S. space program. Their assignment is to collect information from the Internet to answer the question, "Is the U.S. space program an extra or an essential?"

As they hunt, have students record where they visit and what information they find. Work with the class to decide whether the final product is an editorial or a feature story. After the surfing is complete, have students present their findings to the rest of the class.

Be sure to review the use of WWW browsers, FTP tools (Fetch), and telnet — they'll need to pull out all the stops to find information about this one!

Set a reasonable time limit (based on the students' ability to access the Internet) for the project, or it could go on for days!

Starting Point: Try these Web pages: `http://www.infomall.org/kidsweb/` or `http://www.gsfc.nasa.gov/`

Need a great resource for facts and figures? Call the CIA! Have your students point their browser to the CIA World Fact Book at `http://www.ic.gov`

A CyberJourney for 9–12

One of the best ways to help students learn about and identify resources that are available on the Internet is to serve up a scavenger hunt for them to chew on. It's both fun and challenging. You'll be amazed at how many different sources students tap as they answer questions.

This doozy of an activity comes from Terry Mansell, a journalism teacher from Tucson. She has been using the Internet for less than a year, but she is already a supersurfer. Here's a list of 10 questions, appropriate for grades 9-12, that encourage the use of lots of Internet resources and the tools to access them.

CNN on the Web: The ultimate starting point for cyberjourneys

I admit it. I'm a CNN junkie. There's simply no better place to go for up-to-the-minute news. Now CNN offers a suite of Internet services for you and your students to use as a starting point for your Internet research journeys. Here is the pathway to a document that provides a bit of background:

Internet CNN Newsroom: A Digital Video News Magazine and Library

`http://www.cnnnewsroom.com`

This paper discusses the development of *CNN Newsroom* on the Internet, a new multimedia newsmagazine based on *CNN Newsroom* (an educational newsprogram produced by Turner Broadcasting and distributed by cable television operators nationwide). The multimedia program is assembled automatically on a daily basis as a digital video newsmagazine distributed via the Internet. High-quality 1.5 Mbit/second MPEG-I video is used in the program, giving the video clips VHS-level quality. Potential advantages of *Internet Newsroom* are outlined, and innovative plans for its network deployment are discussed.

Here are a few "must-see" sites to visit:

Internet CNN Newsroom

`http://www.cnnnewsroom.com`

This is the home page for choosing which day's programming you wish to view. Programs are listed by date, and you'll find links to archives and daily lesson plans on this page also.

CNN Newsroom Guide

`http://www.nmis.org/`

This site is a repository for the popular CNN Newsroom Classroom Guides.

CNN's Main News Site

`http://www.cnn.com/`

So point those browsers to CNN, the world's most important (Inter)Network.

Enjoy "The Great Internet Scavenger Hunt."

Turn students loose with a Web browser (Netscape Navigator, Mosaic, and so on) and see how they track down the following information. Be sure to ask them to record and share the sources that they use to locate each answer.

1. What is the first line in L. Frank Baum's *The Wizard of Oz?*
2. In how many movies did both Martin Sheen and his son Charlie star?
3. How old was artist Salvador Dali when he did his first painting?
4. Who discovered the element lithium? What is lithium's atomic number?
5. What is the destination of the JasonVI Island Earth Project? (Hint: use WebCrawler.)

6. The MARVEL server offers lots of information from the catalogs of the Library of Congress. What does the acronym MARVEL stand for?
7. What's the ZIP code for Pig, Kentucky?
8. What is the WWW address (URL) for *Bloom County* (the comic strip)?
9. How many sailing magazines are on the Internet?
10. List four education-related businesses that have home pages on the WWW.

Starting point: WebCrawler: `http://www.webcrawler.com`

Don't miss this 9-12 Web site that features CNN Newsroom and other news resources. Point your browser to CNN News at `http://www.cnn.com`

A CyberJourney for College Students and Educators

One of the neat things about the Internet is that you can find sources of information that represent virtually every imaginable point of view. This activity, designed for pre-service or in-service teachers, focuses the learners' attention on using Internet resources to collect and analyze information about an issue that they feel strongly about. The lesson title is "Fighting for a Cause."

Think about an issue that you feel strongly about. It can be an issue related to education, the environment, politics, or students' rights. Surf the Net and collect ideas and facts that help you put together a presentation about Internet resources that are available on your subject. Present the final results of your search to your classmates. As you make your presentation, cite the sources and explore the issue of information bias.

Starting point: Here are some WWW stops (use Netscape or another Web browser) that you might visit to help you get ideas:

Site	*Web address*
A real rush . . .	`http://www.clark.net/pub/jeffd/rushpage.html`
Greenpeace International (Amsterdam)	`http://www.greenpeace.org`

The folks at NASA have put together a special Web page called "Internet in the Classroom" that offers pre-service and in-service teachers hundreds of online activities. Point your browser to NASA at `quest.arc.nasa.gov`

CyberPlanning for the Teacher

It's 4:30 p.m. on a Friday afternoon and I've just spent nearly two hours separating pebbles, sand, gravel, and stones from a marvelous stream-table experiment that dazzled and educated my students earlier that day. Just as I seal my last container, the principal comes in smiling like the cat that ate the canary.

"Have a good day?" she asks, still grinning.

"Sure! Great experiment; we all learned something. Third period even made little boats and sailed them down our model stream," I replied, knowing that these social visits from the principal at this hour of the day were often followed by the dreaded "we really need to . . . " speech.

"How wonderful. You're such a good teacher," she said, grinning even larger now.

"Uh-huh," I said, blushing maybe a bit.

"You know, we really need to update our technology plan," she said, now looking more seriously at me amid the sand, gravel, pebbles, and sand containers.

Aha! I knew it! Even though we just worked on the plan last summer, now it's five months later and she's presented this huge task. Sheesh.

Ready-made cyberjourneys?

Merely having a physical connection to the Internet is not enough for effective K-12 use. What else is there? A company called American Cybercasting Corp. offers a dynamic content package of ready-made cyberjourneys that it calls Educational Structures.

Educational Structures is designed to serve as an up-to-date curriculum component for most subject areas. The program provides more than 70 commercial print publications in hypertext format, ranging from resources suited to the very young (*Ranger Rick*) to those read mainly by older students (*The Washington Post, Discover,* and *Beijing Review*, plus several encyclopedic references).

The company also offers customized organization of Internet-based resources for a school or district, making it easy to incorporate Internet resources into the curriculum. These services include customized lesson plan support and a variety of online activities for students. The product is competitively priced and requires multiple Internet connections at each site for optimum use. For more information, send e-mail to `k12@americast.com`

Okay. So I'm a little dramatic. Actually, I really welcomed those visits from my principal. I knew the technology plan needed to be updated. Technology plans go stale faster than the bread in your pantry. Luckily, I'd planned for this. I'd been doing three things as a "personal cyberjourney" over the last few months that were likely to make the update much simpler:

- Collecting articles from magazines and newspapers about trends
- Collecting samples of other school's technology plans
- Collecting sites on the Web that offered information about technology planning

So, here's a personal cyberjourney that helps you update your school's technology plan. Hopefully, you'll take this as an ongoing task and be ready for when the grinning principal shows up at your door!

Starting point: The U.S. Government Department of Education has published a technology plan that's packed with great statistics, research reports, and a sensible set of steps that can be very helpful. Begin at: `http://www.ed.gov`

One more hint. Visit AltaVista (`http://www.altavista.digital.com`) or Yahoo! (`http://www.yahoo.com`) and use "technology planning" and "education" as keywords. My last search found more than 10,000 potential links!

You'll also discover that many schools now share their tech plans on the Web sites. Visit Web66 (`http://www.web66.coled.umn.edu/`) for a list of schools on the Net.

A CyberJourney for Your School

Here's a cyberjourney that benefits everyone in your community: Develop *your own* Web site.

To establish a Web site, you need two things: disk space on a host computer that has access to the Internet and your own customized home page. A home page contains one or more screens of hypertext-linked graphics and text. Other Internet users reach your home page by using a WWW browser such as Netscape or Mosaic.

Most information providers will grant schools space on their host computer to use for storing a limited amount of WWW information. Some provide the space for free, and some charge a one-time fee. You can create your own home page by using a word processor or a number of software tools that are available on the Internet.

Get set for "Spinning Your Own Web."

Starting point: You can find all you need to start your own site from HomePage Publisher Information at http://www-bprc.mps.ohio-state.edu/HomePage/HPPinfo.html

In case you or your students need a break, it is now possible to order pizza online if you live in certain areas of California (www.pizzahut.com). They're still working on a way to feed the pepperoni through the phone lines, though.

I can't resist! Here's one final Web site that will help you with information about using the World Wide Web and other Net resources in your classroom. This one's packed with more great activities you can use to support your curriculum. Point your browser to Global Online Learning Adventures at http://www.goals.com

The SchoolWeb Exploration Project

Another way to get your own WWW site is to take advantage of a special project in the Internet called "The SchoolWeb Exploration Project." The SchoolWeb Exploration Project is an international consortium of K-12 schools, commercial organizations, nonprofit groups and universities. The mission of the group is to assist K-12 schools by providing them with access to the tools and information they need to develop World Wide Web sites for student use.

SchoolWeb teams up K-12 schools with other Internet users who have access to servers. By using the shared resources, students get a chance to learn about hypertext and publishing on the Internet.

SchoolWeb members are divided into two subgroups: sponsors and school sites. Sponsors are volunteer organizations and individuals who have Web server access and are willing to donate user accounts, disk space, or technical support for K-12 use. The school sites, in turn, design their own Web pages for student academic activities, professional development, and community use; they access the sponsors' servers as a gateway to the Internet.

Want to find out more? Send e-mail to The Corporation for Public Broadcasting at acarvin@k12.cnidr.org

Chapter 22

Building Your Own Web

In This Chapter

- Weaving your own Web page
- Choosing the right tools
- Why build a Web page?

For every educator there comes that special moment, usually within your first two years of teaching, when you get an idea. Not some run-of-the-mill idea that will excite your students for ten minutes — I'm talking about some *insanely great* idea. You know, the kind of idea that keeps you planning until 1:00 a.m. and gets you to the school an hour early just so that you can get things moving. Fortunately, for many educators, these ideas come frequently.

After you come up with the idea and experience the thrill of having your students excited about the learning journey you created, word gets around the school that something wonderful just happened in Mr. Jones or Ms. Smith's classroom, and everyone wants to hop on the bandwagon. (An interesting and positive side-effect is the concurrent decrease in the number of times your name is written next to an expletive on the school's bathroom walls.) You usually spread the word about your great idea through notes in the school's newsletter, sharing handouts with your peers, or by being embarrassed and standing up in front of the faculty, playing show-and-tell. The sad part is that more often than not, the terrific product of teamwork between educator and student usually remains trapped between the classroom walls, a victim of the long-standing tradition that a hidden "mortar-monster" somehow defines and limits the spread of knowledge.

Fortunately, the Web offers an opportunity for you and your students to share your work with millions of people from within the safe confines of the mortar-monster's influence. Now, you and your students can gain well-deserved recognition for your hard work from lots of people you don't even know!

Seriously, and to get a bit philosophical, education has given me much satisfaction over the years. (Maybe that's why I'm a professional student. Is there a degree beyond a doctorate?) Publishing on the Web gives you and your students an opportunity to give back to the body of human knowledge, to become a *producer* as well as a *consumer* of information. The reason so many terrific resources for educators and lifelong learners are already on the Web is that people like you took the time to publish their work. Believe me, the journey itself is part of the reward.

How Do I Weave a Web Page?

To move up the information chain from consumer to producer, you and your students need only four things:

- An idea
- Some concept of how to present the idea
- A word processor or specialized Web page creation tool (even the Mac's Teachtext or your Windows Notepad will do in a pinch!)
- A place to post your Web page

Bodacious ideas

I'll leave the idea-generation part for you and your students to consider. Usually, schools begin with a simple page offering information about the school facility, programs, and the people who work there. Such information is a nice place to begin, but don't stop there. Remember that the purpose of the Web page is to communicate with some *audience*. That audience may be your students, faculty, and administration; your local community; or the whole beach-ball-of-a-planet. It's important, then, as you frame your idea for a Web page, to think about your audience and provide content that compels people to want to visit you. When I recently added a link to an Internet search site to my own home page, for example, traffic increased 10 percent within a week. (Of course, that increase challenges me to play with the rest of the page even more.)

If you want to see a few samples, drop in to Web66 at `http://www.web66.umn.edu` and search sites in your area.

Design and conquer

The design part of creating a Web page is great fun, kind of like designing a yearbook, except that it's interactive. Rather than featuring mug shots and gratuitous photos of the football team, you're featuring original content, student work, links to the outside world, and gratuitous pictures of your principal or department chairperson. You can read lots of specifics about Web design in my book *The World Wide Web For Teachers* (IDG Books Worldwide, Inc.). If you're ready to take the plunge after reading this chapter, I encourage you to visit there.

What tools do I use?

After you've come up with a great idea and have thought about a design theme, it's time to get to work and actually write the Web page. There are basically two ways to create a Web page:

- Learn HTML (the scripting language of the Web) and use your word processor (any word processor will do).
- Use a Web page creation tool like Claris Home Page (my personal favorite; it's included on the CD) or Adobe's PageMill.

Both methods have their benefits. Learning (and teaching) a scripting language like HTML helps you and your students better understand and extend the possibilities of Web scripting. Sure, there are codes to learn and syntax to follow, but you can also do some pretty amazing things by writing HTML raw code that you can't (yet) do with most Web page creation tools.

Web page creation tools like PageMill, Go Live!, or Claris Home Page remove the need for knowing lots of HTML code. Instead, using these tools is more like using a word processor or page layout program. All the commands are reduced to shortcuts, often chosen from a pop-up menu. You can get from zero to Web page in a matter of minutes without knowing a single HTML tag. The downside to these tools is that they've not yet caught up with some of the "bleeding edge" tools like JavaScript and CGI script processing. For that, you need some HTML on your side. (Check out *HTML For Dummies.)*

Finding a home for your page

The last step in creating your own Web page is figuring out where you can post your new creation. If your school, town, or district has its own Web server, you're probably in luck. Just use an FTP (file transfer protocol) program to copy your Web page to the server, and you're in business! If you don't have a server in-house, make a deal with your Internet service provider (ISP) for some space on its Web server, and then use FTP to copy the Web page(s) you've created to the ISP's server. In either case, remember to re-upload the page each time changes are made to it.

A number of online services also offer the opportunity to create a custom Web page. AOL, for example, automates the process of building and posting a rudimentary page. If you or your students want to use a Web page primarily as a jumping-off point to search the Net, some nifty solutions are available. Apple Computer has a neat idea for a personalized search page called MyPage. After inputting some basic information, you're greeted, by name, with a set of "best of" Web resources especially targeted toward your interests. MyPage is great for classroom use, no matter what kind of computer you have! Visit the new `http://myhome.apple.com` (you can use this site if you're a Windows power user, too!).

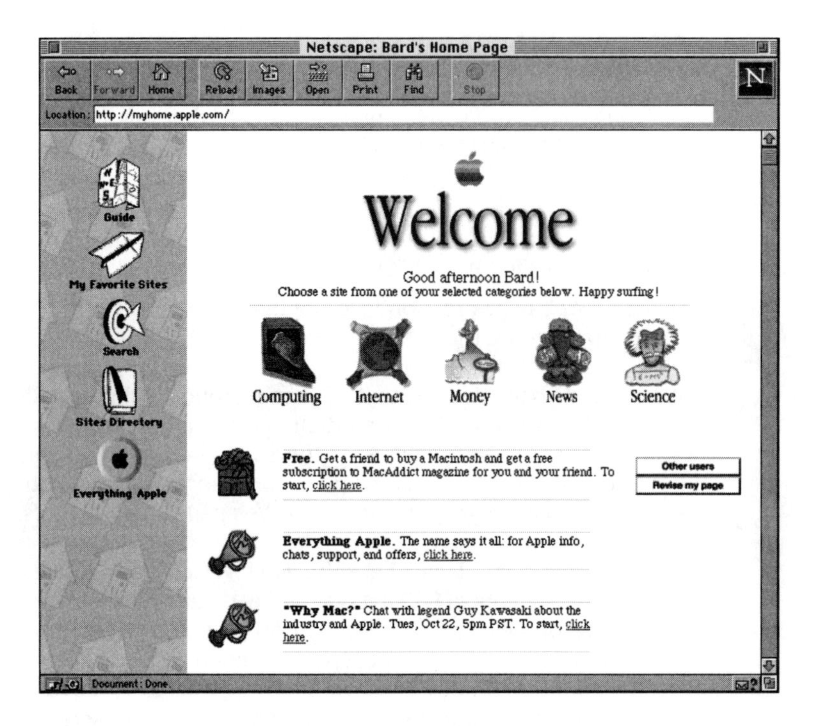

Creating a Web page for yourself, your school, or your classroom represents a logical next step in the evolution of your learning about the Internet. You and your students are literally moving up the information chain from consumer to producer. Above all, don't be intimidated by the tools, HTML code, or anything else involved in Web page creation. They are all much easier to deal with than BASIC or using the first word processors, and you learned those, right? Creating Web pages is definitely worth learning. To borrow a well-worn phrase, it's like "thinking globally and acting locally" at 28.8 Kbps or greater.

Why Web?

Answering the "Why Web?" question is kind of like answering the broader "Why Internet?" question. But just in case you need a few more reasons to get Webbed, think about these points:

- The Web is a very efficient way to present information — organized by nature, cross-platform, and very simple to maintain.
- The Web can be very interactive (take a look at Chapter 19). You'll find that the Web is becoming more multimedia rich and that folks are creating new tools for using it every day.

- The Web offers an opportunity to transfer data from your PC and storage devices to someone else.
- The Web offers an opportunity to teach higher-order thinking skills (à la our buddy Ben Bloom).
- Creating for the Web can be fun.

So what are you waiting for? Get your class Webbed!

Part V

The Part of Tens: The Internet Educator

The 5th Wave By Rich Tennant

"I did this report with the help of a satellite view atmospheric map from the National Weather Service, research text from the Jet Propulsion Laboratory, and a sound file from 'The Barfing Lungworms' new CD."

In this part . . .

Okay. Here's where I admit it. I am an avowed information junkie. When the editors said to come up with some short lists for this part, I figured a couple of thousand sites wouldn't take that much space. Alas, I was forced to choose a Top Ten in each category (but I crammed more in there anyway!). Each of the sites in these lists are teacher-tested and guaranteed (uhm, sort of) to dazzle and excite even the most glassy-eyed video game player. The sites are diverse, but they represent only a tiny fraction of what's available.

Don't be surprised if you find yourself trying all of them. Oops . . . is it 2 a.m. already? Got to go grade those term papers!

Chapter 23

Ten (-Plus) Ideas for E-Mail Exchanges

In This Chapter

- Conduct a survey
- Report the news
- Issue an Olympics challenge
- Have e-mail buddies figure out where you are
- Spin a yarn
- Gleaming the Cube
- Gather newsletter information
- Sponsor a scary-story contest
- Multimedia Mania
- Write to the president
- Find out about a senior citizen
- Exchange ideas with other teachers

Electronic mail makes for a great way to manage your students' time on the Internet because they can do most of the work off-line (without a live Internet connection). Students can use any word processor to create and edit their work, and then you or a student assistant can compile and mail the resulting files. You also can use electronic mail to share ideas with other educators.

Be sure to save your Internet-ready files as *text* (ASCII) files so that anyone can read them, regardless of whether they're using a Macintosh, a computer that uses DOS or Windows, or another kind of computer. ASCII files can be read by word-processing programs.

All the activities in this chapter are adapted from those found on the Internet in idea-rich places such as Syracuse University. (Use Gopher to go to `ericir.syr.edu` and check the `lesson plan` directory.)

Survey Says . . .

Collect e-mail addresses for schools around the country. Have your students design a survey related to a topic of interest and e-mail it to your list. As responses are returned, mark a map to show which part of the country is represented.

Go wild! Possible survey topics might include the following:

- School nutrition
- Attitudes about the use of computers in schools
- Voter registration
- Community history
- Favorite clothes, foods, school subjects, famous persons, and so on
- Most vivid memory
- Favorite periodical
- Best Internet World Wide Web (WWW) site
- . . . and lots more!

News Hounds

Challenge your students to become reporters and provide perspective on local events for e-mail pals around the world. Find an issue in your community that might be of national or global interest and have students write a news story explaining what's happening.

Encourage students to use other Internet resources to help them research their topics before writing. When you send the articles, request that the receiving student give the author constructive and specific feedback, accompanied by their own opinions about the issues or events presented.

Olympic Proportions

Have students develop Olympics-related math "stumper" questions and challenge their peers, via e-mail, to solve them. See who wins the first gold medal in Internet problem-solving.

Here's one to start you off: How many Olympic track and field events involve having the athlete travel more than 15 feet? (Be sure to think vertically *and* horizontally.)

Play "Guess Where"

Create a geographic scavenger hunt. Have your students prepare a list of geographic features and prominent landmarks in your area and challenge other schools across the Internet to identify the location of your school. If students get stumped, have them visit one of the many geographic servers on the Internet. These geographic servers help students match landforms and other characteristics with specific locations; you even learn the latitude and longitude. (Point your Web browser to `www.altavista.digital.com` and use the keyword search term *geography* to find one.)

Story Starters

This tried-and-true activity works on the Internet too. Simply generate 8 or 10 thematically based story starters (prompts) and trade them via e-mail with other schools. For a really interesting twist, have each recipient add only one or two sentences (or paragraphs) and pass it along to the next student. The result is a sort of "global effort."

Gleaming the Cube

The phrase "gleaming the cube" is one known to skateboarders everywhere. It's part of a language born of California culture and skateboarders' wit. The Internet is a particularly good place to explore the jargon of skateboarding and any one of an amazing variety of sports, professions, industries, and activities. Challenge your students to build their own "skateboarder's dictionary," illustrated with information from the Net and information cut from more traditional magazines.

Newsletter Swap

Offer to cross-publish newsletter articles with a school from another area. Have your students create and exchange general interest stories for publication in a special column in your school newsletter. Be sure that in the byline you list the writer's name, e-mail address, and the tag ". . . from the Internet"!

Don't forget to send a copy of your completed newsletter back to the other school via snailmail for inclusion in the school's or class's scrapbook.

Things That Go Bump

Sponsor a scary-story contest via the Internet. Write to several schools and work with teachers and students there to design criteria for the story and the contest. Make arrangements with a local newspaper to publish the winner. Be sure to request a short biography from the winner that includes the author's city, state, and school.

Multimedia Mania

Text isn't the only thing you can send via e-mail. You can attach files too! (See Chapter 11.) Schools everywhere are harnessing the power of multimedia, putting together QuickTime movies and HyperStudio stacks to exchange around the world. How about a "digital snapshot" of your town or school for sharing with others? Who's to say that your next school yearbook won't include some input from international friends!

Send a Letter to the President

Ask your students to draft letters to the president of the United States. As you're reminding them to dot their *i*'s and cross their *t*'s, discuss how to write a persuasive letter. Mail their masterpieces to `president@whitehouse.gov`. They get a response from an automated e-mail answering machine or, occasionally, a real person. Word has it that the president actually sees a few of these electronic letters.

Note that you can also contact most of the folks in Congress via e-mail. Call your congressional offices or check the Internet for their addresses.

Interview a Senior Citizen

Arrange for students to develop a list of questions to ask the oldest person they know. Have them try to find out as much as possible about the person's life and times. Enter the resulting raw data into an e-mail message and zip it to another classroom somewhere on the Internet. The receiver's task is to create a short biographical sketch, based on the data they've received, and return a finished product to its owner. Publish the results in your school or community newspaper or on your own Web site.

Start a Lesson Plan Chain Letter

Sending lots of mail to folks you don't know is a no-no on the Internet. A couple of lawyers plastered the Net with an advertisement once, and they're still getting complaints.

You might try a variation of a multiposted, or chain, letter, though. Simply create a mail message to two of your friends asking for their favorite teaching idea. Mail it along with a note to pass it on and a request to have each subsequent letter sent to your address. Before long, you have more ideas than you can fit on your hard drive. Be sure you include a cut-off date in your letter so you don't still get mail ten years from now.

A Few More Ideas from Other Net-Teachers

I'm warning you, this Internet stuff can get out of hand. Try one project and you and everyone around you are suddenly clamoring for more access and more time to do projects online. There are so many possibilities that you could literally plan an entire curriculum focused on Net-projects like the preceding ones. Below are a few more snippets of activities I've picked up from fellow net-surfing teachers. They tell me that the response from students and participating teachers was overwhelmingly positive. Use them at your own risk. :-)

- **Research exchange:** Exchange research on a given topic that's found on the Internet.
- **Literature swap:** Exchange literature that represents the students' own culture or environment.
- **Poems plus:** Create poetry on a chosen theme and exchange it for illustration by the students who receive it.

- **Electronic Park:** Swap descriptions of the world's first "electronic dinosaur" and have recipients create a name and illustration for each creature. (No fair writing about your first computer — even though it's a dinosaur. One of my first computers, a Mac 512K, is now a real-live fish tank in my den. I'm a firm believer in recycling.)

Chapter 24

Ten (and More) Mailing Lists Not to Miss!

In This Chapter

- Mailing lists for teachers
- Mailing lists for students

Here they are. Especially selected for you by the Friday-Afternoon-at-the-Pub Teacher's Wind-Down Group. All the mailing lists in this chapter are teacher tested and are guaranteed not to have harmful side effects.

Mailing lists are like e-mail newsgroups, except that the comments of fellow mailing list users are delivered directly to your mailbox. You choose the topic and use Eudora Light or another e-mail program to send a subscribe message to the list's owner or moderator, and in short order, your first messages arrive. (For information on how to stop the messages from packing your mailbox, see Chapter 12.)

Try these and you'll be up to your eyeballs in useful classroom ideas before you know it! (Just be sure to substitute your name for the `<your name>` prompt that I give you in the instructions.)

TESL-L

A terrific source of information for Teachers of English to Speakers of Other Languages (TESOL).

Send an e-mail subscribe message to `LISTSERV@cunyvm.cuny.edu`

Message text: `subscribe TESL-L <your name>`

COSNDISC

The Consortium for School Networking presents a discussion about how to set up a schoolwide network, as well as troubleshooting tips and software hints. This is a must-subscribe for every educator with a mandate to "create a network."

Send an e-mail subscribe message to `LISTSERV@bitnic.bitnet`

Message text: `subscribe COSNDISC <your name>`

ALA

The "mother ship" of Library Sciences, the American Library Association's main discussion list.

Send an e-mail subscribe message to `LISTSERV@ua1vm.ua.edu`

Message text: `subscribe ala-serv <your name>`

CURRICUL

Here you find K-12 and higher-education discussions about curriculum and instruction.

Send an e-mail subscribe message to `LISTSERV@saturn.rowan.edu`

Message text: `subscribe CURRICUL <your name>`

MEDIALIST

A list of international media organizations with their e-mail addresses.

Send an e-mail subscribe message to `majordomo@world.std.com`

Message text: `subscribe medialist <your name>`

K12ADMIN

This list provides lively discussion about issues and challenges in K-12 educational administration.

Send an e-mail subscribe message to `LISTSERV@suvm.bitnet`

Message text: `subscribe K12ADMIN <your name>`

KIDLINK

You can find a wide variety of cool telecommunications projects here.

Send an e-mail subscribe message to `LISTSERV@ndsuvm1.bitnet`

Message text: `subscribe KIDLINK <your name>`

SPEDTALK

An open, unmoderated list that's a forum for current issues about practices, policies, and research in special education.

Send an e-mail subscribe message to `majordomo@virginia.edu`

Message text: `subscribe SPEDTALK <your name>`

LM_NET

You can find great information about school library and media resources here.

Send an e-mail subscribe message to `LISTSERV@suvm.bitnet`

Message text: `subscribe LM_NET <your name>`

Y-RIGHTS

This mailing list is a discussion group on the rights of kids and teens. It is open to kids, teens, young adults, adults, senior citizens, teachers, students, and anyone else interested in enlightening today's youth.

Send an e-mail subscribe message to `LISTSERV@SJUVM.BITNET`

Message text: `subscribe Y-RIGHTS <your name>`

GC-L

The Global Classroom Discussion List offers a discussion of online projects and ideas with a decidedly international flavor.

Send an e-mail subscribe message to `LISTSERV@uriacc.uri.edu`

Message text: `subscribe GC-L <your name>`

EDTECH

Subscribe to this list for discussions about educational technology.

Send an e-mail subscribe message to `LISTSERV@ohstvma.bitnet`

Message text: `subscribe EDTECH <your name>`

According to a study by the U.S. Government Accounting Office, 25 percent of U.S. schools lack the computers and other technology infrastructure they need to implement school reform.

IECC

Subscribe to IECC to access a meeting place for teachers seeking school-to-school connections for e-mail exchanges and projects.

Send an e-mail subscribe message to `craigd.ricecdr@stolaf.edu`

Message text: `subscribe IECC-request <your name>`

SUPER K-12

SUPER K-12 provides an information exchange for educators with high-speed connections (56 Kbps or greater).

Send an e-mail subscribe message to `LISTSERV@suvm.syr.edu`

Message text: `subscribe superk12 <your name>`

NET-RESOURCES

Subscribe to NET-RESOURCES for a great list of new Internet resources.

Send an e-mail subscribe message to `LISTSERV@is.internic.net`

Message text: `subscribe NET-RESOURCES <your name>`

EDUPAGE

EDUPAGE is an educational newsletter that is delivered via e-mail. To subscribe to EDUPAGE, send a note to `edupage@educom.edu` with your name, institution name, and e-mail address. To unsubscribe, respond to EDUPAGE surveys, or offer news items, send mail to `edupage@educom.edu`

Bonus: Ten Great Mailing Lists for Students

When you are logged on and scanning the list of mailing lists out there, watch for these student-tested lists:

AMWEST-H	History of the American West
KIDZMAIL	Issues and interests relating to children
PEN PALS	Develop writing skills and meet other students
PHYSICS	Students chatting about physics
SABB-L	Student athlete bulletin board
SCOUTS-L	Discussions relating to various youth groups

TALKBACK	Discussion group for children
WISENET	Women in science, math, and engineering
WX-TALK	Chatting about everybody's favorite subject, the weather
YOUTHNET	Discussions about kids and the Internet

Chapter 25

Ten Groups of Newsgroups Any Educator Could Love

In This Chapter

- About your computer
- Groups about other newsgroups, Gopher sites, and WAIS servers
- Groups that discuss graduate work
- Groups about online projects
- General groups for educators and students
- Math and science groups
- Miscellaneous education groups
- `alt.` education groups

'Round these parts, folks like things in tens. Choosing ten newsgroups for this chapter is a bit like choosing ten M&Ms from a one-pound bag. So I've hunted around and found ten *groups* of newsgroups for your reading pleasure. Bet you can't read just one.

Remember that you use a newsreader (such as NewsWatcher) or your browser (Netscape Navigator) to view and post to newsgroups. Also remember that many of these groups are *unmoderated;* that is, anything goes. Be vigilant for posts in any newsgroup that are inappropriate for classroom use.

About Your Computer

These newsgroups give you information about your computer, and there are plenty more `comp` groups representing any platform you can imagine (and some you've probably never heard of).

comp.sys.apple2

comp.sys.ibm.ps2.hardware

comp.sys.mac.announce

comp.os.ms-windows.announce

comp.os.ms-windows.misc

comp.sources.apple2 (Yes, those workhorses are still alive and well!)

misc.forsale.computers.mac

misc.forsale.computers.pc-clone

misc.kids.computer

Newsgroups, Gopher Sites, and WAIS Servers

In these newsgroups you find information about other newsgroups, Gopher sites, or WAIS servers. A quick read of these groups can save you and your students hours of searching.

comp.infosystems.wais

comp.infosystems.gopher

news.announce.newgroups

Graduate Work

These newsgroups are great for educators who want to chat about the wild and woolly world of graduate work. (You even find ideas for dissertation topics here!)

soc.college.teaching-asst

soc.college.gradinfo

Online Projects

Need a source for information about projects for students on the Internet? Try these newsgroups.

finet.freenet.kidlink.kidlink	Find a project for your students
finet.freenet.kidlink.kidproj	Participate in projects that are under way
finet.freenet.kidlink.kidplan	Propose new projects

General Groups for Educators and Students

These newsgroups are custom designed for educators and students. The k12 groups are generally posts by teachers for teachers. In these groups you find project ideas, software reviews, lesson plans, opportunities to collaborate with other educators, and much more.

k12.chat.elementary
k12.chat.junior
k12.chat.senior
k12.chat.teacher
k12.ed.art
k12.ed.business
k12.ed.comp.literacy
k12.ed.health-pe
k12.ed.life-skills
k12.ed.math
k12.ed.music
k12.ed.science
k12.ed.soc-studies
k12.ed.special
k12.ed.tag
k12.ed.tech
k12.lang.art
k12.lang.deutsch-eng
k12.lang.esp-eng
k12.lang.francais
k12.lang.russian
k12.library
k12.news

A 1996 RAND study indicates that in 1995 there was one computer for every nine students in K-12 schools in the U.S.

Back to Basics

The following newsgroups contain discussions that are centered around science and mathematics. Note that in some cases you're chatting with other educators, and in other cases you're chatting with scientists or researchers who are using the subject area discussion to further their work.

Interact with *real live scientists* in these newsgroups.

`sci.edu`

`sci.answers`

Only serious mathematics students (grades 6-12) need tackle this group. It's the ultimate online math challenge.

`geometry.puzzles`

Miscellaneous

Here are a couple of miscellaneous education-related newsgroups and one great source for information about grants to support all those items on your technology shopping list!

`misc.education`

`misc.education.home-school.misc`

`info.nsf.grants`

`alt.uu.lang.misc` (the USENET Univ. Language Department)

`alt.` Groups

The `alt.` groups are the breeding ground for wannabe newsgroups. They've received a bad reputation because `alt.` groups are generally unmoderated and are sometimes the repository for all those naughty graphics you've been warned about.

No hardware solution can substitute for the watchful eye of a vigilant teacher. Be aware that you and your students will inevitably stumble upon off-topic and off-color posts, especially in `alt.` groups. Take care to watch that your students don't veer their Net-surfboards into a wave they can't handle.

These groups represent unmoderated discussions that are focused on education topics such as research and student organizations.

`alt.education.alternative`	Explore nonstandard educational models
`alt.education.research`	Great place to discuss hot topics in education research
`alt.education.higher.stu-affairs`	For college deans and organizations
`alt.education.email-project`	Pen-pal projects, unmoderated
`alt.education.distance`	Distance learning and satellite technology
`alt.education.disabled`	Talk about teaching students with special needs

Chapter 26

Ten Gopher Sites

In This Chapter

- Weather, or not
- Ask ERIC
- To the moon!
- Disabilities
- Adult literacy

A furry little creature is hiding in your classroom computer. He's inquisitive, he's curious, and he's ready to jump on the Internet and work for you. He's Gopher.

It's time to put him to work. This chapter lists ten interesting Gopher sites for you and your students to access. To get to these sites, fire up TurboGopher, HGopher, or your Web browser and enter the domain names that are listed.

The Weather Machine

Access current maps, satellite photos, and forecasts for the United States.

Gopher to `wx.atmos.uiuc.edu`

Ask ERIC

This Education Resource Information Clearinghouse site at Syracuse University has tons of lesson plans, as well as resources and reference materials for teachers.

Gopher or telnet to `ericir.syr.edu`

NASA (Marshall)

Find out everything you always wanted to know about NASA from the Marshall Space Flight Center. You can get lesson plans, shuttle schedules, mission patches (graphics), and much more.

Gopher to `spacelink.msfc.nasa.gov`

U.S.D.O.E.

The U.S. Department of Education offers update information about a variety of national and local educational issues.

Gopher to `gopher.ed.gov`

The White House

Explore thousands of government documents and resources.

Gopher to `gopher.whitehouse.gov`

Dana College Campus Gopher

This great collection of K–12 resources includes CNN Newsroom and FreeNet access information, brought to you from Nebraska.

Gopher to `gopher.dana.edu`

Canada's SchoolNet

An amazing collection of resources, both Canadian and educational.

Gopher to `gopher.schoolnet.carleton.ca`

Disability Information

This site is a super source of information, statistics, network resources, and government documents that are related to disabilities.

Point your Web browser to `http://codi.buffalo.edu` for instructions on the Gopher site.

A 1996 RAND study indicated that K-12 schools spent about $70 per student on technology during the 1994-1995 school year. (The study recomends $300 per student.)

National Center on Adult Literacy

Here you can find research and literacy resources that are related to adult learning and literacy, courtesy of the University of Pennsylvania. A searchable server makes information retrieval very efficient.

Gopher to `litserver.literacy.upenn.edu`

ERIC Clearinghouse on Assessment and Evaluation (Washington, D. C.)

The resources here include information and tests from the Educational Testing Service (ETS) and noncommercial test sources. You can also find an index to the *Mental Measurements Yearbook* and *Tests in Print*.

Gopher to `gopher.cua.edu`

National Center for Adult Literacy

A fabulous collection of print and software resources to support adult literacy.

Gopher to `gopher.litserver.literacy.upenn.edu`

More Great Gophers

Here are more education Gopher sites for you to explore. Point your Gopher to these URLs:

`chronicle.merit.edu`	Chronicles of Higher Education
`gopher.peachnet.edu`	Georgia Educational Network
`gaia.sci-ed.fit.edu`	Florida Technical Education Gopher
`informns.k12.mn.us`	Internet for Minnesota Schools
`goldmine.cde.ca.gov`	California Department of Education
`nysernet.org`	Empire Schoolhouse, New York

Chapter 27

Ten Great FTP Sites

In This Chapter

- The Smithsonian
- Stanford University
- Music from Wisconsin
- Internet guide
- Stock prices
- More FTP sites
- Net information
- Files for Macs, DOS, and Windows
- Recipes
- The Supreme Court rules!
- ¿Que Pasa?
- Internet maps
- VOA

FTP is *File Transfer Protocol,* Internet-speak for retrieving (copying) files from another computer (host) to your computer or copying files from your computer to a host (for example, copying Web pages to a server). You can use Fetch (or other FTP software) or access these sites from within most Web browsers. (Just type **ftp://** followed by the FTP location in the Open dialog box.)

Each of the sites included in this chapter has lots of files for your classroom or personal use. Remember to screen all files by using a virus detection program (such as Virex, S.A.M., or Disinfectant). Better safe than sorry!

In each of the example sites, use the *ftp to* address to open the connection and then search the directory that follows. When in doubt, look for the `/pub` (public) directory.

Visit the Smithsonian

The graphics and text files at this site describe and illustrate the vast collection of the Smithsonian Institution in Washington, D.C.

ftp to `photo1.si.edu`
in the directory `/pub/`

Check Out Stanford University

Lots of education and reference materials are here for downloading.

ftp to `sumex-aim.stanford.edu`

Make Some Music

The University of Wisconsin maintains a huge library of song lyrics, tablature, music pictures, and more.

ftp to `ftp.uwp.edu`
in the directory `/pub/music/`

Get Stock Prices, Not Quite Live

There's no such thing as free *real-time* quotes on the Internet. You can get 'em, but you pay dearly. This *quote-dump* is an acceptable alternative. The delay in posting quotes seems to be about 15 minutes.

ftp to `ftp.dg.com`
in the directory `/com/pub/misc.invest/quote-dump/`

FTP and Me

Get a list of FTP sites, updated regularly.

ftp to `ftp.funet.fi`
in the directory `/pub/`

The Net on the Net

The Clearinghouse for Networked Information Discovery and Retrieval (CNIDR) offers lots of information about the Internet, including statistics, policies, and tutorial information.

ftp to `ftp.cnidr.org`

Tons of Mac Files

The University of Michigan has a large library of Macintosh files that you can download.

ftp to `mac.archive.umich.edu`

Tons of Files for DOS and Windows

Washington University in St. Louis maintains a ton of software for downloading to most popular computer systems, including more GIF and JPEG pictures than you can ever imagine.

ftp to `wuarchive.wustl.edu`

Get Cookin'

You'll have so many recipes that the home economics teacher will think you're a professional chef.

ftp to `gatekeeper.dec.com`
in the directory `/pub/recipes/`

Supreme Court Rulings

At this popular FTP site, you can get most rulings within 24 hours of the decision.

ftp to `ftp.cwru.edu`
in the directory `/hermes/`

¿Que Pasa?

Explore Internet resources for foreign language teachers at the Clearinghouse for Subject-Oriented Internet Resource Guides.

ftp to `una.hh.lib.umich.edu`
in the directory `/inetdirsstacks/get lang:kovacsd`

Map of the Net

PostScript-format maps of the Internet. Use PageMaker (or another PostScript viewer) and a PostScript printer to view/print.

ftp to `ftp.merit.edu`
in the directory `/maps/`

Voice of America

The Voice of America offers CNN Headlines, European news, and even audio programs.

ftp to `ftp.voa.gov`
in the directory `/pub/`

Chapter 28

Ten Great Educational Telnet Targets

In This Chapter

- Media and reference
- Science
- History and geography
- Sports and P.E.
- Economics and mathematics
- General educational interest

Telnet can be a powerful tool in your classroom, no matter what the subject. Here are a few of my favorite educational places to visit, organized by subject. Note that some telnet sites send a page or two of information about the site and then log you off. You have to either look quickly or open a session-log file (from the File menu).

Remember that when you telnet, you're using valuable resources on someone else's (the host) computer, so don't be surprised if things are slow or you get the online equivalent of a busy signal.

To access a telnet site, use NCSA Telnet or WinTel (use the addresses as shown) or Netscape (click the Open button and type `telnet:` before each address).

Media and Reference

The Library of Congress

Telnet to: `dra.com`

This mirror site for the Library of Congress is a very busy place. Mirror sites provide "alternate doorways" into busy servers and sometimes allow access to exact copies of programs or data that were once available only on the original host computer.

Worldwide library access

Telnet to: `laguna.epcc.edu`
Login: `library`

This Hytelnet server offers access to university and public library catalogs from around the world.

The Bible (and more)

Telnet to: `library.dartmouth.edu`

Dartmouth offers everything from the full text of the Bible to Shakespeare's plays to Dante.

Dictionary

Telnet to: `cs.indiana.edu`
Login: `anonymous`

Full-text version of a popular dictionary. Type `help` at any prompt if you get stuck.

U.S. Government Programs and Information

Telnet to: `kids.ccit.duq.edu`
Login: `gopher`

A link to International Educational Grants and Resources, bibliographies, and more.

Science

Earthquake information

Telnet to: `geophys.washington.edu`
Login: `quake`

Did you realize that hundreds of quakes occur around the globe each week? This site offers the time, latitude, longitude, and more for quakes, seconds after they occur. It's a valuable source for earth science activities.

EPA Online

Telnet to: `epaibm.rtpnc.epa.gov`

There's a great chemistry database available through the "CH" menu.

NASA Spacelink

Telnet to: `spacelink.msfc.nasa.gov`
Login: `guest`

Find out everything from what's in the current shuttle payload to what the logo for the Apollo 4 mission looks like. Classroom activities and much more make this a great telnet destination.

The National Institutes of Health

Telnet to: `nih-library.nih.gov`

This clearinghouse for health and medical information is an important source of information for health, biology, or life science classes.

Air pollution

Telnet to: `ttnbbs.rtpnc.epa.gov`

A gateway to various computers on the Internet that contain information and statistics about air pollution.

Weather

Telnet to: `wind.atmos.uah.edu 3000`
`downwind.sprl.umich.edu 3000`

Up-to-the-minute weather forecasts, current conditions, earthquake reports, ski conditions, water temperatures, and much more.

History and Geography

University of Kansas history

Telnet to: `ukanaix.cc.ukans.edu`
Login: `history`

From Peru to Pasadena, there's history about every place you can think of, and quite a few you couldn't think of. Search archives by place or event. You can pick up little-known history facts, too, and use them to make your lessons more interesting.

Geography server

Telnet to: `martini.eecs.umich.edu 3000`

Believe it or not, you can type in a zip code or the name of any U.S. city, and this humongous database returns information about the city, county, state, telephone area codes, elevation, features, latitude/longitude, census data, time zone, postal codes, and *more*. Where was all this when I took geography in the dark ages? Talk about a time saver!

Archaeology

Telnet to: `cast.uark.edu`
Login: `nadb`

Explore the wonders of the past through the National Archeological Database Information Management System.

FedWorld

Telnet to: `fedworld.gov`

More than 100 databases with everything you could possibly want to know about the U.S. government.

Former USSR

Telnet to: `ukanaix.cc.ukans.edu`
Login: `ex-ussr`

Explore new and historical information from the former Soviet Union.

Sports and P.E.

Visit these sites as a carrot for a terrific statistics activity or just to find out how your favorite team is doing.

NBA scores

Telnet to: `culine.colorado.edu 859`

NHL scores

Telnet to: `culine.colorado.edu 850`

Baseball scores

Telnet to: `culine.colorado.edu 862`

NFL scores

Telnet to: `culine.colorado.edu 863`

Economics and Mathematics

Stock market information

Telnet to: `a2i.rahul.net`
Login: `guest`
Choose: `n`
Choose: `Current System Info`
Choose: `Market Report`

Give your students $10,000 in bogus bucks and have them play the market. This site supplies them with up-to-the-minute information.

General Educational Interest

The Learning Link

Telnet to: `sierra.edu`
Login: `newuser`
Password: `newuser`

This must-see site has current information for educators about computers, technology, and more. Lesson plans and ideas for collaboration abound.

KidLink

Telnet to: `kids.ccit.duq.edu`
Login: `kidlink`

This site is packed with information about ongoing telecommunications projects aimed at students in grades 4-9.

Grant information

Telnet to: `fedix.fie.com`

Information on scholarships, minority assistance, grants available for technology, and more.

Chapter 29

Ten Educational and Reference Web Sites Not to Miss

In This Chapter

- Education Web sites
- Reference Web sites

There are literally thousands of sites on the Web that are potentially useful for you and your students. Of course, I've found *way* more than ten sites that I thought you'd enjoy. I've even added a few new exemplary sites since the first edition of this book. All the sites listed in this chapter are excellent teacher-tested classroom resources and provide links to other sites that have an educational focus. (See Chapter 30 for even more sites!)

To travel the World Wide Web (WWW), launch your Web browser (Netscape Navigator, MacWeb, Mosaic, and so on) and use the Open command to enter each of the addresses (URLs) in this chapter. Enter all the information that you see after the word *Address:*

Educational Sites

Set your tractor beams on these sites and you'll find lots of ideas to enhance or enrich your curriculum. Each site contains information appropriate for K-12 and college students.

Apple Computer Education Page

Information about Apple products, software solutions, and more.

Address: `http://education.apple.com`

Earthquakes

Find out how the Earth's moving today at this site operated by the U. S. Geological Survey (U.S.G.S.).

Address: `http://quake.wr.usgs.gov/QUAKES/CURRENT/current.html`

Genome

The Human Genome Database is a vast storage area for data about the genes and chromosomes in your body. Fascinating and challenging!

Address: `http://www.ornl.gov/TechResources/Human_Genome/home.html`

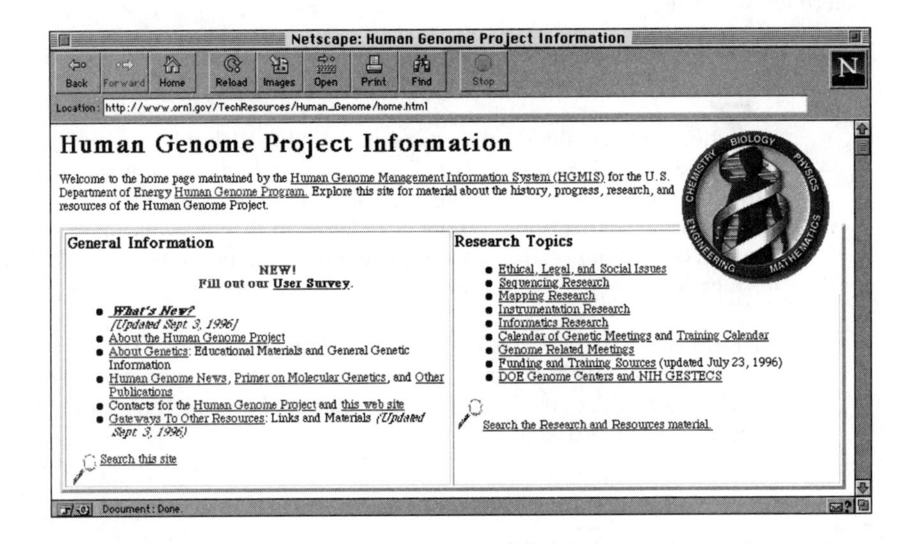

LiveText: K–12 Resources

Educational project ideas and other resources abound at this site sponsored by Columbia University.

Address: `http://www.ilt.columbia.edu/k12/index.html`

National Aeronautics and Space Administration

Visit NASA and tap its wealth of online educational resources.

Address: `http://www.nasa.gov/`

The NSF Grants Database

This National Science Foundation Web page is chock-full of ideas for grants and funding.

Address: `http://medoc.gdb.org/best/stc/nsf-best.html`

The Planets

Explore the Milky Way without ever leaving your classroom!

Address: `http://seds.lpl.arizona.edu/nineplanets/`

United States Department of Education

Access educational policies and U.S. D.O.E. publications.

Address: `http://www.ed.gov/`

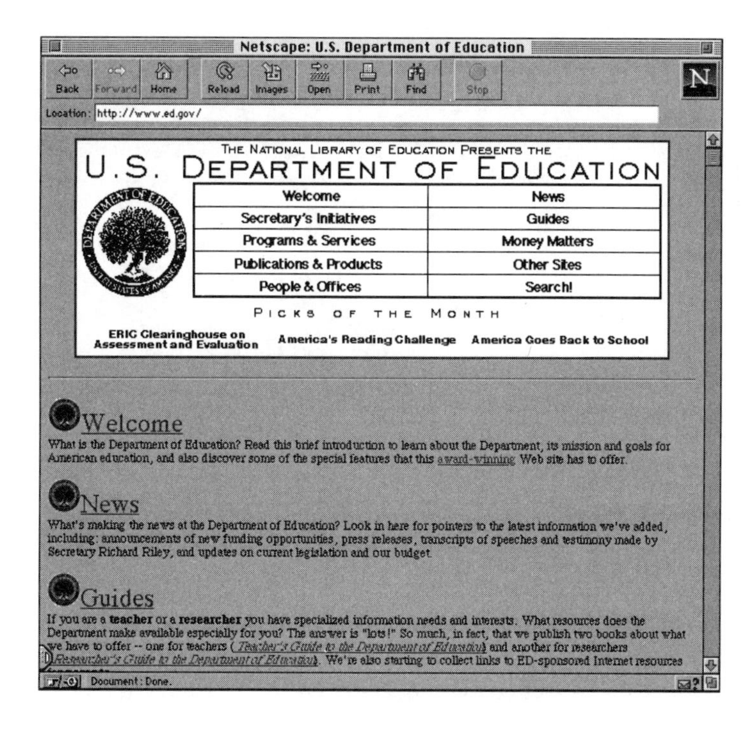

Virtual Frog Dissection Kit

You won't even miss the smell of formaldehyde when your students sample this page.

Address: `http://george.lbl.gov:80/vfrog/`

Vose School Educational Resources

Here's what happens when creative teachers create their own Web site. Excellent!

Address: `http://www.teleport.com:80/~vincer/`

Virtual Museums

Visit museums from the Louvre in France to Atlanta's High Museum. The sites included here typically include online art and lots of historical data.

Address: `http://www.icom.org/vlmp`

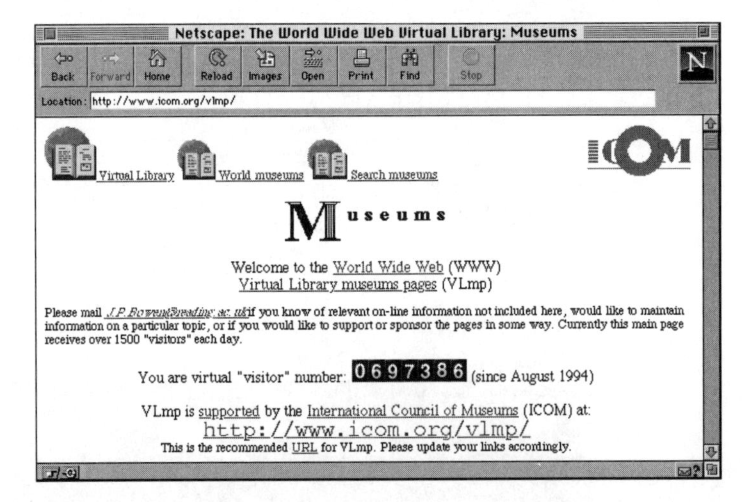

Web66

A terrific resource for educational resources and creating your own Web page.

Address: `http://web66.coled.umn.edu/`

What's Hot and Cool

Check out the *education* category on this constantly updated catalog page.

Address: `http://kzsu.stanford.edu/uwi/reviews.html`

Reference Sites

You'll find literally thousands of reference sites on the World Wide Web. Most have hypertext links to other sites that are just as rich in information. Here are a few that come highly recommended by teachers from around the globe.

ArchNet

A simple, elegant resource page for archaeologists. Great content for exploration by amateurs and professionals alike.

Address: `http://www.lib.uconn.edu/ArchNet/`

CIA

Visit the Central Intelligence Agency's home page to access the *World Factbook,* an almanac packed with facts and figures.

Address: `http://www.odci.gov/`

Complete Works of Shakespeare

The *other* Bard speaks — through the Internet.

Address: `http://the-tech.mit.edu/Shakespeare/works.html`

The Corporation for Public Broadcasting

Visit Big Bird and friends at this information-rich site.

Address: `http://www.cpb.org/`

EdWeb

A top resource for teachers in the field of educational technology.

Address: `http://edweb.cnidr.org:90/`

Library Resources

This site, sponsored by Calvin College, provides a broad base of cross-disciplinary reference resources.

Address: `http://gopher.calvin.edu/Lib_Resources/`

Periodic Table

From Hydrogen to Americum — all the elements and their properties are here for the clicking.

Address: `http://www2.shef.ac.uk/chemistry/web-elements/web-elements-home.html`

The Scoop Children's Book Review

You won't believe all the rich information here! Reviews of the latest in children's literature, an Educator Resource Center, Top Ten List, Activity Center, even a chatroom.

Address: `http://www.friend.ly.net/scoop/`

TENET

Visit the Texas Educational Network (TENET), one of the most resource-rich state networks.

Address: `http://www.tenet.edu/`

University of California Museum of Paleontology

Dinosaurs lurk in this Berkeley archive site.

Address: `http://ucmp1.berkeley.edu/`

Weather Map

Is it raining in Peoria? A satellite map or weather graphic gives your students enough information to give the network weather forecasters a run for their money.

Address: `http://home.ucar.edu/wx.html`

Chapter 30

Ten (and More) Sites That Are Educational, Interesting, Fun, or Great Places to Begin

In This Chapter

- Learning and reference sites
- Fun sites
- Jump sites

I just couldn't resist sharing a list of some very useful Internet resources that I found while doing research for this book. The sites in this chapter are educational, interesting, or just plain fun to explore. I've also tagged a few WWW *jump sites* onto the end. A jump site provides hundreds (and sometimes thousands) of links to other Web pages or a search engine to help you find the resources you need on the Web. So whether you need a lesson plan, a chuckle, or just want to be amazed, fire up your computer and try out these sites.

Learning and Reference

The Web has quickly become the resource of choice on the Internet. New educational sites are popping up daily. The sites in this chapter contain specific information that may be of particular interest to educators or contain resources for your classroom or links to other resources that can help you brighten any lesson plan.

Remember, you can enter a URL directly in the Address line of your Web browser. Just type `http://`, `ftp://`, `news://`, or `mailto://` in the command line along with the rest of the URL, and you're good to go!

Bugs, bugs, bugs!

More than you and your students could ever want to know about creepy-crawly things.

Address: `http://www.orkin.com`

Commercial vendors online

A list of commercial vendors with Web pages. Updated regularly.

Address: `http://www.slac.stanford.edu/comp/vendor/vendor.html`

Demographic summaries 1994

Look here for an impressive amount of information about the people of our world. The 1995 data should be available by the time you read this book.

Address: `http://www.digimark.net`

ESSP: Educational Space Simulations Project

Jump on board this site for exciting educational space simulations projects for teachers and students.

Address: `http://chico.rice.edu/armadillo/Simulations/simserver.html`

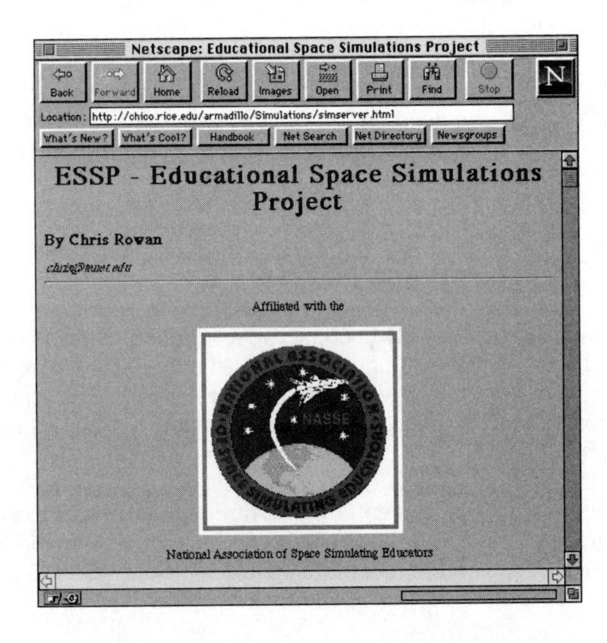

Go ask Alice

Is this a live person or a computer? Check out this fascinating experiment in intelligent computer conversation *live* from Canada!

Address: telnet to `debra.dgbt.doc.ca 3000`

Choose `alice` from the main menu.

Greenpeace

Dedicated to creating a green and peaceful world.

Address: `http://www.greenpeace.org/`

Guide to the Internet

A comprehensive guide for your technically minded students.

Address: `http://www.nova.edu./Inter-Links/`

How far is it?

You won't believe this site! Enter two places, just about anywhere on the earth, and this site computes the distance.

Address: `http://gs213.sp.cs.cmu.edu/prog/dist/`

Internet statistics

A gold mine for information about the growth of the Internet.

Address: `http://www.cs.indiana.edu/internet/internet.stat.html`

Libraries on the Net

Log in to the library at Boston University, Harvard, and others with the following addresses.

Address: telnet to `library.bu.edu (login: library)`

Address: telnet to `pac.carl.org`

Address: telnet to `pennlib.upenn.edu`

Address: telnet to `gopher.harvard.edu`

K–12 WWW menu

A link to K-12 resources around the world.

Address: `http://k12.cnidr.org:80/janice_k12/k12menu.html`

Kids Web

A worldwide digital library for kids.

Address: `http://www.npac.syr.edu:80/textbook/kidsweb/`

Newsgroup search

Search either of these sites for information about newsgroups and what they contain.

Address: `http://www.lycos.com`

Search `Newsgroups`

Address: `http://alpha.acast.nova.edu/cgi-bin/lists/`

Online reference works

A solid list of reference resources.

Address: `http://198.214.57.13/tec/reference.html`

Parenting

References, bibliographies, and "how-to" manuals for parenting.

Address: `http://www.internet-is.com/parent/`

Project Gutenberg

Files containing full text of hundreds of books, articles, and speeches.

Address: `http://www.vuw.ac.nz/non-local/gutenberg/works/`

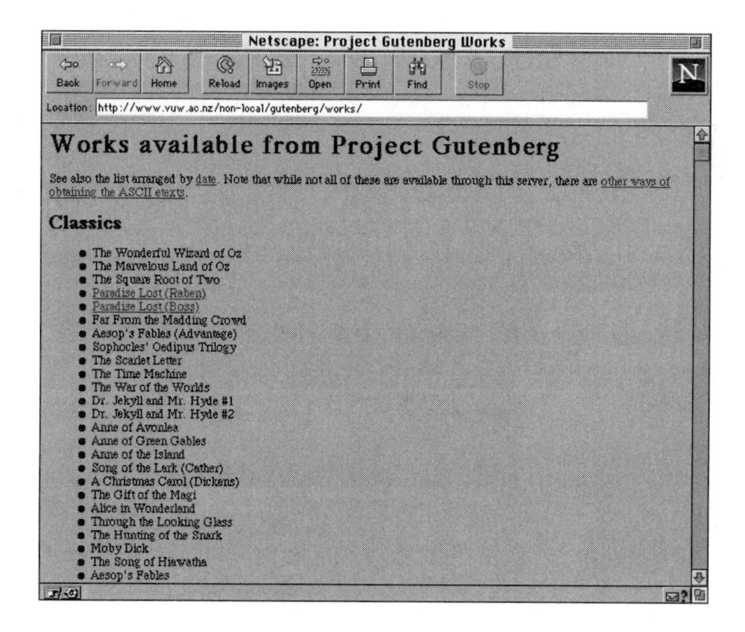

Sports Page

Every statistic imaginable for almost any sport.

Address: `http://www2.nando.net/SportServer/moresports/`

The Weather Unit

Worldwide atmospheric information, including maps, charts, and statistics.

Address: `http://faldo.atmos.uiuc.edu/WEATHER/weather.html`

The Well

(Whole Earth 'Lectronic Link) An Internet provider's home page that's brimming with information about education, the environment, and much more.

Address: `http://www.well.com/`

The USA CityLink Project

Find out amazing things about your own city.

Address: `http://www.NeoSoft.com:80/citylink/`

THOMAS: Legislative Information on the Internet

The official government site for Congress. Jam-packed with information.

Address: `http://thomas.loc.gov`

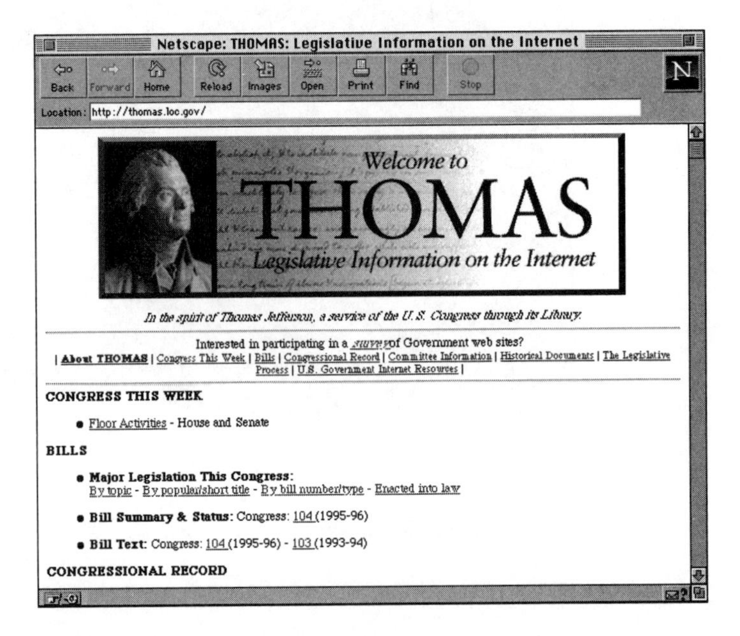

Time Magazine

Read it here *before* it hits the news stands!

Address: `http://www.time.com`

Toll-free phone numbers

Search the database to find the toll-free number of your choice.

Address: `http://att.net/dir800/`

U.S. Department of the Treasury

From money to taxes, this site has it all.

Address: `http://www.ustreas.gov/treasury/homepage.html`

U.S. Patent Information

Find information about all the latest inventions.

Address: `http://www.law.cornell.edu/usc/`

Virtual Library

A library of libraries, including the Library of Congress.

Address: `http://www.nasa.gov/`

Wentworth Communications

Packed with practical ideas for your classroom.

Address: `http://www.wentworth.com/classroom/edulinks.html`

Just Plain Fun!

If you want to kill a few hours or just impress your friends, check out these sites, selected because they are unique, fun, or addictive.

Walt Disney World — Lake Buena Vista, Florida

Meet Mickey and his friends on the information superhighway.

Address: `http://www.best.com/~dijon/disney/parks/waltdisneyworld/`

SeaWorld/Busch Gardens

Address: `http://www.seaworld.com`

Star Trek: The Next Generation (STTNG)

Beam yourself to outer space via the information superhighway.

Address: `http://www.ugcs.caltech.edu:80/~werdna/sttng/`

Address: `http://voyager.paramount.com/`

Trojan Room coffee machine

Regular or decaf?

Address: `http://www.cl.cam.ac.uk/coffee/coffee.html`

Interesting Devices Connected to the Net

Monitor the position of a chameleon or the status of a robot arm — and much more!

Address: `http://www.yahoo.com/Computers_and_Internet/Internet/Entertainment`

The ultimate TV list

An extensive listing of television shows for those rare times when you're *not* surfing the Internet.

Address: `http://www.tvnet.com/UTVL/utvl.html`

Buena Vista MoviePlex marquee

Address: `http://www.wdp.com/BVPM/MooVPlex.html`

Welcome to Pizza Hut

Address: `http://www.pizzahut.com/`

Useless WWW pages

Address: `http://www.chaco.com/useless`

Origami

Address: `http://www.datt.co.jp/Origami/`

David Letterman

Address: `http://www.yahoo.com`

Search for `Letterman` (this one changes often!).

The Power Rangers

Address: `http://kilp.media.mit.edu:8001/power/homepage.html`

Jumping-Off Points

These Web pages give you access to powerful search engines that search the Web for the resources you need or offer thousands of preprogrammed links, usually sorted by subject, to make accessing information as easy as the click of a mouse.

AltaVista

Address: `http://www.altavista.digital.com`

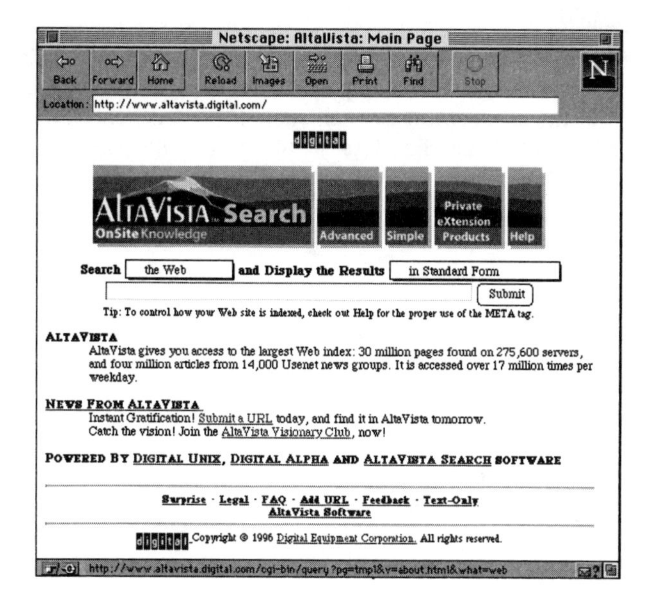

WebCrawler

Address: `http://webcrawler.com`

WWWW — the World Wide Web Worm

Address: `http://www.cs.colorado.edu/home/mcbryan/WWWW.html`

Hooked.Net Launchpoint

Address: `http://www.hooked.net/`

Netsurfer Digest

Address: `http://www.netsurf.com/nsd/index.html`

The Whole Internet Catalog

Address: `http://gnn.com/wic/wics/index.html`

The well-connected Mac

Address: `http://www.macfaq.com/`

What's cool

Address: `http://home.mcom.com/home/whats-cool.html`

ElNet Galaxy

Address: `http://www.einet.net/`

Yahoo!

I've saved one of the best for last! Here's the granddaddy of all link sites. Yahoo! provides *thousands* of subject-sorted links to Web pages from around the globe. The education category at this site is an excellent place to begin most any search. You'll also find lots of Yahoo! spin-offs, like the popular kid-ready search site, Yahooligans!

Address: `http://www.yahoo.com/`

Part VI
Appendixes

"I don't mean to hinder your quest for knowledge, however it's not generally a *good* idea to try to download the entire Internet."

In this part . . .

I once asked a 6th grade Life Science student, "What's your appendix do?" His reply was, "I don't know, but my mom just had hers taken out, and we're waiting around to see what doesn't work anymore." (You should've heard what the same kid said when we talked about the brain!)

These appendixes are designed for those of you who, like me, occasionally stare at the computer and think, "It doesn't work anymore." I've stuffed into these chapters a huge list of what to do when things go wrong, some cyberterms defined in plain English, and a brand-new mega-list of international Web sites for you to visit.

At least we can all escape to Europe on the Web! (How many days until summer vacation?)

Appendix A

When Things Go Wrong

Murphy's Laws are alive and well in the classroom. From time to time, hardware and software seem to become possessed by mischievous spirits that are bent on making your life miserable.

When you are using the Internet and Internet tools, you find that some things are unavoidable — problems such as busy signals and data that just doesn't move from place to place the way it should.

Here are a few basic tips that can save you some trouble. I've divided the tips into the Internet, hardware, software, and a special section for modems (*Nightmare on Internet Street*).

The Internet

You guessed it. Sometimes there's absolutely nothing wrong with your hardware or your software. It's the network. This situation may be the most frustrating kind of problem, because you're pretty helpless to do anything about it. Caution: These errors usually occur right in the middle of a major project, a major presentation, or anytime your principal or superintendent or department chairperson signs on to the Net.

Is it busy, or is it dead?

Web browsers like Netscape Navigator often display a message like this:

```
A network error occurred: unable to connect to server [TCP
Error: EBADF] or "Error 404 - Server not available." The
server may be down or unreachable.
```

Argggghhh! This can mean one of four things:

- The server is too busy. Your connection's fine, but a couple thousand folks are ahead of you, clicking their hearts out to get to the site.
- The server is temporarily or permanently "sick" because of technical problems.
- The pipeline is clogged (the network's just too busy).
- You mistyped the URL (this one you CAN do something about!).

In general, if you get the error described above, try retyping the URL or waiting a few minutes before you try logging on again.

Picture pains

Sooner or later you run into an icon that looks like a "broken picture." That means the images are unreadable because of bad or missing data, or because your connection is flaky.

Usually, you can just click the "broken picture" icon and the picture reloads. Sometimes you can also click the "re-load" button in Netscape and it reloads the entire page, "fixed" graphics and all.

Troubleshooting the Hardware

If you've been teaching for any time at all, you know that the number-one rule in troubleshooting a classroom computer is to check for mischief. Curious students who are well meaning, or not so well meaning, can wreak havoc with a click of the mouse or a kick of a plug.

It's dark in here!

When nothing shows up on your monitor, check the power plug and the physical computer-to-monitor connection and make sure that everything's OK. Also check the display controls to make sure that someone hasn't put you in the dark with a twist of the brightness or contrast knobs.

Crash and burn

Sometimes your computer will "freeze" while it is connected to the Internet. This problem usually indicates some kind of memory conflict or a corruption in your software. The solution varies according to what type of computer you're using and how you're accessing the Internet.

If you are using a PC that is running Windows and it freezes, the best thing to do is restart it. Turning your machine off breaks the telephone/network connection and frees up whatever was blocking your transmission. If a simple reboot doesn't work, the next step is to try reinstalling your Internet software program. Still having trouble? Check to make sure that you're not running too many programs at once.

If crashes or screen-freezes happen frequently and you're using a Macintosh, try increasing the memory allocation for the program.

Here's how to increase the memory allocation for a Macintosh program (application):

1. **Single-click the program icon.**
2. **Choose Get Info from the File menu.**
3. **Increase the number in the bottom Preferred size box by about 200 or so.**
4. **Close the dialog box.**
5. **Double-click the program icon to restart the program.**

Ultimately, the solution may be to purchase more RAM for your Macintosh or Windows-compatible computer. I recommend a minimum of 8MB for today's Internet applications, and 16MB is optimum on a Power Mac or a PC running Windows 95.

Troubleshooting the Software

If things just aren't going well as your Internet journey begins, you should examine your software and the settings that enable you to make a connection to the Net. Check to make sure you've entered the correct IP address and other information into your PPP/SLIP or network connection software. (The Cheat Sheet in the front of this book gives you a good idea of what questions to ask.)

If you are connected to the Net through a commercial online service, visit the online support areas or call the toll-free help lines for assistance. If you're connected via a commercial Internet service provider (ISP), give them a call and seek their advice. Because much of the software for SLIP or PPP connections is freeware or shareware, ready assistance from the programmers may not be available. Your ISP has probably heard your question a thousand times before and can probably help you.

Undeliverable mail

Four things can cause your mail to be returned. Look for the reason in the "bounce" message that you receive from the host computer. Here are the most common reasons that mail doesn't get through and some ways to correct the problems.

- **Host unknown:** The Internet doesn't recognize the domain name that you entered. Check to make sure that you entered the correct address. Check your spelling, spacing, and punctuation!
- **User unknown:** The mail made it to the host computer but not to the person's address in the memory banks. Again, check to ensure that you haven't made a spelling boo-boo and resend the mail. Also, try sending a request for a correct address to `postmaster@domain` (see Chapter 10 for information on how to do this e-mail stuff).
- **Can't send:** Something's up, and the host is down. The best way to fight this problem is to wait an hour or so and try to resend your mail.
- **Service unavailable:** You've addressed your mail correctly, but the electronic postmaster is out to lunch. Sometimes this message means that the postmaster is just too busy to pay attention to your mail. Resend it later.

Network nasties

If you're connecting to the Internet through a computer that's in a network, problems in accessing the Internet may be the result of improperly configured network software. These problems can occur if you abort the program unexpectedly (thunderstorms, children tripping over cables, or turning off your computer after it freezes). Check with your network administrator to make sure that you have all the software, as well as rights and privileges, that you need to make the connection.

The Modem and the Phone Line

Several problems can ruin your day when it comes to working with your modem and phone lines. Call-waiting, noise on the line, and software that's configured incorrectly for your modem are a few of the more common problems.

Custom calling features

If your school has call-waiting, you can temporarily disable it by adding *70 or 1170 before the phone number. The resulting dial-up number may look like this:

```
1170,555-1212
```

This trick disables call-waiting only for the time that you're online. After you hang up, call-waiting resumes as usual.

Can't connect

If your dial-up connection doesn't seem to work, check the software settings described in the documentation for your modem. Do they include a set of configurations (drivers) for your specific modem type? If so, are those configurations properly set up on your computer?

If you're connecting via SLIP or PPP, check to see that all the numbers (IP address and so on) look correct. (After you get the information that you need from your Internet provider, use the form provided in Chapter 4 to record it.) Double-check to see that your modem cable is plugged in to the correct port on your computer.

If you're using a dial-up connection that's made via a telecommunications program, problems with software settings can often be signaled by random characters transmitted to your screen. That on-screen gibberish usually indicates that something in your modem setup is incorrect. Compare the settings with those provided by your Internet provider and correct them before you redial.

Noisy things

Noise can come from poorly installed wiring; cheaply constructed modems, interference from radios, TVs, and other electronic equipment; or even from the phone company itself. Now, everyone knows that schools traditionally have the highest quality phone wiring, right? If you're always getting dropped (or in computer terms, *punted*), you can ask the phone company to check for noise on your lines. The faster the connection speed, the more important a clean (noise-free) line becomes.

Phone extension roulette

If more than one phone in your school uses the same line, consider purchasing an in-use indicator box. These handy boxes are available at most electronics stores and can save you lots of grief. When someone else in the school is on the line, an indicator light shows that the line is unavailable.

Moving too slowly

Sometimes things just don't seem to be moving fast enough. In that case, the software may not be set to recognize your modem or connection speed. Dial-up numbers are different for some modem speeds. A 2400 bps number, for example, won't support faster connections. Check with your Internet service provider or commercial online service to make sure that the dial-up number you're using matches the speed that you want to use.

No dial tone

If you have everything connected but can't get a dial tone when your modem attempts to dial, something's up with your phone line. If you have an in-line switch that controls who accesses a telephone line, make sure that it's switched so that your extension is hot.

If you are dialing out for the first time and can't get a dial tone, your school's phone system may not support direct dial out. Check with the maintenance folks; you may need a dedicated phone line.

Appendix B
Glossary

address

A bunch of letters and/or numbers that tell the world who you are, followed by more letters and numbers that tell them where you are. Your Internet address looks something like this: `username@domain name`. The username is your login name or account number. The domain name is the name of the computer through which you're connected to the Internet. The domain name can be a few words strung together with periods. An Internet address usually doesn't have any spaces between words or symbols, but when there are spaces, they are indicated by an "underscore" character, as in `fredf@bedrock_slate.com`

alt

A newsgroup that deals with "alternative" topics. It's often thought of as the place where topics are born. When they grow up, they move to other classifications. Beware when you are stomping around in `alt.` territory; some things in the bushes shouldn't be in your classroom.

America Online

AOL. A public online service that has access to the Internet. AOL has the largest U.S. subscription base of any of the commercial online services. Many of its subscribers are educators.

Anarchie

A Macintosh shareware FTP program that does Archie searches. Find it on most commercial online services, or check popular FTP sites.

anonymous FTP

When you log on to someone else's computer, you may need to provide a login name and password. On some systems, logging in as "anonymous" and using your e-mail address as a password are enough to give you access to public files.

Archie

A bunch of servers that keep track of all the files that are available for downloading on the Internet. It's also the name of a program that you use to search these servers. After Archie finds a file, you can get it by using FTP.

ARPAnet

The granddaddy network of the Internet. An acronym for Advanced Research Project Administration Network.

ASCII

American Standard Code for Information Interchange. Another word for characters (letters and numbers) in a text file.

baud

A unit of transmission speed. The greater the baud rate, the faster data moves from point to point.

BBS

Bulletin Board System. A system that lets people post messages and read others' messages. Usenet newsgroups are kind of like the world's largest distributed BBS.

binary file

A file that may contain words, sounds, pictures, and even movies in its "raw form." Because binary code is the most basic form of digital information interchange, it can be read or executed by many different types of computers.

binhex

A program that converts a binary file, specific to a particular machine, to a text file so it can be transferred over the Net. The program can then be used to convert it back to binary for use on your computer.

bounce

When you send e-mail and it comes back marked as undeliverable.

browser

A program that enables you to explore the World Wide Web (WWW).

CGI (Common Gateway Interface)

A programming standard used by Web servers for handling user input in forms. A CGI is an extension to a Web server that gives the server some functionality that it doesn't already have (such as database access).

chat

The electronic equivalent of CB radio. Person-to-person real-time conferencing.

communications program

A program that enables you to dial through a modem and access another computer. Examples are Microphone and Z-Term for Macintosh computers and CrossTalk and Procomm Plus for computers that are running Windows.

CompuServe

The granddaddy of all online communications networks. Focuses mostly on the business user.

cyberspace

The digital world of computers and the information that passes between them. Comes from the sci-fi novel *Neuromancer* by William Gibson.

dial-up connection

You've got one of these if you access a network or the Internet by dialing a telephone number. The opposite, a *direct* connection, means the computer is always hooked into the Net.

digest

A compilation of a bunch of messages posted to a mailing list. The mailing list's moderator puts all the messages together periodically, by topic, and sends them out to all subscribers.

DNS

Domain Name Server. Geek-speak for converting Internet IP addresses, like `182.156.12.24`, to Internet addresses like `mit.edu`. If you have your own DNS server, you can subdivide your site into your own unique domain names (`phs.edu` or `maryvillemiddle.edu`, for example).

domain name

Internet-speak for a computer on the Net. The part of an Internet address that comes after @.

dotted quad

The techno-weenie words that describe a numerical Internet address such as this one: `128.33.43.55`.

download

To move data from another computer to yours. Compare with *upload*.

edu

An Internet identifier for a college, university, or K–12 school.

elm

A UNIX mail program. Compare to *pine*.

e-mail

Electronic mail. Messages sent via modem or over a network.

Eudora

A terrific mail program for Macintosh or Windows computers. Both a shareware and a commercial version are available.

FAQ

Frequently Asked Questions. Commonly asked questions about a variety of topics, including learning the Internet. Reading FAQs saves you a great deal of time and embarrassment. You find FAQs in public areas of most FTP sites and in the Internet areas of commercial online services.

Fetch

A handy Macintosh FTP program from Dartmouth that enables you to transfer files.

Finger

A program that displays information about people on the Internet. If you're on a UNIX network, the finger command tells you who's currently using the system. On an Internet host computer, running the program lets you know a user's full name and the last time that user logged on to the Net.

flame

A sarcastic, critical, or obnoxious message posted to a newsgroup or sent via e-mail. Flames are neither nice nor necessary.

FTP

File Transfer Protocol. A method of transferring files across the Internet from one computer to another. Also refers to the name of a program that transfers files.

gateway

A computer that connects one network with another network when the two networks use different protocols.

GIF

Graphics Interchange Format. A kind of universal picture file that Macintoshes, computers that are running Windows, and most other computers running most other operating systems can read by using a program called a GIF Viewer.

Gopher

A program that runs on Internet host computers and helps you find information on the Net. The results are displayed via menus and can include documents and links to other computers. To get to Gopher, either launch a program such as TurboGopher or telnet to a Gopher server.

Gopherspace

That great area that Gopher searches on the Internet.

HGopher

A Microsoft Windows program that enables you to gopher information in a graphics-based environment.

home page

The first page you see when you launch your Web browser.

host

A computer that offers resources that are usable by Internet users. You can access a host computer via telnet, FTP, or the World Wide Web. Technically, in TCP/IP, any machine connected via IP is considered a *host* computer.

HTML

HyperText Markup Language. The language used to create a page for the World Wide Web. The commands enable users to specify different fonts, graphics, hypertext links, and more. You can use a word processor to create a Web page if you know the HTML commands to embed.

HTTP

HyperText Transfer Protocol. The way World Wide Web pages are transferred over the Web. Every Web address begins with `http://`

hypertext

Text found on Web pages that you can click to go to another location, page, or document, or to be linked to sounds, graphics, or movies.

information superhighway

This is a goodie. It means lots of things. Most people think that the Internet *is* the information superhighway. They're mostly right. Stuff such as cable TV and phone company networks also qualify, though.

Internet

A bunch of computers hooked together by high-speed telephone lines and networks. The whole is greater than the sum of the parts.

IP

Internet Protocol. Techno-speak for the language that computers use to route information from computer to computer on the Internet.

IRC

Internet Relay Chat. A system that enables Internet users to *chat,* or talk in real-time, by using an Internet link (rather than after a delay, as with e-mail messages).

Java

A programming language that gives your browser added functions (such as animated icons and text) and that can also be translated to your computer's hard drive in the form of little programs (called *applets*) that make Web pages "live" and interactive.

JPEG

A compressed file format for pictures.

Jughead

A program that helps you search Gopherspace. Compare to *Veronica.*

k12

A type of newsgroup that contains lots of great stuff for educators.

LISTSERV

A family of programs that automatically controls, sorts, and distributes incoming messages on a mailing list server.

MacTCP

An extension that enables your Macintosh to connect to the Internet. (On newer Macintosh computers, this control panel is replaced with TCP/IP.)

MIME

A standard for attaching binary files for sending across the Internet. MIME stands for Multipurpose Internet Mail Extensions.

mirror site

A duplicate of a Web or FTP site. Mirror sites help reduce the traffic by enabling users to choose from sites geographically closer to them.

modem

A marvelous piece of electronics that translates what you type and create on your computer into a signal that can be sent through a phone line and recreated by another modem on the other end.

moderated

In newsgroups and mailing lists, it means that someone's watching the list or newsgroup to ensure that people don't go crazy and get off the topic or start flaming other users.

MPEG

A compressed file format for movies.

network

Basically, a bunch of computers strung together by wire. They could be wired together at one site (local area networks, or LANs) or be connected via telephone or satellite (wide area networks, or WANs).

newbie

Someone who's new to the Internet. I must still be a newbie, because I discover something new every time I log on.

newsgroup

A bulletin board system on the Internet that's organized by topic.

newsreader

A program that enables you to read and respond to newsgroups on the Internet easily.

node

A computer that's hooked to the Internet.

NREN

National Research and Education Network. An effort to bring high-speed computing to schools everywhere.

pine

A UNIX mail program that's based on elm.

ping

A program that searches to see whether an Internet site is still active.

PKZIP

A file-compression program for DOS and Windows.

PPP

Point to Point Protocol. An alternative to SLIP for dial-in access to the Internet. It's more reli-able, and sometimes faster, than SLIP. A control panel called MacPPP is used to connect to the Internet if you have a dial-in connection.

Project X

An amazing Web organization tool from the gurus at Apple's Advanced Research Labs. Get it free at `http://www.atg.apple.com`

protocol

A set of rules that controls communications on or between networks.

Real Audio

An amazing Web tool that enables you to hear stereo-quality sound through your computer's speakers from downloaded sound files or from "streaming" (continuous) audio from a Web site. (Visit `www.realaudio.com` for more information.)

service provider

A company that supplies you with the connection that you need to access the Internet.

shareware

Software that you download and try out. If you keep the software, you're honor bound to send the author a small fee.

Shockwave

A Netscape Navigator "plug-in" (add-on tool) that enables you to view, in real-time, animation and movies made with Macromedia Director. (Visit `http://www.macromedia.com` for more information.)

SLIP

Serial Line Internet Protocol. A way to connect directly to the Internet so that programs you download come to your local hard drive and not to your information service provider's. If you have a SLIP account, your computer is actually *on* the Internet; it's not just a dumb terminal. If you're SLIP (or direct or PPP) connected, others can telnet to *your* computer, too. A control panel called MacSLIP or InterSLIP is used to connect to the Internet if you have a dial-in connection.

spam

Posting commercial messages to lots of unsuspecting users. A huge no-no on the Internet. (Also a mysterious luncheon meat and the topic of Monty Python skits.)

StuffIt

A Macintosh file-compression program.

StuffIt Expander

A Macintosh file-decompression program.

TCP/IP

Transmission Control Protocol/Internet Protocol. The system or language used between computers (hosts) on the Internet to make and maintain a connection.

telnet

A way to log in to someone else's computer and use their computing resources.

terminal

A stupid, brainless front-end machine that relies on the computing power of a host computer. You can run programs on your computer that make it act like a stupid, brainless computer to enable you to dial in to some host computers.

TurboGopher

A program that enables Macintosh users to access Gopher servers by using a familiar (and friendly) point-and-click interface.

UNIX

A computer operating system. Get *UNIX For Dummies* by John R. Levine and Margaret Levine Young (IDG Books Worldwide, Inc.) to become an instant expert.

upload

To move data from your computer to a host computer. Compare with *download*.

URL

Uniform Resource Locator. Basically, the address of any Gopher, FTP, telnet, or WWW site. URLs for Web pages look like this: `http://www.domain.top-domain`; for a Gopher site, it might be `gopher://domain.top-domain`

Usenet

User's Network. A collection of thousands of newsgroups.

Uuencode/uudecode

Programs that encode and decode newsgroup (and some other) files for sending over the Internet.

Veronica

A Gopherspace search program.

VT100

The thing you enter when a host computer asks for "terminal type."

WAIS

(Pronounced *wayz*). Wide Area Information Server. A system of servers that enables you to search for documents on the Internet.

WinSock

A program that conforms to a set of standards called the Windows Socket API. WinSock programs control the link between Windows software and a TCP/IP program. You need this API if you're using a computer running Windows to connect to the Internet.

World Wide Web

Also known as WWW or the Web. A graphics-rich hypermedia system that enables you to move from site to site with the click of a mouse, collecting great (and not-so-great) information at every step.

Appendix C

International Schools on the WWW

Since the first edition of *The Internet For Teachers,* over 10,000 more schools have created Web pages and posted them to the Internet. In the first edition, I featured a list of hundreds of U.S. schools that had already made the switch from *information consumers* to *information providers* by publishing their own Web pages. In this edition, I supply a partial list of international sites for you and your students to explore. Virtually all are high schools, but a few have links to elementary/primary sites. For an updated list, try visiting a great general education site: `http://www.collegebound.com/keypals/`

If you're interested in a full list of U.S. schools on the Web, visit the Web66 site at `http://web66.coled.umn.edu/`

Be sure to type **http://** before each address given in this list, if you need to do so for your Web browser.

Australia

`www.as.edu.au/`

The Armidale School, Armidale, New South Wales

`www.world.net/~camphigh/`

Campbelltown Performing Arts High School, Campbelltown, New South Wales

`www.magna.com.au/~langy/wcc_top.html`

William Clarke College, Sydney, New South Wales

`impulse.hawkesbury.uws.edu.au/CHS/`

Colo High School, New South Wales

`www.arch.unsw.edu.au/coverdale/`

Coverdale Christian School, Riverstone, New South Wales

`www.ozemail.com.au/~cbrook/`

Cranbrook School, Sydney, New South Wales

`www.ozemail.com.au/~loretonh/`

Loreto Normanhurst, Sydney, New South Wales

`www.ozemail.com.au/~mghslib/`

Macarthur Girls' Technical High School, Parramatta, New South Wales

`www.ozemail.com.au/~pictonhs/index.html`

Picton High School, Picton, New South Wales

`www.ozemail.com.au/~ranbhs/`

Randwick Boys' High School, Randwick, New South Wales

`impulse.hawkesbury.uws.edu.au/JRAHS/`

James Ruse Agricultural High School, New South Wales

`godzilla.zeta.org.au/~stpauls/`

St. Paul's Grammar School, Penrith, New South Wales

`www.opennet.net.au/schools/shoalhavenhs/`

Shoalhaven High School, Nowra, New South Wales

`www.magna.com.au/~wshs/`

Westfields Sports High School, Sydney, New South Wales

`Godzilla.zeta.org.au/~mojo/WileyPark.html`

Wiley Park Girls' High School, Sydney, New South Wales

`www.acgs.qld.edu.au/`

Anglican Church Grammar School, East Brisbane, Queensland

`www.gil.com.au/ozkidz/bac/`

Brisbane Adventist College, Brisbane, Queensland

`www.uq.edu.au/ggs/`

Brisbane Girls' Grammar School, Brisbane, Queensland

`www.uq.edu.au/~zzbrisgr/`

Brisbane Grammar School, Brisbane, Queensland

`www.OntheNet.com.au/~shselano/homepage.html`

Elanora State High School, Elanora, Queensland

`cq-pan.cqu.edu.au/schools/local-schools/ghs/ghs.html`

Glenmore State High School, Rockhampton, Queensland

`www.bushnet.qld.edu.au/schools/herberton_secondary/index.htm`

Herberton Secondary School, Herberton, Queensland

`proteas.client.uq.edu.au/index.htm`

John Paul College, Brisbane, Queensland

`www.uq.oz.au/~zzjoxley/index.html`

Moreton Bay College, Wynnum, Queensland

`www.uq.oz.au/~zzredshs/`

Redcliffe High School, Redcliffe, Queensland

`peg.pegasus.oz.au/~maxlink/stpauls/`

St. Paul's School, Bald Hills, Queensland

`www.opennet.net.au/schools/sote/welcome.html`

The School of Total Education, Warwick, Queensland

`www.onthenet.com.au/~somerset/info.htm`

Somerset College, Mudgeeraba, Queensland

`www.uq.oz.au/~zzlibrar/index.html`

Springwood Central State School, Logan City, Queensland

`www.ozemail.com.au/~stuascho/`

Stuartholme School, Brisbane, Queensland

`www.ozemail.com.au/~bps/`

Blackfriars Priory School, Adelaide, South Australia

`www.ozemail.aust.com/~cbc/index.html`

Christian Brothers College, Adelaide, South Australia

`www.ozemail.com.au/~loretosa/`

Loreto College, Marryatville, South Australia

`www.ozemail.com.au/~reed/mcc/mcchome.html`

Mt. Carmel College, Adelaide, South Australia

`www.ozemail.com.au/~pacslib/index.htm`

Prince Alfred College, Adelaide, South Australia

Austria

`www.iguw.tuwien.ac.at/~brg1/`

BRG, Schottenbastei

`www.cso.co.at/bg19/`

Bundesgymnasium Wien 19, Vienna

`www.borg-graz.ac.at/`

Bundesoberstufenrealgymnasium, Graz

`www.vol.at/HS_Markt/`

Hauptschule Hard-Markt Hard

`www.stams.ac.at/meinhardinum/`

Meinhardinum Stams, Tyrol

`www.geocities.com/Athens/4817/index.html`

Oberstufenrealgymasium der Dioezese, Linz

Belgium

```
www.argo.be/scholen/argo010
```

Atheneum Keerbergen, Keerbergen

```
www.euregio.net/bsstvith/bs.htm
```

Bischofliche Schule Sankt Vith, Sankt Vith

```
www.tornado.be/~euro_mol/index.html
```

European School, Mol

```
www.INet.net/hemaco/
```

Helige-Maagdcollege Dendermonde, Dendermonde

```
www.kuleuven.ac.be/~hchrist/ihfen.htm
```

Holy Family Institute, Tielt

```
www.club.innet.be/~pub00953/
```

Instituut Berkenboom, Sint Niklaas

```
www.club.innet.be/~pub01229/
```

Instituut Stella Michelbeke, Matutina

```
www.argo.be/scholen/argo011/index.htm
```

Koninklijk Antheneum Merksem, Antwerp

```
www.club.innet.be/~ind1428
```

Lemmensinstituut, Louvain

```
www.kuleuven.ac.be/~hchrist/olvct
```

O.L.V. College, Tienen

```
ns.hookon.be/St-Lievens
```

Oudercomite Sint-Lievenscollege Ghent, Ghent

```
www.kuleuven.ac.be/~hchrist/slc.htm
```

Sint-Lievenscollege, Antwerpen

```
www.club.innet.be/~pub00841
```

Vrije Handelsschool St. Isidorus, Sint Niklaas

```
www.club.innet.be/~pub.006281/
```

Vris Handelsinstituut Deinze-Michiels-Brugge

Bermuda

```
www.bbsr.edu/~gprep/homepage.html
```

St. Georges Prep School

Czech Republic

```
www.cuni.cz/zborovska/
```

High School Zborovska, Prague

Denmark

```
www.aalborges.dk
```

Aalborg Handelsskole, Aalborg

```
www.aats.dk
```

Aalborg Tekniske Skole, Aalborg

```
www.cybernet.dk/users/frbarfod/
```

Frederik Barfods Skole, Copenhagen

```
www.herningts.dk
```

Herning Tekniske Skol, Herning

```
www.nrsbgym.dk/
```

Noerresundby Gymnasium

```
www.n-kh.dk/
```

Nyborg-Kerteminde, Nyborg

```
inet.uni-c.dk/~rung-gym/
```

Rungsted Gymnasium, Rungsted

`www.skivets.dk/`

Skive Tekniske, Skive

Estonia

`www.keila.edu.ee`

Keila Gumnaasium

`www2.edu.ee/~cougar/`

Kohila

`www2.edu.ee/~klas/rrg.html`

Rakvere Reaalgumnaasium, Laane-Virumaa

`www.oesel.ee/kg/index.html`

Kuressaare Gumnaasium, Saaremaa

`www2.edu.ee/~sven/ppeda.html`

Tallinna Pedagoogiline Seminar, Tartumaa

`www2.edu.ee/~georg/nrg/`

Tartu M. Harma Gumnaasium, Tartumaa

Finland

`kala.jyu.fi/vkoulu/aki/honkolaa/index.html`

Honkola Primary School, Äänekoski

`www.mankkaaya.fi/`

Mankkaa Comprehensive School, Espoo

`voimax.voima.jkl.fi/`

Voionmaan Koulu, Jyväskylä

France

`www-inln.unice.fr/~delerue/college/`

College de Menton, Menton

```
sunsite.unc.edu/isp/
```

International School of Paris, Paris

Germany

```
www.educat.hu-berlin.de/schulen/avh
```

Alexander von Humboldt Gymnasium, Berlin

```
www.uni-stuttgart.de/External/chf/chf-home.html
```

Barufskolleg fuer Chemie und Umwelt, Stuttgart

```
www.uni-duisburg.de/HRZ/BBS/bbs.htm
```

Berufliche Schulen, Moers

```
www.informatik.uni-oldenburg.de/~reinfel/caeci.html
```

Cacilienschule Oldenburg, Oldenburg

```
www.hh.schule.de/christianeum/
```

Christianeum, Hamburg

```
www.educat.hu-berlin.de/schulen/coubertin/
```

Coubertin Gymnasium, Berlin

```
members.aol.com/uberger/www/mgf.htm
```

Das Maristengymnasium Fuerstenzell, Fuerstenzell, Bavaria

```
www.uni-karlsruhe.de/~za220/htm/dbs.htm
```

Dietrich Bonhoeffer Schule, Weinheim, Wuerttemberg

```
www.est.fn.bw.schule.de/
```

Elektronikschule Tettnang Baden-Wuerttemberg

```
ourworld.compuserve.com/homepages/els/
```

Ernst-Ludwig-Schule, Bad Nauheim

```
www.rz.uni-frankfurt.de/~fxfdg227/
```

Friedrich Dessauer Gymnasium, Frankfurt

`www.Worms.Fh-Rpl.DE/Gauss-Gymnasium`

Gauss Gymnasium, Worms

`www.geocities.com/RainForest/1335/`

Gewerbliche und Hauswirtschaftlich-Sozialpflegerische Schulen, Emmendingen

`www.uni-karlsruhe.de/~za101/index.html`

Leopold-Feigenbutz-Realschule, Oberderdingen

`abulafia.osgo.ks.he.schule.de/Lichtenberg/`

Lichtenberschule, Kassel Hessen

`www.zfn.uni-bremen.de:80/~oegym`

Oekumenisches Gymnasium, Bremen

`192.253.114.31/Home.html`

Patch American High School, Stuttgart

`www.belwue.de/rs-renningen/home.html`

Realschule Renningen, Renningen

`www.uni-karlsruhe.de/~za204/`

Theodor-Heuss-Gymnasium, Muehlacker

`www.tu-chemnitz.de/~fischer/wbg1.html`

Waldenburg High School, Waldenburg

Greece

`www.ellinogermaniki.gr/`

Ellinogermaniki Agogi High, Athens

Hungary

`www.jate.u-szeged.hu/csongrad/niifp/bethlen/index.htm`

Bethlen Gabor Reformatus Gimnazium, Szonyi

Iceland

`rvik.ismennt.is/~manic/fva`

Fjolbrautaskoli Vesturlands a Akranesi, Reykjavik

`rvik.ismennt.is/~sigbern/fa/forsida.html`

Fjolbrautaskolinn vid Armula, Reykjavik

`rvik.ismennt.is/~hlynur/`

Heradsskolinn High, Reykholt

`rvik.ismennt.is/~mh/`

Menntaskolinn vio Hamrahlio, Reykjavik

Indonesia

`www.lava.net/~fsaelan/kemang/kemang.htm`

Al-Azhar Kemang High School, Jakarta

`web.mit.edu/user/r/h/rhandojo/www/PL/PL.html`

Pangudi Luhur High School, Jakarta

`futon.sfsu.edu/%7emartinw/CC/cc.html`

Canisius High School, Jakarta

Ireland

`www.iol.ie/~ckgrlsck`

Christ King Girls Secondary School, County Cork

`www.iol.ie/esp/webpages/colennad.html`

Colaiste Eannan, Dublin

`classroom.broadcom.ie/gsns`

Good Shepherd National School, Dublin

`www.iol.ie/~frcost`

Grange Community College, Dublin

`www.iol.ie/~frcost/`

Grange Community College, Dublin, Leinster

`www.iol.ie/~kingshos`

The King's Hospital, Dublin

`www.iol.ie/~mtstmchl`

Mount Saint Michael Secondary School, County Mayo

`www.iol.ie/esp/webpages/pressec.html`

Presentation Secondary School, Wexford

`www.iol.ie/~stdavids`

Saint David's Boys National School, Artane

`www.iol.ie/~stopscod`

Saint Oliver Plunkett School, Malahide

Israel

`www.amhsi.com/html/page4.html`

The Alexander Muss High School

`www.gilo.jlm.K12.il`

Gilboa High School

`www1.snunit.k12.il/snunit_e/hatzor/sch2.htm`

Hatzor HaGlilit High School

`www.leyada.jlm.k12.il/`

Hebrew University High School

`www1.snunit.k12.il/snunit_e/school/main.htm`

High School for Environmental Studies, Midreshet Ben Gurion, Negev

`http://www.leyada.jlm.K12.il`

Leyada High School

```
http://www1.snunit.k12.il/snunit_e/reut.htm
```

Reut

Italy

```
sit.iuav.unive.it/~mfosc/index.html
```

Giunasio Liceo MarcoFoscarini, Venice

```
omeganet.italnet.it/itis/pysellis.htm
```

Instituto Industriale Statale "E Fermi" Montava, Lombardia

```
www.verbania.alpcom.it/scuole/ferrini/ferrini.html
```

InstitutoTechnico Contardo Ferrini, Verbania

```
www.clio.it/sr/vr/deledda/homedele.html
```

Instituto TecnicoStatale "G. Deledda," Puglia

```
alberti.crs4.it/engl-welcome.html
```

Leon Battista Alberti High School, Cagliari Sardinia

```
www.unibs.it:80/~lunardi/
```

Astolfo Lunardi, Brescia

```
www.mclink.it/n/citrag/
```

Citta' dei Ragazzi di Roma, Rome

```
www.fis.unipr.it./HP_Parma/scuola/itis_pr/
```

ITIS Leonardo Da Vinci, Parma

```
www.alaska.net/~knutson/Naples/Index.html
```

Forrest Sherman High School, Naples

Japan

```
www.daimon-hs.daimon.toyama.jp/
```

Daimon High, Daimon Toyama

```
www.kyoto-chs.fushimi.kyoto.jp/index-e.html
```

Kyoto Commercial High School, Kyoto

```
www.bekkoame.or.jp/~futagami/
```

Futagami Technical High School, Toyama

```
www.hamako-ths.hamamatsu.shizuoka.jp/index-e.html
```

Hamamatsu Technical High School, Hamamatsu Shizuoka

```
www.iino-hs.suzuka.mie.jp/
```

Iino High School, Suzuka Mie

```
www.bekkoame.or.jp/~johoku/
```

Johoku Junior High School, Okazaki Aich

```
inetsv1.kaizukita-hs.hirata.gifu.jp/
```

Kaizukita High School, Hirata Gifu

```
inetsv1.kawashima-jhs.kawashima.gifu.jp/
```

Kawashima Junior High School, Kawashima Gifu

```
fzkjhss.fzk.yamanashi.ac.jp/
```

Kofu Junior High School, Kofu Yamanashi

```
www.komatsu-ths.komatsu.ishikawa.jp/
```

Komatsu Technical High School, Komatsu Ishikawa

```
www.educa.nagoya-u.ac.jp/huzoku/index-e.html
```

Nagoya University School of Education Affiliated Junior-Senior High School, Nagoya Aichi

```
www.tokai-ic.or.jp/Schoolnet/Contribution/Billings-Nakamura/
            Nakamura/indexE.html
```

Nakamura High School, Nagoya Aichi

```
www.nanzan-intlhs.toyota.aichi.jp/index.html
```

Nanzan Kokusai High School, Toyota Aichi

```
www.ed.niigata-u.ac.jp/niigata_jh/home.html
```

Niigata Junior High School, Niigata Niigata

```
marcer.nagaokaut.ac.jp/kumagai/
```

Sakae Junior High School, Sakae Niigata

```
www.seiryo.ac.jp/koukou.html
```

Seiryo High School, Kanazawa Ishikawa

```
www.skg.shimizu.shizuoka.jp/index.html
```

Shimizu Kokusai High School, Shimizu Shizuoka

```
www.tcp-ip.or.jp/~tahara/index.html
```

Tahara Junior High School, Tahara Aichi

```
www.city.joetsu.niigata.jp/education/tchs/tchs.html
```

Takada Commercial High School, Jyoetsu Niigata

```
pathy.fujita-hu.ac.jp/taki-net/
```

Taki High School, Konan Aichi

```
oakserv.nishi-hs.fuchu.toyama.jp/
```

Toyama-nishi High School, Fuchu Toyama

```
yamura-ths.tsuru.yamanashi.jp/
```

Yamura Technical High School, Tsuru Yamanashi

```
www.chofu-jhs.shimonoseki.yamaguchi.jp/
```

Chofu Junior High School, Shimonoseki Yamaguchi

```
www.ipc.hiroshima-u.ac.jp/~rose/
```

Fukuyama Junior-Senior High School, Fukuyama Hiroshima

```
133.62.191.5/Default-E.HTML
```

Hikari Junior High School, Hikari Yamaguchi

```
www.bekkoame.or.jp/~asahinam/
```

Miyoshi Technical High School, Miyoshi Hiroshima

`muscat.okadaifu-jhs.okayama.okayama.jp/`

Okayama University Junior High School, Okayama Okayama

`www.urban.or.jp/home/goldryu/pta.html`

Shiratake Junior High School, Kure Hiroshima

`taisya.taisya-jhs.taisha.shimane.jp/welcomee.html`

Taisya Junior High School, Taisya Shimane

`www1.meshnet.or.jp/konan/`

Tamano Kohnan Senior High School, Tamano Okayama

`202.249.136.2/`

Yonago Minami Commercial High School, Yonago Tottori

`kids.glocom.ac.jp/netcloak.acgi$arekinai_OP`

Arekinai Junior High School, Shibecha Hokkaido

`ice.iwa.hokkyodai.ac.jp/schools/miruto/miruto_e.html`

Miruto Junior High School, Kurisawa Hokkaido

Luxembourg

`www.restena.lu/ecole_europ/ee_home.html`

European School

`www.restena.lu/al/alhome.html`

Lycée Athénée de Luxembourg

`www.restena.lu/lce/`

Lycée Classique d'Echternach

`www.restena.lu/lge/home.html`

Lycée de Garçons Esch-sur-Alzette

`www.restena.lu/lmr/lmrhome.html`

Lycée de Michel-Rodange

`www.restena.lu/lrsl/lrshome.html`

Lycée Robert-Schuman

`www.restena.lu/ltecg/ecghome.html`

Lycée Technique Ecole de Commerce et de Gestion

Macau

`www.macau.net/~liceu/liceumacau.html`

Macau High School

Malaysia

`www.jaring.my/iskl/`

International School of Kuala Lumpur, Kuala Lumpur

Marshall Islands

`http://www.aloha.net/~spartan/`

Kwajanlein Junior/Senior High School

Netherlands

`www.iaehv.nl/users/apla/guusschool.html`

Bijenkorfschool r.k.Jenaplan-basisschool, Eindhoven Noord-Brabant

`www.dsl.nl/davinci/`

Da Vinci College, Leiden

`dse.iaehv.nl/onderwijs/voortgezet/eckart/basis.htm`

Eckart College, Eindhoven

`www.dse.nl/onderwijs/voortgezet/lorentz/`

Het Lorentz Lyceum

`www.abc.nl/ISA/`

International School of Amsterdam, Amsterdam

`www.publishnet.nl/~maerlant/`

Maerlant College, Brielle

`www.eur.nl/ROTAN/vwo/montessori/index.htm`

Montessori Lyceum Rotterdam, Rotterdam

`www.pi.net/~grundel/home.html`

Scholengemeenschap De Grundel, Hengelo

`ddh.bart.nl/digischool/`

SG Dalton-Vatel, Voorburg

`www.cs.vu.nl/~mmeijers/Jansenius.html`

SG Jansenius, Hulst

Norway

`soliton.wave.no/edu/birralee/`

Biralee International School, Trondheim

`www.tjener.uninett.no/~hosltops/`

Hosletoppen Skole, Baerum

`www.nls.no/viking/ostersund/ostersund-intro.html`

Østersund Middle School, Fetsund

`gudmund.vgs.no/ytrebygda/`

Ytrebygda, Skole, Bergen

Poland

`idsserv.waw.ids.edu.pl/ids/school/liceum2/.index.html`

Batory High School, Warszawa

`www.v-lo.krakow.pl/`

Fifth Secondary School, Cracow

`idsserv.waw.ids.edu.pl/ids/school/lolopole/.index.html`

First Secondary School, Opole

```
www.waw.pdi.net/~pslo/
```

I Spolecznc Liceum Ogolnoksztalcace, Warsaw

```
iris.ids.uni.wroc.pl/lo9/index.html
```

IX Liceum Ogolnoksztalcace imenia Juliusza, Slowackiego, Wroclaw

```
idsserv.waw.ids.edu.pl/ids/school/loolecko/loolecko.html
```

Jan Kochanowski Grammar School, Olecko

```
www.vlo.ids.gda.pl/
```

V Liceum Ogolnoksztalcace, Gdansk

```
pcl.xlo.torun.pl
```

X Liceum Ogolnoksztalcac

Portugal

```
educom.fct.unl.pt/~ebiahrcl/
```

Escola Alexandre Herculano

Romania

```
ldc.sfos.ro/
```

Dimitrie Cantemir High School

Russia

```
www.ort.spb.ru/school_e.htm
```

International School of General Education, St. Petersburg

Singapore

```
www.acs.ac.sg/
```

Anglo-Chinese School

```
www.commerceasia.com/germanctre/gschool/index.htm
```

German School

```
raffles.org/rgspage.html
```

Raffles Girls School

`www.raffles.org/ripage.html`

Raffles Institution

`www.moe.ac.sg/schools/srjc/welcome.html`

Serangoon Junior College

`www.moe.ac.sg/schools/vs/index.html`

Victoria School

Slovakia

`www.upjs.sk/Gymnazia/Trebisovska/index.html`

Gymnazium Trebisovska 12, Kosice

Slovenia

`www.s-gimb.lj.edus.si/`

Gimnazija Bezigrad, Lubljana

`stenar.arnes.si/guest/sskkssb2s/index.html`

Gimnazia Brelice

`stenar.arnes.si/guest/smsgfmls/index.html`

Gimnazia Franca Miklosica

`www.s-gms.ms.edus.si/`

Gimnazia Murska Sobota

`stenar.arnes.si/guest/gljpoljane7/index.html`

Gimnazia Poljane, Ljubljana SI, Trbovlje

`stenar.arnes.si/guest/glvic2s/index.html`

Gimnazia Vic, Ljubljana

South Africa

`www.dc.wcape.school.za"`

Diocesan College, Cape Town

```
www.mc.pmb.school.za"
```

Maritzburg College, Pietermaritzberg

```
www.shaka.iafrica.com/~uthong/"
```

Uthongathi School, Durban

South Korea

```
seoul-ahs.dsi.net:70/0/HOME.html
```

Seoul American High School, Seoul

Spain

```
www.ocea.es/bis/bis.htm
```

Baleares International School, Baleares

```
www.lander.es/~ealemanm/index.html
```

Deutsche Schule, Madrid

Sweden

```
www.algonet.se/~adalen/
```

Adalsskolan High, Kramfors

```
www.bor.skolinternet.telia.se/
```

Bor's Högstadieskola, Värnamo

```
www.botfri.se/
```

Botkyrka Friskola

```
194.17.52.2/
```

Dragonskolan Gymnasieskola

```
linnea.asogy.stockholm.se/~eriksdal/
```

Eriksdal School, Stockholm

```
www.odata.se/hotel/friab/fria.htm
```

Friaborgsskolan, Simrishamn Scania

`www.hedbergska.sundsvall.se/`

Hedbergska Skolan, Sundsvall Vesternorrland

`www.geocities.com/Athens/2595/index.html`

Hogsatra School, Stockholm

`www.jakgym.se/`

Jakobsbergs Gymnasium, Stockholm

`www.netg.se/~lovgarde/le-home.html`

Lövgärdesskolan, Gothenburg

`www.pedc.se/borgar/mbsidet.htm`

Malmo Borgarskola

`www.algonet.se/~matteus/`

Matteus School, Stockholm

`www.mjolner.adbc.se/`

Mjölnerskolan, Torsas

`ledung.roden.se/`

Rodengymasiet, Norrtalje

`www.algonet.se/~sirius/school.htm`

Saltsjöbadens Samskola, Stockholm

`www.algonet.se/~ellenkey`

Secondary Waldorf School

`www.svaneskolan.lund.se/`

Svaneskolan, Lund

`www.tycho.helsingborg.se/`

Tycho Brahe School, Helsingborg

Switzerland

```
www.unil.ch/CESSM
```

CessMorges, Gymnase Cantonel, Morges

```
www.cdl.ch
```

College du Leman International School, Geneva

Taiwan

```
www.ck.tp.edu.tw/
```

Chien-Kuo Senior High School, Taipei

Thailand

```
taygate.au.ac.th/web/isb/
```

International School of Bangkok, Bangkok

Trinidad and Tobago

```
www.caribinfo.com/bahs/
```

Bishop Antsey Girls High School

```
www.wow.net/fatima/
```

Fatima College

Turkey

```
www.bups.bilkent.edu.tr/
```

Bilkent University Preparatory School, Ankara

United Kingdom

```
www.rmplc.co.uk/eduweb/sites/abbhall/
```

Abberley Hall School, Abberley Hall, Worcestershire

```
www.shef.ac.uk/~as/
```

Abbeydale Grange School's Home Page, Sheffield, South Yorkshire

```
www.rmplc.co.uk/eduweb/sites/abschool/index.html
```

Abingdon School, Abingdon

`www.rmplc.co.uk/eduweb/sites/ackworth/index.html`

Ackworth School

`www.rmplc.co.uk/eduweb/sites/ahhs/index.html`

Alec Hunter High School, Braintree, Essex

`www.webzone1.co.uk/www/brainstorm/aveley.htm`

Aveley School, Essex

`www.infm.ulst.ac.uk/~neelb/ballee/ballee.html`

Ballee Community High School, Ballymena

`www.infm.ulst.ac.uk/~neelb/ballycla/ballyhs.html`

Ballyclare High School, Ballyclare

`www.rmplc.co.uk/eduweb/sites/blatch/index.html`

Blatchington Mill School, Hove, Sussex

`www.brakenhale.berks.sch.uk/`

Brakenhale High School, Bracknell, Berkshire

`www.rmplc.co.uk/eduweb/sites/butupper/index.html`

Buttershaw Upper School

`www.infm.ulst.ac.uk/~neelb/carrick/carrhome.html/`

Carrickfergus College, Carrickfergus

`www.tcns.co.uk/cedar/`

The Cedar School, Nursling, Southampton

`www.rmplc.co.uk/eduweb/sites/cherwell/index.html`

Cherwell School, Oxford

`schools.sys.uea.ac.uk/schoolnet/sec/cbs/`

Christian Brothers Secondary School, Belfast

`www.rmplc.co.uk/eduweb/sites/clifton/index.html/`

Clifton High School, Bristol

`user.itl.net/~dhautree/index.html`

d'Hautree School, Jersey Channel Islands

`www.deacons.cambs.sch.uk/`

Deacon's School, Peterborough

`www.iol.ie/esp/webpages/downhigh.html`

Down High School, Downpatrick

`www.cityscape.co.uk/users/dp01/index.html`

Downham Market High School, Norfolk

`www.doc.mmu.ac.uk/EXT/schools/ducie/`

Ducie High, Manchester

`schoolnet.sys.uea.ac.uk/schoolnet/cns/index.html`

Eaton City of Norwich School, Norwich

`www.u-net.com/set/ellenwilkinson/ellen.html`

Ellen Wilkinson High School for the Arts, Manchester

`www.rmplc.co.uk/eduweb/sites/emanuel/index.html`

Emanuel High School

`www.rmplc.co.uk/eduweb/sites/felsted/`

Felsted School, Felsted

`www.rmplc.co.uk/eduweb/sites/libfsl/index.html`

Friends School, Lisburn

`www.efr.hw.ac.uk/heriots/`

George Heriot's School, Edinburgh

`www.infm.ulst.ac.uk/~neelb/glengorm/glengorm.html`

Glengormley High School, Belfast

`www.rmplc.co.uk/eduweb/sites/hatchend/index.html`

Hatch End High School, Harrow, Middlesex

`www.cityscape.co.uk/users/eq48/index.html`

Hemel Hempstead School, Hemel Hempstead

`www.rmplc.co.uk/eduweb/sites/highfi/index.html`

The Highfield School, Letchworth, Hertfordshire

`www.rmplc.co.uk/eduweb/sites/jags/index.html`

James Allen's Girls School, London, England

`www.rmplc.co.uk/eduweb/sites/keschool/index.html`

King Edward's School, Birmingham

`www.i-way.co.uk/~jchapman/lps.htm`

Leighton Park School, Reading, Berkshire

`www.lsst.lincs.sch.uk`

Lincoln School for Science and Technology

`turnpike.net/metro/vollans/lecs.html`

Long Eaton Community School, Nottingham

`www.digital-yorkshire.co.uk/mount/`

The Mount School, York, Yorkshire

`www.rmplc.co.uk/eduweb/sites/oakham/index.html`

Oakham School, Rutland

`www.iol.ie/esp/webpages/omagh.html`

Omagh High School, Omagh

`www.liv.ac.uk/~pensbyb/pensbyboys.homepage.html`

Pensby High School for Boys

`www.rmplc.co.uk/eduweb/sites/qbadmin/index.html`

Queensbridge School, Moseley

`www.infm.ulst.ac.uk/~neelb/rainey/rainey.html`

Rainey Endowed School, Londonderry

`ourworld.compuserve.com/homepages/Richard_Paul/`

Rannoch School, Perthshire

`www.airtime.co.uk/ribblesdale/`

Ribblesdale School, Lancashire

`www.tcns.co.uk/davidw/first.html`

Sandon School, Great Baddow, Chelmsford, Essex

`www.rmplc.co.uk/eduweb/sites/stfelix/`

St. Felix School, Southwold

`ireland.iol.ie/esp/webpages/stlouise.html`

St. Louise's Comprehensive College, Belfast

`www.infm.ulst.ac.uk/~neelb.maghera/pmmaghera.html`

St. Patrick's College, Maghera

`www.infm.ulst.ac.uk/~neelb.stpiusxi/index.html`

St. Pius X School, Maherafelt

`diana.ecs.soton.ac.uk/~pm/StV.html`

St. Vincent College, Gosport

`www.rmplc.co.uk/eduweb/sites/suttonvs/index.html`

Sutton Valence School, Kent

`giraffe.rmplc.co.uk/eduweb/sites/taunton/`

Taunton School, Taunton Somerset

`www.ftech.net/~brit`

The BRIT School for Performing Arts and Technology, Croydon

`www.rmplc.co.uk/eduweb/sites/highfi/index.html`

The Highfield School, Letchworth, Hertfordshire

`www.zynet.co.uk/maynard/Welcome.html`

The Maynard School, Exeter

`user.itl.net/~viccol/`

Victoria College, Jersey

`www.rmplc.co.uk/eduweb/sites/mpjones/index.html`

West Houghton School, Westthoughton, Bolton

Virgin Islands

`http://146.226.202.75/`

Sts. Peter and Paul School

Higher Education

For a list of American and international universities with Web pages, visit the Web site located at:

`www.clas.ufl.edu/`

Appendix D

About *The Internet For Teachers*, 2nd Edition, CD

System Requirements

Your Apple Macintosh, PC, or reasonable facsimile thereof needs to meet the following system requirements. If your computer doesn't meet at least most of these requirements, you may experience problems using this CD.

- A Macintosh with a 68030, 68040, or PowerPC processor or a PC with a 386SX or faster processor
- At least 8MB of total RAM on a PC (Windows 95 users will have better performance with 16MB total RAM) or at least 4MB of free RAM on a Mac. (*Free RAM* is the amount of memory available to the Mac when no other programs are running.)

  In some cases, turning on virtual memory (Macintosh only) helps you if you are a little short of memory, but some demos may run erratically.
- Mac System 7.5 or higher (System 7.1 may be used, but some programs may require System 7.5's special features) or Microsoft Windows 3.1*x*, or Windows 95 installed
- A CD-ROM drive — double speed (2x) or faster
- A monitor capable of displaying at least 256 colors or grayscale
- A modem with a speed of at least 14,400 bps (28,800 bps is recommended)
- A digital camera (optional; needed for videoconferencing software)
- A microphone (optional; needed for videoconferencing and telephony software)
- A sound card with speakers (Macs have this capability built in.)
- A direct Internet connection (AT&T WorldNet Service setup software is included on the CD as a sign-on option.)
- About 30MB (Mac) or 40MB (Windows) of free hard disk space available to install all the software from this CD (You need less space if you don't install every program.)

Before using this CD, I recommend that you install Adobe Acrobat Reader and StuffIt Expander. These programs make it easier for you to install some programs and read the manuals for some of the software. See the installation instructions for StuffIt Expander and Adobe Acrobat Reader in the following section, "What's on the CD."

What's on the CD

Before you install any software, be sure to save any documents you are working on, and close any programs that are currently running.

Windows users need to use their Run command to install most of the software. For most of the programs below, I tell you what to type in the Run dialog box. With the CD inserted in your CD-ROM drive, follow these steps to open the Run dialog box in Windows 3.1 and Windows 95 to begin installation.

1. **Windows 3.1x: From the Program Manager, choose File⇨Run.**

   Windows 95: Click the Start button and then choose Run.

2. **In the Run dialog box that appears, type in the command line for the program you want to install as shown with each description.**
3. **Click OK to begin installation.**

Throughout the installation instructions, I assume that your Windows PC assigns your CD-ROM drive with the letter D. Be sure to substitute your correct drive letter if your CD-ROM drive uses a different letter.

AT&T WorldNet℠ Service, from AT&T

For Windows 3.1, Windows 95, and Macintosh. If you don't have an Internet service provider, I've provided setup software to get you on the Internet with AT&T WorldNet Service. Included with AT&T WorldNet Service is a special version of Netscape Navigator™, a popular World Wide Web browser, and more. A special version of Microsoft Internet Explorer is also included for use with Windows 95.

AT&T WorldNet Service asks you to pay a fee for their service. Before you register for an account, have your credit card handy, and have your modem connected to your computer and phone line.

If you already have an Internet service provider, installing AT&T WorldNet Service may affect your computer's current Internet connection settings, particularly any Netscape Navigator settings. Be sure to back up your settings and your BOOKMARK.HTM file before continuing.

Installing AT&T WorldNet Service registration software

Windows 95 installation (with Netscape Navigator): In the Run dialog box, type in **D:\WORLDNET\WIN95NN\SETUP.EXE**

Windows 95 installation (with Microsoft Internet Explorer): In the Run dialog box, type in **D:\WORLDNET\WIN95IE\SETUP.EXE**

Windows 3.1 installation: In the Run dialog box, type in **D:\WORLDNET\WIN31\SETUP.EXE**

Macintosh installation: On the CD, open the AT&T WorldNet Service folder. Double-click the Install AT&T WorldNet icon.

Follow the on-screen instructions. I recommend that you choose Typical installation. After copying is complete, you're notified that the setup has made necessary changes in your computer's system configuration files to recognize your new software. When you're asked to restart your computer, do so.

Completing account setup

After restarting your computer, you can set up your account:

1. **Windows users: In the AT&T WorldNet Service program group, double-click the icon named, aptly, Double Click to Set Up Account, or Double Click to Register.**

   Mac users: Double-click the Account Setup icon in the AT&T WorldNet Service folder created on your hard disk.

2. **If you have an existing AT&T WorldNet account, be sure to choose the Use Existing Account button. Otherwise, choose Create New Account.**

3. **Click the User Information button when it appears and fill in the necessary personal information.**

4. **In the Modem Setup window, let your computer detect your modem (be sure to have it connected and switched on first). If your computer can't find your modem, choose your modem from the list shown in the window.**

5. **Click the Complete Registration button in the main window when you are done.**

   A window appears, asking you for some details of your phone line. Supply the necessary information and then click the Continue button. The Account Setup program calls an 800 number to connect you to AT&T WorldNet Service to complete the final details.

   If you *don't* get connected, make sure that your modem is connected and switched on and that your phone lines are clear and ready. Also, click the Back button in Account Setup to check your settings. If you still can't connect, call AT&T WorldNet Customer Service at 800-400-1447.

6. **After you're connected, several registration forms appear. Complete these forms and double-check any personal information that you find. Use the PgDn and PgUp keys to snoop around the various options.**

Mac users should pay close attention to the personal information screens, because your version of the Account Setup software may have a bug that places your city, state, and zip code information in the wrong locations in these registration screens. Just retype the information in the correct boxes if you spot such a problem.

7. **Locate the Registration Code text box near the top of the window and click in the box. If you're an AT&T long-distance customer, type the code** L5SQIM631. **If you don't use AT&T as your long-distance carrier, type the code** L5SQIM632.

In the final screens, you are asked to create an e-mail address for yourself, as well as make decisions on other services. After you've completed these items, you're done!

Adobe Acrobat Reader, from Adobe Systems, Inc.

For Windows and Macintosh. Adobe Acrobat Reader is a free program that opens portable document format (PDF) files. PDFs are handy ways to publish electronic documents that contain the same formatting and graphics of a printed document.

Windows 95 installation: In the Run dialog box, type in **D:\ACROBAT\AR32E30.EXE**

Windows 3.1 installation: In the Run dialog box, type in **D:\ACROBAT\AR16E30.EXE**

Macintosh installation: Open the Acrobat folder, double-click the Install Acrobat Reader 3.0 icon, and follow the on-screen instructions.

Claris Emailer Trial, by Claris Corporation

For Macintosh. Claris Emailer is a versatile e-mail program that can handle your e-mail needs not only from the Internet but also from online services such as America Online and CompuServe. This trial version is fully functional but works for only 30 days. More information on Claris Emailer can be found on the Web at `http://www.claris.com`

Installation: Open the Claris Emailer Trial folder on the CD, double-click the Emailer Trial Installer 1.0v3 icon, and follow the on-screen instructions.

Claris Home Page Trial, by Claris Corporation

For Windows 95 and Macintosh. Claris Home Page is one of a brave new line of programs that enable you to create full-featured Web pages quickly and conveniently. This trial version is fully functional for 30 days. More information about Home Page can be found at the Claris Web site at `http://www.claris.com`

Windows 95 installation: In the Run dialog box, type in
D:\HOMEPAGE\CHPDEMO.EXE

Macintosh installation: Open the Claris Home Page folder and double-click the Claris Home Page 30 Day Trial icon to begin.

Enhanced CU-SeeMe 2.0, by White Pine Software

For Windows and Macintosh. Enhanced CU-SeeMe 2.0 is a nifty program that lets you use the (relatively free) Internet to talk to and see other Internet users. To use this software, you need at least a microphone, a PC with a sound card, and speakers. If you like, you can attach a digital camera to your computer. You don't need a camera to see other users with cameras, however. The software is good for a 30-day trial. For more information on Enhanced CU-SeeMe, visit the White Pine Software Web site at `http://www.wpine.com`

Note: Enhanced CU-SeeMe also comes with a copy of Adobe Acrobat Reader. If you choose to install Acrobat Reader during this process, you won't need to install Acrobat Reader again.

Windows 95 installation: In the Run dialog box, type in
D:\CUSEEME\WIN95\C211W32X.EXE

Windows 3.1 installation: In the Run dialog box, type in
D:\CUSEEME\WIN31\C211W16X.EXE

Macintosh installation: Open the Enhanced CU-SeeMe folder and double-click the Install 1 Enhanced CU-SeeMe icon. When asked to enter a serial number, type **DCBE01100KDCWWCA**

Eudora Light, from Qualcomm Incorporated

For Windows and Macintosh. Eudora Light is a popular freeware Internet e-mail program. The latest version of Eudora Light and more information on it's commercial sibling, Eudora Pro, can be found at the Eudora Web site at `http://www.eudora.com`

Windows installation (all versions): In the Run dialog box, type in
D:\EUDORA\EUL301.EXE

After you have Adobe Acrobat Reader installed, you can read the Eudora Light manual EUL3MANL.PDF.

Macintosh installation: Open the Eudora Light folder on the CD, and double-click the Eudora Light 3.0.2 Installer icon. The manual for Eudora Light is a PDF document you can open and read with Adobe Acrobat Reader (included on the CD). After Acrobat Reader is installed, just double-click on the Eudora Light 30x Manual.PDF icon to read it.

Free Agent 1.1, from Forté Corporation

For Windows. Free Agent is a popular freeware Usenet newsgroup reader for PCs. Like Eudora Light, Check out Forte's Web site for more information on Free Agent and its commercial sibling, Agent, at `http://www.forteinc.com`

Windows 95 installation: In the Run dialog box, type in **D:\FREEAGNT\WIN95\AF32-230.EXE**

Windows 3.1 installation: In the Run dialog box, type in **D:\FREEAGNT\WIN31\AF16-230.EXE**

Hampson's Gopher 2.3 (HGOPHER), from Martyn Hampson

For Windows. HGOPHER 2.3 is a neat, free utility to search Gopher sites on the Internet. To install Hgopher, follow these steps:

1. ***Install StuffIt Expander for Windows first.*** **(See the section on StuffIt Expander for its installation instructions).**
2. **Run StuffIt Expander, and choose File⇨Expand.**
3. **In the dialog box that appears, click on the Drives list box at the bottom center and choose your CD-ROM drive (drive D for most of you).**
4. **In the Directories list window, open the HGOPHER folder.**
5. **In the Files window on the left, select HGOPH23.ZIP, and then click OK.**
6. **StuffIt Expander will ask you where to place the program. Select a location on drive C using the dialog box provided, and click OK to finish.**

HyperFTP 1.4, from Douglas Hornig

For Macintosh. HyperFTP is a simple utility to link to FTP sites.

This utility is a HyperCard stack, so you need HyperCard 2.*x* or HyperCard Player to run it. HyperCard Player is a free utility that can be found with older versions of the Mac OS, or you can download the program from the Web site at `http://mirror.apple.com`

Macintosh installation: Open the HyperFTP folder on the CD and double-click the HyperFTP14.sea icon to begin installation.

Internet Coach: Mission to Planet X Lite, by APTE

For Windows. Mission to Planet X Lite is a demo version of APTE's full-featured Internet teaching program for kids. This demo contains audio and video, so you need a sound card to use this software. For more information on APTE's products, check out the Web site at `http://www.apte.com`

This demo runs completely from the CD. You don't need to install the program to your hard disk (you wouldn't want to — the program's over 80MB in size!).

Windows 95: In the Run dialog box, type in **D:\PLANETX\MLITE32.EXE**

Windows 3.1: In the Run dialog box, type in **D:\PLANETX\MLITE16.EXE**

Ircle, from Onno R. Tijdgat

For Macintosh. Ircle is a neat shareware program that enables you to use Internet Relay Chat. The software has an evaluation period of 15 days from installation to your hard disk. Updated versions of Ircle can be found on the Web at `http://www.xs4all.nl/~ircle`

Macintosh installation: To install, drag the Ircle 2.5 folder from the CD to your Mac's hard disk.

JPEGView, from Aaron Giles

For Macintosh. JPEGView is a great way to view the most popular image formats available on the Internet. JPEGView is "postcardware," so send the author a postcard from your hometown if you like the software.

Macintosh installation: Open the JPEGView folder, and drag the JPEGView 3.3.1 folder from the CD to your Mac's hard disk. Inside the JPEGView 3.3.1 folder is an extension named JPEGView JFIF Preview. Place this item in your Mac's Extensions folder, located inside the System Folder.

mIRC, from Khaled Mardam-Bey and mIRC Co. Ltd.

For Windows. Like Ircle for the Mac, mIRC helps you chat away with your PC via Internet Relay Chat. mIRC is shareware.

Windows 95 installation: In the Run dialog box, type in **D:\MIRC\MIRC452T.EXE**

Windows 3.1 installation: In the Run dialog box, type in **D:\MIRC\MIRC452S.EXE**

NSCA Telnet, from the University of Illinois at Urbana-Champaign

For Macintosh. This is versatile terminal emulator for telnet access on your Macintosh. NSCA Telnet is in the public domain (that is, it's free).

Macintosh installation: Open the NSCA Telnet folder on the CD and double-click the NCSA Telnet 2.6 icon. You can also install the documentation by double-clicking the NCSA Telnet 2.5 Docs icon.

Nuntius, by Peter Speck

For Macintosh. Nuntius is a useful, free Usenet newsgroup reader.

If you're in the mood to shop around for other news readers, check out NewsWatcher. You can find it and more software on the Web at `http://www.shareware.com`

Macintosh installation: Drag the Nuntius folder from the CD to your Mac's hard disk.

Paint Shop Pro, from JASC, Inc.

For Windows. Paint Shop Pro is a shareware graphics editing program with versions for Windows 95 and Windows 3.1. You can try out the software for 15 days. The latest version of this and other JASC products can be found on the Web at `http://www.jasc.com`

Windows 95 installation: In the Run dialog box, type in **D:\PSP\WIN95\SETUP.EXE**

Windows 3.1 installation: In the Run dialog box, type in **D:\PSP\WIN31\SETUP.EXE**

StuffIt Expander, from Aladdin Systems

For Windows and Macintosh. StuffIt Expander is a very popular freeware file decompression utility for the Macintosh. The Windows version, also freeware, can decompress not only StuffIt archives from a Mac but also PKZIP and UNIX archive formats. It can also decode some Internet binary formats. Aladdin Systems makes many other file management products, primarily for the Mac. Visit the Web site at `http://www.aladdinsys.com`

Windows installation (all versions): In the Run dialog box, type in **D:\STUFFIT\SITEX10.EXE**

After you install StuffIt Expander for Windows, follow these instructions to configure the program to ask you where to install decompressed items.

1. **Open StuffIt Expander.**
2. **Choose Options⇨Destination.**
3. **In the dialog box that appears, under the section "Destination Directory for Expanded Files," click the Ask button.**
4. **Just below, in the section marked "Create a subdirectory with the same name as the archive," choose the button next to When the archive contains more than one file or directory.**
5. **Click OK.**

Macintosh installation: Open the StuffIt Expander folder on the CD and double-click the StuffIt Expander 401 Installer icon to begin.

Surfboard Demo, from Abbott Systems

For Macintosh. Now you can open your Internet Web sites from your desktop with the convenience of a TV remote control. This demo version of Surfboard has all the features of the commercial product except that saving is disabled. Visit the Abbott Systems Web site at `http://www.abbottsys.com`

Macintosh installation: Open the Surfboard Demo folder and then double-click the Surfboard Demo Installer icon.

TurboGopher, from the University of Minnesota

For Macintosh. A spiffy Gopher search program, TurboGopher is a shareware product. The latest version can usually be found on the Web at `http://www.shareware.com`

Macintosh installation: Drag the TurboGopher folder from the CD to your Mac's hard disk.

VuePrint, by Hamick Software

For Windows. VuePrint is another PC graphics viewer and editor. This shareware program has a 15-day trial period. Updates can be found at `http://www.hamrick.com`

Windows installation (all versions): In the Run dialog box, type in **D:\VUEPRINT\VUEPRI46.EXE**

WebPhone 2.01, from NetSpeak Corporation

For Windows. WebPhone is another tidy Internet phone program for Windows. Until you register and pay for the program, you are limited to a talk time of 3 minutes and other features of the software are also limited. For the latest version, drop by the `http://www.netspeak.com` Web site.

Windows installation (all versions): In the Run dialog box, type in **D:\WEBPHONE\WP201.EXE**

WinZip 6.2, from Nico Mak Software

For Windows. WinZip is a shareware file compression utility which creates and extracts files saved in the popular PKZIP file compression format.

Windows 95 installation: In the Run dialog box, type in **D:\WINZIP62\WIN95\WINZIP95.EXE**

Windows 3.1 installation: In the Run dialog box, type in **D:\WINZIP62\WIN31\WINZIP31.EXE**

WS_FTP, from Ipswitch, Inc.

For Windows. WS_FTP is a powerful Windows FTP program designed for the novice user. This limited edition has a 15-day free trial and comes in a Windows 95 and Windows 3.1 version.

Windows 95 installation: In the Run dialog box, type in **D:\WS_FTP\INST32.EXE**

Windows 3.1 installation (all versions): In the Run dialog box, type in **D:\WS_FTP\INSTALL.EXE**

Index

• Symbols •

• A •

• B •

• C •

• N •

• O •

• X •

• Y •

• Z •

AT&T WorldNet℠ Service

A World of Possibilities…

Thank you for selecting AT&T WorldNet Service — it's the Internet as only AT&T can bring it to you. With AT&T WorldNet Service, a world of infinite possibilities is now within your reach. Research virtually any subject. Stay abreast of current events. Participate in online newsgroups. Purchase merchandise from leading retailers. Send and receive electronic mail.

AT&T WorldNet Service is rapidly becoming the preferred way of accessing the Internet. It was recently awarded one of the most highly coveted awards in the computer industry, *PC Computing*'s 1996 MVP Award for Best Internet Service Provider. Now, more than ever, it's the best way to stay in touch with the people, ideas, and information that are important to you.

You need a computer with a mouse, a modem, a phone line, and the enclosed software. That's all. We've taken care of the rest.

If You Can Point and Click, You're There

With AT&T WorldNet Service, finding the information you want on the Internet is easier than you ever imagined it could be. You can surf the Net within minutes. And find almost anything you want to know — from the weather in Paris, Texas — to the cost of a ticket to Paris, France. You're just a point and click away. It's that easy.

AT&T WorldNet Service features specially customized industry-leading browsers integrated with advanced Internet directories and search engines. The result is an Internet service that sets a new standard for ease of use — virtually everywhere you want to go is a point and click away, making it a snap to navigate the Internet.

When you go online with AT&T WorldNet Service, you'll benefit from being connected to the Internet by the world leader in networking. We offer you fast access of up to 28.8 Kbps in more than 215 cities throughout the U.S. that will make going online as easy as picking up your phone.

Online Help and Advice
24 Hours a Day, 7 Days a Week

Before you begin exploring the Internet, you may want to take a moment to check two useful sources of information.

If you're new to the Internet, from the AT&T WorldNet Service home page at `www.worldnet.att.net`, click on the Net Tutorial hyperlink for a quick explanation of unfamiliar terms and useful advice about exploring the Internet.

Another useful source of information is the HELP icon. The area contains pertinent, time saving information-intensive reference tips, and topics such as Accounts & Billing, Trouble Reporting, Downloads & Upgrades, Security Tips, Network Hot Spots, Newsgroups, Special Announcements, etc.

Whether online or off-line, 24 hours a day, seven days a week, we will provide World Class technical expertise and fast, reliable responses to your questions. To reach AT&T WorldNet Customer Care, call **1-800-400-1447**.

Nothing is more important to us than making sure that your Internet experience is a truly enriching and satisfying one.

Safeguard Your Online Purchases

AT&T WorldNet Service is committed to making the Internet a safe and convenient way to transact business. By registering and continuing to charge your AT&T WorldNet Service to your AT&T Universal Card, you'll enjoy peace of mind whenever you shop the Internet. Should your account number be compromised on the Net, you won't be liable for any online transactions charged to your AT&T Universal Card by a person who is not an authorized user.*

*Today, cardmembers may be liable for the first $50 of charges made by a person who is not an authorized user, which will not be imposed under this program as long as the cardmember notifies AT&T Universal Card of the loss within 24 hours and otherwise complies with the Cardmember Agreement. Refer to Cardmember Agreement for definition of authorized user.

Minimum System Requirements

IBM-Compatible Personal Computer Users:

- IBM-compatible personal computer with 486SX or higher processor
- 8MB of RAM (or more for better performance)
- 15–36MB of available hard disk space to install software, depending on platform (14–21MB to use service after installation, depending on platform)
- Graphics system capable of displaying 256 colors
- 14,400 bps modem connected to an outside phone line and not a LAN or ISDN line
- Microsoft Windows 3.1x or Windows 95

Macintosh Users:

- Macintosh 68030 or higher (including 68LC0X0 models and all Power Macintosh models)
- System 7.5.3 Revision 2 or higher for PCI Power Macintosh models: System 7.1 or higher for all 680X0 and non-PCI Power Macintosh models
- Mac TCP 2.0.6 or Open Transport 1.1 or higher

- 8MB of RAM (minimum) with Virtual Memory turned on or RAM Doubler; 16MB recommended for Power Macintosh users
- 12MB of available hard disk space (15MB recommended)
- 14,400 bps modem connected to an outside phone line and not a LAN or ISDN line
- Color or 256 gray-scale monitor
- Apple Guide 1.2 or higher (if you want to view online help)

  If you are uncertain of the configuration of your Macintosh computer, consult your Macintosh User's guide or call Apple at 1-800-767-2775.

Installation Tips and Instructions

- If you have other Web browsers or online software, please consider uninstalling them according to the vendor's instructions.
- If you are installing AT&T WorldNet Service on a computer with Local Area Networking, please contact your LAN administrator for setup instructions.
- At the end of installation, you may be asked to restart your computer. Don't attempt the registration process until you have done so.

IBM-compatible PC users:

- Insert the CD-ROM into the CD-ROM drive on your computer.
- Select ***File/Run*** (for Windows 3.1x) or ***Start/Run*** (for Windows 95 if setup did not start automatically).
- Type ***D:\setup.exe*** (or change the "D" if your CD-ROM is another drive).
- Click ***OK***.
- Follow the onscreen instructions to install and register.

Macintosh users:

- Disable all extensions except Apple CD-ROM and Foreign Files Access extensions.
- Restart Computer.
- Insert the CD-ROM into the CD-ROM drive on your computer.
- Double-click the *Install AT&T WorldNet Service* icon.
- Follow the onscreen instructions to install. (Upon restarting your Macintosh, AT&T WorldNet Service Account Setup automatically starts.)
- Follow the onscreen instructions to register.

Registering with AT&T WorldNet Service

After you have connected with AT&T WorldNet online registration service, you will be presented with a series of screens that confirm billing information and prompt you for additional account set-up data.

The following is a list of registration tips and comments that will help you during the registration process.

I. Use one of the following registration codes, which can also be found in Appendix D of *The Internet For Teachers, 2nd Edition* Use L5SQIM631 if you are an AT&T long-distance residential customer or L5SQIM632 if you use another long-distance phone company.

II. During registration, you will need to supply your name, address, and valid credit card number, and choose an account information security word, e-mail name, and e-mail password. You will also be requested to select your preferred price plan at this time. (We advise that you use all lowercase letters when assigning an e-mail ID and security code, since they are easier to remember.)

III. If you make a mistake and exit or get disconnected during the registration process prematurely, simply click on "Create New Account." Do not click on "Edit Existing Account."

IV. When choosing your local access telephone number, you will be given several options. Please choose the one nearest to you. Please note that calling a number within your area does not guarantee that the call is free.

Connecting to AT&T WorldNet Service

When you have finished installing and registering with AT&T WorldNet Service, you are ready to access the Internet. Make sure your modem and phone line are available before attempting to connect to the service.

For Windows 95 users:

- Double-click on the ***Connect to AT&T WorldNet Service*** icon on your desktop.

  OR
- Select ***Start, Programs, AT&T WorldNet Software, Connect to AT&T WorldNet Service.***

For Windows 3.x users:

- Double-click on the ***Connect to AT&T WorldNet Service*** icon located in the AT&T WorldNet Service group.

For Macintosh users:

- Double-click on the ***AT&T WorldNet Service*** icon in the AT&T WorldNet Service folder.

Choose the Plan That's Right for You

The Internet is for everyone, whether at home or at work. In addition to making the time you spend online productive and fun, we're also committed to making it affordable. Choose one of two price plans: unlimited usage access or hourly usage access. The latest pricing information can be obtained during online registration. No matter which plan you use, we're confident that after you take advantage of everything AT&T WorldNet Service has to offer, you'll wonder how you got along without it.

Explore our AT&T WorldNet Service site at `http://www.att.com/worldnet`.

IDG BOOKS WORLDWIDE, INC.
END-USER LICENSE AGREEMENT

Read This. You should carefully read these terms and conditions before opening the software packet(s) included with this book ("Book"). This is a license agreement ("Agreement") between you and IDG Books Worldwide, Inc. ("IDGB"). By opening the accompanying software packet(s), you acknowledge that you have read and accept the following terms and conditions. If you do not agree and do not want to be bound by such terms and conditions, promptly return the Book and the unopened software packet(s) to the place you obtained them for a full refund.

1. **License Grant.** IDGB grants to you (either an individual or entity) a nonexclusive license to use one copy of the enclosed software program(s) (collectively, the "Software") solely for your own personal or business purposes on a single computer (whether a standard computer or a workstation component of a multiuser network). The Software is in use on a computer when it is loaded into temporary memory (i.e., RAM) or installed into permanent memory (e.g., hard disk, CD-ROM, or other storage device). IDGB reserves all rights not expressly granted herein.

2. **Ownership.** IDGB is the owner of all right, title, and interest, including copyright, in and to the compilation of the Software recorded on the CD-ROM. Copyright to the individual programs on the CD-ROM is owned by the author or other authorized copyright owner of each program. Ownership of the Software and all proprietary rights relating thereto remain with IDGB and its licensors.

3. **Restrictions on Use and Transfer.**

   (a) You may only (i) make one copy of the Software for backup or archival purposes, or (ii) transfer the Software to a single hard disk, provided that you keep the original for backup or archival purposes. You may not (i) rent or lease the Software, (ii) copy or reproduce the Software through a LAN or other network system or through any computer subscriber system or bulletin-board system, or (iii) modify, adapt, or create derivative works based on the Software.

   (b) You may not reverse engineer, decompile, or disassemble the Software. You may transfer the Software and user documentation on a permanent basis, provided that the transferee agrees to accept the terms and conditions of this Agreement and you retain no copies. If the Software is an update or has been updated, any transfer must include the most recent update and all prior versions.

4. **Restrictions on Use of Individual Programs.** You must follow the individual requirements and restrictions detailed for each individual program in the "About the CD" appendix (Appendix D) of this Book. These limitations are contained in the individual license agreements recorded on the CD-ROM. These restrictions may include a requirement that after using the program for the period of time specified in its text, the user must pay a registration fee or discontinue use. By opening the Software packet(s), you will be agreeing to abide by the licenses and restrictions for these individual programs. None of the material on this CD-ROM or listed in this Book may ever be distributed, in original or modified form, for commercial purposes.

5. **Limited Warranty.**

   (a) IDGB warrants that the Software and CD-ROM are free from defects in materials and workmanship under normal use for a period of sixty (60) days from the date of purchase of this Book. If IDGB receives notification within the warranty period of defects in materials or workmanship, IDGB will replace the defective CD-ROM.

(b) **IDGB AND THE AUTHOR OF THE BOOK DISCLAIM ALL OTHER WARRANTIES, EXPRESS OR IMPLIED, INCLUDING WITHOUT LIMITATION IMPLIED WARRANTIES OF MERCHANTABILITY AND FITNESS FOR A PARTICULAR PURPOSE, WITH RESPECT TO THE SOFTWARE, THE PROGRAMS, THE SOURCE CODE CONTAINED THEREIN, AND/OR THE TECHNIQUES DESCRIBED IN THIS BOOK. IDGB DOES NOT WARRANT THAT THE FUNCTIONS CONTAINED IN THE SOFTWARE WILL MEET YOUR REQUIREMENTS OR THAT THE OPERATION OF THE SOFTWARE WILL BE ERROR FREE.**

(c) This limited warranty gives you specific legal rights, and you may have other rights which vary from jurisdiction to jurisdiction.

6. **Remedies**.

(a) IDGB's entire liability and your exclusive remedy for defects in materials and workmanship shall be limited to replacement of the Software, which may be returned to IDGB with a copy of your receipt at the following address: Disk Fulfillment Department, Attn: The Internet For Teachers, 2nd Edition, IDG Books Worldwide, Inc., 7260 Shadeland Station, Ste. 100, Indianapolis, IN 46256, or call 1-800-762-2974. Please allow 3-4 weeks for delivery. This Limited Warranty is void if failure of the Software has resulted from accident, abuse, or misapplication. Any replacement Software will be warranted for the remainder of the original warranty period or thirty (30) days, whichever is longer.

(b) In no event shall IDGB or the author be liable for any damages whatsoever (including without limitation damages for loss of business profits, business interruption, loss of business information, or any other pecuniary loss) arising from the use of or inability to use the Book or the Software, even if IDGB has been advised of the possibility of such damages.

(c) Because some jurisdictions do not allow the exclusion or limitation of liability for consequential or incidental damages, the above limitation or exclusion may not apply to you.

7. **U.S. Government Restricted Rights**. Use, duplication, or disclosure of the Software by the U.S. Government is subject to restrictions stated in paragraph (c) (1) (ii) of the Rights in Technical Data and Computer Software clause of DFARS 252.227-7013, and in subparagraphs (a) through (d) of the Commercial Computer—Restricted Rights clause at FAR 52.227-19, and in similar clauses in the NASA FAR supplement, when applicable.

8. **General**. This Agreement constitutes the entire understanding of the parties and revokes and supersedes all prior agreements, oral or written, between them and may not be modified or amended except in a writing signed by both parties hereto which specifically refers to this Agreement. This Agreement shall take precedence over any other documents that may be in conflict herewith. If any one or more provisions contained in this Agreement are held by any court or tribunal to be invalid, illegal, or otherwise unenforceable, each and every other provision shall remain in full force and effect.

Installation Instructions

Well, almost. *The Internet For Teachers,* 2nd Edition CD-ROM contains software for Windows users, software for Mac users, and plenty of things for both Windows and Mac users. The installation instructions for each program are too long to summarize here. Just turn to Appendix D to find detailed instructions on all that you get on the CD . . . and how to put these wonderful things on your computer.

Before using this CD, however, I recommend that you install Adobe Acrobat Reader and StuffIt Expander. These programs make it easier for you to install some programs and read the manuals for some of the software.

Adobe Acrobat Reader, from Adobe Systems, Inc.

Windows installation (all versions): In the Run dialog box, type in **D:\ACROBAT\ACROREAD.EXE**

Macintosh installation: Open the Adobe Acrobat Reader folder, double-click the ACROREAD.MAC icon, and follow the on-screen instructions.

StuffIt Expander, from Aladdin Systems

Windows installation (all versions): In the Run dialog box, type in **D:\STUFFIT\SITEX10.EXE**

After you install StuffIt Expander for Windows, follow these instructions to configure the program to ask you where to install decompressed items.

1. **Open StuffIt Expander.**
2. **Choose Options⇨Destination.**
3. **In the dialog box that appears, under the section "Destination Directory for Expanded Files," click the Ask button.**
4. **Just below, in the section marked "Create a subdirectory with the same name as the archive," choose the button next to When the archive contains more than one file or directory.**
5. **Click OK.**

Macintosh installation: Open the StuffIt Expander folder on the CD and double-click the StuffIt Expander Installer icon to begin.